A Patchwork Shawl

A Patchwork Shawl

CHRONICLES OF SOUTH ASIAN WOMEN IN AMERICA

EDITED BY

SHAMITA DAS DASGUPTA

Rutgers University Press

New Brunswick, New Jersey, and London

Frontispiece photo by Jaishri Abichandani

Excerpt from "Freedom-bound" in *Rabindranath Tagore: Selected Poems,* translated by William Radice (Penguin Books, 1985) translation copyright © William Radice, 1985. Reproduced by permission of Penguin Books Ltd.

Excerpts from "Tourism" by Shahida Janjua and "I-Dentity" by Prachi Momin from *Charting the Journey: Writings of Black and Third World Women,* edited by Shabnam Grewal, Jackie Kay, Liliane Landor, Gail Lewis, and Pratibha Parmar. London: Sheba Feminist Publishers, 1988.

Excerpts from "Osakan/Mother" by Sakae S. Roberson, "In Remembrance" by Janice Mirikitani, and "For the Poets of 'Firetree' on the Second Anniversary of the Death of Benigno Aquino" by Valorie Bejarno
from *Making Waves* by Asian Women United of California
© 1989 by Asian Women United of California.
Used by permission of Beacon Press, Boston.

Excerpt from "Introduction" by Minal Hajratwala used by permission of the author. Poem first published in *Forkroads: A Journal of Ethnic-American Literature* 5 (fall 1996).

Library of Congress Cataloging-in-Publication Data

A patchwork shawl : chronicles of South Asian women in America /
   [editor] Shamita Das Dasgupta.
      p. cm.
   Includes index.
   ISBN 0-8135-2518-7 (alk. paper). — ISBN 0-8135-2517-9 (alk. paper)
    1. South Asians—United States—Social conditions. 2. Minority
women—United States—Social conditions. 3. Women immigrants—
United States—Social conditions. I. Dasgupta, Shamita Das.
E184.S69P38 1998
305.48'8914073—dc21   97-49650
                                                   CIP

For my mother, Biva,
who taught me to dream
and
my daughter, Sayantani,
who showed me how to make dreams come true

CONTENTS

Who Am I? Re-Questing Identity

Me and We: Family and Community

Nation and Immigration: Rethinking the "Model Minority"

PREFACE

A Patchwork Shawl is the culmination of a journey that began nearly three decades ago. I immigrated to the United States then and inadvertently became a participant-observer in the making of our diasporic communities, a work still in progress. It dawned on me much later how fortunate I have been to be a witness to this historic process.

I came to this country in the late 1960s, a young wife following her husband, without much of an idea about what it would mean to be in a country where I could not readily dig into my own history for sustenance. Everyone and everything was forcing change on me. I remember the arguments that wracked our small community in the Midwest: whether to adopt Western clothing, whether to insist that our children speak our native languages at home, whether to teach them our traditional songs, dances, and rituals, and whether to become involved in political issues and controversies in our adopted country. With the passing of years, these primitive queries took concrete shape and the negotiations around them have intensified. *A Patchwork Shawl* documents this ongoing debate.

For the beginning of this book I have extracted four lines of a poem by Rabindranath Tagore, translated by William Radice. The lines express the mood of the book more than anything I can say. Tagore's poem, "Muktapathey" (On the open path), translated by Radice as "Freedom-bound," celebrates a female lover who has rejected the rules of a ritual-bound society to find autonomy. Tagore's metaphor for freedom is the road, and home symbolizes restrictive socialization. The collection of essays in *A Patchwork Shawl* represents this unlimited woman, the diasporic woman who gladly renounces security within the confines of four walls to walk the path of freedom. The road is the process, a struggle that carries within it the sweet promise of justice.

A Patchwork Shawl is a collective effort. It would never have been a reality without the loving support of many people, too numerous to list here. First and foremost are the women who have contributed their imaginations and analyses to the book. Their encouragement and patience through various revisions have been invaluable to me. Three of the essays, Rinita Mazumdar's, Naheed Islam's, and Sayantani's and mine, were presented at the first South Asia Women's Conference in Los Angeles, California. I am indebted to Sangeeta Gupta, who convened the conference and helped with the beginning phase of this project. Many authors have voluntarily sent me their creative writings and essays for this volume. Although I could not include their contributions because of obvious space limitations, their enthusiasm has convinced me of the need for more such documentation.

This book would never have been finished without Martha Heller, whose skill as an editor is matched only by the warmth of her personality. Her excitement and belief in the project and my abilities to complete it have guided me through various ups and downs that, I suppose, are part of any such work. I am indebted deeply to my friend Martha. I am also thankful for the facilitative assistance that so many individuals with Rutgers University Press have given me, especially Paula Kantenwein. Susmita Bando, an artist and a friend, has enhanced the book by contributing her art for the cover. I am completely in awe of her work and her generosity.

A Patchwork Shawl owes its cogency in organization to Kamala Visweswaran, a dear friend. I have adopted the order of chapters which she suggested for this book. I cherish the encouragement and inspiration Kamala has offered me through the completion of this project.

As always, my daughter, Sayantani, has been a source of support and constructive criticism. I thank her for helping me make *A Patchwork Shawl* what it is today. Thanks also to my husband, Sujan, for not letting me give up, and to Mishty, for being a joy in my life.

A Patchwork Shawl carries within it my amazement at the resilience of our communities and the second-generation women and men who are challenging and rewriting the old rules. The book, ultimately, is a celebration of their work.

Shamita Das Dasgupta

A Patchwork Shawl

To sit where orthodoxy rules
Is not her wish at all—
Maybe I shall seat her on
A grubby patchwork shawl.
Rabindranath Tagore, "Freedom-bound"

Introduction

SHAMITA DAS DASGUPTA

So we, each one
Unfold our lives.
A feast of difference.
Richly varied.
Rainbow coloured.
      S. Janjua, "Tourism"

A New Earth under Our Feet

More than anything, this book is a collection of stories: the stories of women's lives, our lives. Our stories span different worlds: Bangladesh, Sri Lanka, Nepal, India, Pakistan, and the United States. Our lives are diverse and different, yet they are tied together with a common thread: experiences we have shared as immigrants from South Asia and women of color living in the United States of America.

Who are we? Who are South Asian immigrant women? Any political or research attention leveled at our communities has rarely focused on women. The general populace still tends to perceive us in stereotypes: docile, subservient, passive, politically unaware, asexual, and bound by traditions.[1] Parmatma Saran, an Indian immigrant scholar, reinforces this mainstream viewpoint about Indian womanhood: "Generally, Indian women are less assertive than their American counterparts and the majority feel that relations cannot be changed by being too assertive. They recognize that being too assertive and demanding is not the right approach to correct things."[2] Despite such convenient categorizing, the realities of our life experiences do not allow simple caricatures. Our lives go beyond images of the proverbial "good"

1

daughter, the asexual, all-enduring mother who walks three steps behind her man. Passive and insulated womanhood is not our reality.

Our foremothers came to the United States at the tail end of the 1800s, when our natal lands were still intact under British colonial rule. Much of the detail about these pioneers' lives and experiences is now lost to us. We can only imagine their lives amid an atmosphere of virulent racism and scanty women's communities. However, we can be certain that these women did not lead sheltered lives hidden within their homes. One of the early South Asian women in the United States was Kanta Chandra Gupta of Delhi. She arrived in San Francisco in 1910 and became the first South Asian woman to apply for citizenship, at the age of nineteen. Kanta, like many of her contemporaries, supported India's independence movement and organized against British rule in India. In addition to taking care of a family, she became a chiropractor with her own established practice.[3] Like Kanta, the few women who were allowed to join their families in the United States worked alongside men to establish a firm financial footing, raise children, develop a community, and end colonization of their motherland.[4]

Setting Up a New Home

twenty-five years she's been here
and still
    a-me-ri-ka makes her mouth sour tight
    sticks in her mind like spit-wet thread
    caught in the eye of a needle.
           S. S. Roberson, "Okasan/Mother"

"When will you be going back?" This question, put to us in various ways and multiple times, makes us ask another: "Where is our home?" If the psychological feeling of "home" is created by an illusion of safety within boundaries and by erasing the histories of oppression and resistance, then we South Asian women can claim no place as our home.[5] On the other hand, we can perhaps count the entire world as our home. To assume home in terms of fixed geography belies our experiences of physical as well as psychological movement. Challenging any sense of constancy, our home has long been fluid and ever-changing owing to political, demographic, and economic travelings in and out of the physical space we now call South Asia. Jasbir K. Puar, a South Asian scholar exploring the notion of home in the United States, writes, "An oversimplified understanding of home as birthplace and not home as displace(ment) mocked the tensions I was feeling with my 'Americanness' and the strong emotions I had about India."[6] This tension is endemic in our communities in America, where the push and pull of going and staying, claiming and rejecting, being and not being continuously sway our definitions of home.

This journey to spaces beyond our "assigned" place is not new to us. As South Asians, we are legatees of a long history of overseas migration. This migratory trend was the by-product of British colonization, as the preponderance of emigration to colonies and other places—Fiji, Guyana, West Indies, the United Kingdom, Canada, Europe, various African countries, and the United States—indicates. This movement began with indentured labor, persisted with free passage, and culminated in (in)voluntary emigration, or the "brain drain," from the subcontinent to North America.[7] During as well as after colonial rule, Indians left their natal land and spread all over the globe in search of new homes. Thus, for us, the concept of home and the search for it have become more and more complex with time.

The answer to the puzzling question "Who are we?" becomes even more complicated as we, South Asian immigrants, nest ourselves within our communities in America. Despite U.S. immigration policies' efforts to homogenize our population, we are no longer a monolithic middle- and upper-class group.[8] Since the late 1970s, a significant number of women have entered the country and struggled to make space for themselves in the working class. These are the women we buy our Indian spices and vegetables from, they "man" the urban newspaper booths and sell us bunches of flowers through car windows at traffic lights, they roll *rotis* (a flat bread) for our nearest Indo-Pak grocery store, they cook and serve at Bangladeshi restaurants, they clean motel bathrooms, and they may even be the undocumented housekeeper or nanny in many a South Asian home. This new group disputes the homogeneity of the South Asian community in America and has remodeled the population to a bimodal demographic distribution.

Naima is such a woman, a South Asian working woman in America.[9] She came to America, sponsored by her husband, with a five-year old daughter, a suitcase full of saris, and little English. Her husband worked at a newspaper stand in a big city. A month after Naima and her daughter arrived, her husband was shot by teenage muggers and was permanently paralyzed. For the past twelve years, Naima has supplied cooked meals to South Asian families and fried samosas to three local grocery stores. She is the main breadwinner of her family.

A New Face in the Mirror

In the mirror—the face of an unnamed person
Me
Skin the colour of eyes, roots all conflict.
Call me P- . . . .
I endure like a lamb
Spit on my back
I seek help from my heritage,
Adhere to a culture in my imagination.

P. Momin, "I-Dentity"

Martin and Mohanty describe a community as "the product of work, of struggle; it is inherently unstable, contextual; it has to be constantly re-evaluated in relation to critical political priorities; and it is the product of interpretation, interpretation based on an attention to history, to the concrete."[10] One's true community thus, cannot be that which one is born into, the birth space. Rather, it is the workplace that is achieved by constant clarification of one's political position. However, just as the concept of home tends to become artificially bound by mountains, oceans, and places that are not home, the notion of a community is conjured up through conformities, similarities, and an illusion of harmony among people who may have little in common. The popular idea of "community" denies conflicts within a potentially differing group while accentuating frictions with all outside. In South Asian American communities, this differentiation between inside and outside is stringently maintained. Members of the community whose behaviors do not comply with the approved referent standards are perfunctorily ostracized. Elaborating on such community power and the mechanisms that maintain it, Hongo writes: "Power constantly maintains itself and polices those under its domination. And power is insidious—it often masquerades as resistance to power, inverting principles, exchanging roles, proliferating in a cultural hall of mirrors that distort, multiply, and disguise its operations."[11]

For instance, in the 1995 India Day Parade in New York City, the organizing umbrella agency, the Federation of Indians in America (FIA), banned all groups that worked with battered women, gays and lesbians, and taxi drivers or groups that focused on communal (dis)harmony from the march celebrating India's independence. Obviously, these organizations were highlighting conflicts that the community had labored to deny.

The appearance of a monolithic community is maintained not only publicly but privately also. In homes, families, and marriages, differences are actively repressed by a call for cultural purity. Being loyal to the traditional "culture" is an immigrant's ticket to belonging, our communities' acknowledgment of someone as Pakistani, Bangladeshi, Sri Lankan, Nepali, or Indian. However, South Asian cultures that are reformulated and disseminated in the United States are neither traditional nor natural. The powerful of the communities' leaders have endeavored to create counterfeit authenticity by denying culture's essential flux and inherent disparities. By controlling the religious, social, cultural, and informational institutions such as temples, mosques, newspapers, televisions, and cultural organizations in the community, the male bourgeoisie have managed to suppress intracommunity dissension and manipulated its public image. Contradictions and intricacies that emerge in a lived culture, as in South Asia, are obliterated deliberately in the United States in the name of unity, coherence, and formal presentation to the dominant mainstream.

To be fair, this intolerance for heterogeneity among immigrant South Asians is partially a result of the need to display a flawless public face to a mainstream that is derisive of diversity. Creating a mythical South Asian culture that is homogeneous, uncontentious, and resistant to outside corruption is a way of assuaging the host nation's fear of differences. This fictitious construction of culture is further reinforced when the mainstream affirms the community's characteristics by branding it a "model minority."

During the 1970s, the idea of the model minority was created by the U.S. media as an argument against including South Asians in social welfare programs. They propagated the myth that South Asians were exempt from social problems such as unemployment, poverty, racism, delinquency, and familial conflict. This myth not only biased the general populace but was also internalized by the communities themselves. Thus, in addition to their own efforts to mask intracommunity diversity, South Asians became obsessed with living the model minority stereotype.

The main casualty of our communities' efforts to reformulate homogeneous "authenticity" are women. In their efforts to immortalize the traditional "culture," South Asians have placed an inordinate burden on community women. Since this culture is an outdated version of the original, South Asian women in America are given the task of perpetuating anachronistic customs and traditions. A young South Asian writer expresses this problem succinctly: "Often when South Asians emigrate from their country of origin they attempt to preserve the culture by rigidly holding to the values that were prevalent at the time of their departure."[12] That is, immigrants become frozen in time.

The practice of making women emblematic of a nation's cultural survival is in the tradition of locating family *izzat* (Urdu for honor) in its female members. In the new country, women not only carry this antiquated responsibility but have also been assigned the role of bearers, as well as transmitters, of culture and traditions to the next generation. They alone have been made accountable for the safekeeping of an ancient culture: "The discourse . . .—America vs. India, West vs. East, Modernity vs. Tradition—has a long and complex history for Third World women. . . . Briefly, questions of tradition and modernity have, since the nineteenth century, been debated on the literal and figurative bodies of women. It thus comes as no surprise that the burden of negotiating the new world is borne disproportionately by women, whose behaviour and desires, real or imagined, become the litmus test for the South Asian Community's anxieties or sense of well-being. . . . Women . . . are quite frequently policed with the stick of tradition: it is women who are called on to preserve the ways of the old country."[13]

As a consequence, the conduct of both immigrant and second-generation women is monitored closely.[14] Women who transgress in thought, action, or behavior are marked as "Westernized" (read: traitors to the culture/community) and brought back into the fold. Mothers who do not confine their daughters within the prescribed role of "good girl" and daughters whose behavior proclaims autonomy are psychologically exiled for their betrayal.[15] By the same token, lesbians, social change activists, and cultural critics are peremptorily dismissed from communities as non-Indian/Pakistani/Bangladeshi, and so on.[16]

Learning to Name, Speaking of Names

Tell me your name.
Tell me about your name.
Tell me the ways you understand your name,
all the blue nuances of your name
                    M. Hajaratwala, "Introductions"

Although a sense of self and community is forever tied together for women of South Asian descent, our very identification as South Asian is problematic: "The use of the term 'South Asia' has become interchangeable with the term 'India.'"[17] Whatever this political and historical alliance implies, as Naheed Islam points out, it does not signify "equal space and voice within and between" the categorized.[18] That is, Indians dominate in any South Asian coalition, while Pakistanis, Bangladeshis, Sri Lankans, and Nepalis are relegated to the role of the "other," their inclusion an afterthought. Frequently, the reductionist affiliative label of "South Asian" (read: Indian) is adopted for the convenience of the organizers, and incorporation of the others is considered an act of the host's generosity. With each conference, anthology, research project, academic department, and organization labeled South Asian in which Indians dominate, we reconstruct and consolidate this unequal power relationship. The marginalized South Asians in the United States recreate margins themselves.

The debate here is on the issue of true inclusion. Yet the bulk of information available to us about immigrants from South Asia, especially women, focuses on Indians. To discard this information for the sake of balanced representation may not be viable at this time. In addition, all such discussions serve only to problematize the issue rather than to find a solution. Perhaps the path lies in discarding the label itself and adopting a new one that would allow us to forge a more equal relationship, similar to the amalgamated "black" identity in Britain.

However, a contentious process of South Asian diasporic identity (re)formation is not an anomaly. Multiple, fluid, overlapping identities can only be crystallized by negotiating color, class, nation, and tradition, real and imaginary markers of our contexts. Our identities are affected intensely by our location and relocation in physical as well as psychological worlds. The conflicts and concords that emerge as these worlds interact and collide can only facilitate the process of creation. Marie Gillespie's discussion on identity formation among London Punjabi teenagers addresses this complex dialectic process: "These young people's identities are both formed and transformed by their location in history and politics, language and culture. Through their material and cultural consumption and production, they are also constructing new forms of identity, shaped by but at the same time reshaping the images and meanings circulated in the media and in the market."[19]

A New Voice Ringing Loud

Our tongues are sharp like blades.
We overturn furrows of secrecy.
>   Yes, we will harvest justice. . . .
>   And yes,
the struggle continues on
with our stampede of voices.
>   J. Mirikitani, "In Remembrance"

Historically, the family has been the primary social refuge for South Asian women. A woman's identity in South Asia has never been conceived of in individual terms; rather it was always fused with that of the men in her life: father, brother, husband, and son. Thus, a South Asian woman is generally defined by her familial roles: daughter, sister, daughter-in-law, wife, mother, and grandmother. This inordinate dependence on the family is a source of strength as well as vulnerability for the South Asian woman in America. Away from traditional structure of the extended family, which affords some protection, South Asian women in the United States are being victimized in unique ways. Like her community, family also can be a source of oppression for a South Asian woman, and yet her life is inexorably embedded in it.

In my capacity as a counselor with Manavi, the pioneering South Asian organization in New Jersey that focuses on violence against women, I met Sudha. She called Manavi to seek assistance after her husband had been arrested on domestic violence charges the previous night. She had been beaten by him over the course of a decade, ever since her marriage and immigration to this country. This time, she secured a restraining order against him and wanted him out of her life forever. In the end, this did not happen. Although Sudha was not an overly dependent or weak person, a few community leaders intervened and insisted that she withdraw all charges. Two of them even came to take her to the police station so that she could remove the temporary restraining order. Sudha could not withstand this barrage of community pressures and capitulated. Her experiences are not unique. The majority of South Asian victims of domestic violence indicate that they are afraid of the community's responses if they take any actions against their abusers.

The violence that women suffer at home is fervently denied much of the time by community members in order to maintain an unblemished image in the eyes of the mainstream world. This disallowance of women's negative experiences is part of the male fantasy of an idyllic family and perfect wife, a family that is affable and conflict free and a wife who is mother, friend, lover, supporter, all rolled into one. Within this fabrication of ideal womanhood, there is, of course, no space allocated for the lesbian, the activist, the protester, the different and individual woman.

As South Asians began to claim spaces in the United States in the 1980s, the male bourgeoisie who dominated the institutions of the budding communities expended efforts to construct a public face that rested, in part, on a tame and passive image of womanhood.[20] They defined the South Asian American woman as heterosexual, chaste, obedient, faithful, and a constant nurturer.[21] Women as the symbol of "family values" is another way that South Asians validate their stereotype of a model minority to the mainstream community.

In the last fifteen years, numerous women's organizations working on violence, sexuality, disease, racism, and communal disharmony have been formed in the United States. The majority are led by women who question traditions and the presumed safety of females within families, as well as their communities, and challenge the powers that be. Anthologies such as *Our Feet Walk the Sky*, *Contours of the Heart*, and *A Lotus of Another Color* speak to our varied experiences as women in the new world.[22] Authors such as Ameena Meer, Chitra Banerjee Divakaruni, and Ginu Kamani encapsulate our knowledge of living here in fiction and short stories. Most of these writings are unequivocally subversive, cutting at the roots of the prevalent order and organizing principles of our family, community, nation, and state.

Locating ourselves as Third World feminists living in the First World is an exacting task. Mainstream Western feminism allows little space for activists who contest its essentially insulated political position, forcing us to choose between being South Asians and being feminists. Simultaneously, our geographical location in the West raises serious suspicions about the sincerity, as well as feasibility, of our commitment to social change in South Asia. Yet our communities in the United States tend to dismiss our political consciousness as "Western" or "foreign" and, therefore, a betrayal of our heritage.

Unfortunately, not only do the South Asian communities marginalize women activists, but progressive South Asian women often actively reject the communities of their origin: "We hold up to the culture the shame of what its traditions and cultural practices have so often done to its women, the deaths, the brutalities, and the more mundane and quotidian sufferings of women within 'our' culture, that 'our' culture is complicitous with."[23] This schism between the "progressive" and the "traditional" South Asians is nurtured by both parties to the extent that both end up believing the categories are mutually exclusive.

Nevertheless, the majority of South Asian activists struggle to keep their work "contextualized" within their cultures. Uma Narayan writes about this ambivalence: "Despite these accusations of 'westernization,' our sorts of voices will not quietly vanish, shamed into silence. We are the sisters, the wives, the daughters of those who dismiss us, and our points of view are no more able to be 'outside' that culture and those traditions than the perspectives of those who label us 'westernized.'"[24]

This equation of cultural criticism with cultural betrayal is even more pronounced for the second generation. Since the community feels that its integrity depends on the faithfulness of its children, indoctrinating this group into the manufactured culture has become a priority. Teaching traditional gender relations to U.S.-reared youth, especially to community daughters, is at the core of this education program. Thus, "the second generation Indian woman feels that old-world gender roles are still rigidly being upheld for her."[25] Consequently, two distinct voices of South Asian women are emerging from the second generation: one that accepts the absolute glorification of traditions mediated by the parents' generation and another that vilifies the culture as an impediment to its growth as progressive activists. The first group tends to homogenize and essentialize "the culture" as a monolithic Hindi-film-based vision of upper-caste and -class Hindu glory, whereas the second takes an ahistoric position that is oblivious to the long tradition of South Asian women's strength and activism.

All cultures contain elements that disenfranchise women as well as ones that empower them. It is for us to recognize by whose machinations and for whose benefit the former become reified as tradition and the latter exiled to obscurity. As activists we need to salvage those parts of our culture that uplift women as a group.

Walking a New Path

I hear their voices chanting a new song
Strong and demanding
Take my hand now and we will join them
Never mind the miles. . . .

> V. Bejarno, "For the Poets of 'Firetree'
> on the Second Anniversary of the Death
> of Benigno Aquino"

The path we walk is both new and old. Resistance and activism have been central to South Asian women's history. Radha Kumar recounts only a part of this history of activism in her book on the nineteenth-century movements for social justice.[26] South Asian women have been educators, workers, and movers and shakers who were not necessarily confined within their geographic boundaries. Their activism spread across the diaspora, choosing to make a difference wherever they found themselves.

Interestingly, the icon of the strong South Asian woman is lost in the Western stereotype of her. The mainstream views South Asian cultures as inherently restrictive and confining, especially for women. Many young second-generation South Asian women I have met on America's college campuses claim that their own cultures have only limited them and that they have gained strength as activists by rejecting their traditions. This I call the *Mississippi Masala* syndrome.[27] The young heroine in the film is the assimilated immigrant who represents all that is rebellious, adventurous, and free, presumably characteristics of the West. She can find herself only by rejecting her family and community. Her foil is her mother, an immigrant of the old order who, although Madonna-like in her nurturance, wants to drag the daughter back in the darkness of traditionalism. It is only by embracing Westernization that the heroine finds deliverance.[28] Bharati Mukherjee echoes similar sentiments in her fiction. Her heroine, Jasmine, transforms her name from Jyoti to Jasmine to Jane in search of liberation as she physically and psychologically travels from Hasnapur, India, to Iowa, from the old to the new world.[29] This wanton neglect of South Asian women's activism has the dangerous potential of falsifying their histories in the diaspora.

Indeed, I would argue that instead of encouraging and accommodating South Asian women's activism, Westernization actually denies variability in women's roles. In the Western conceptualization, we have choices between two roles: traditional (read: backward, oppressive, sexist, uneducated, passive, and docile) and progressive (read: enlightened, egalitarian, active, vocal, and

Westernized). The pervasiveness of these dichotomous images has obliterated any other viable models from our minds. Such linear and dualistic concepts are, of course, typical of Western thinking.

Within South Asian cultures, alongside the oppositional models of good and bad girls, there is a well-accepted third ideal of femininity; that of the *virangana*, or brave, mythic warrior-woman. The *virangana* is a well-respected and revered role that crosses religious boundaries. The role is represented by the numerous women leaders who throughout history have taken us into battles with the enemy and have led us in the struggle for justice. From Lakshmibai, the warrior queen of Jhansi, to women who fought in the nationalist movements, to Pakistani Prime Minister Benazir Bhutto, South Asia's history abounds in activist women. Nor is it only a Hindu model. Within Islamic cultures, there are many women leaders who exemplify this warrior role. Khadija, Fatima, and Ayesha from the time of the Prophet; Noorjehan, Jahanara, and other heroines from the Mughal period; Rokeya Sakhawat Hussain, Halima Khatun, Badrunnessa Begum, and numerous other freedom fighters during the colonial time; and, in recent years, women organizers in South Asian countries are all *virangana*s.

It is not that we have to learn a new role to become activists; rather, we have to retrieve our collective memory. Part of this process is being reintroduced to our own heroines and becoming reacquainted with our foremothers: women who fought in the nationalist movements, who participated in the Telangana uprising, who started the Chipko and Narmada Bachao movements, women in Bangladesh, Pakistan, Sri Lanka, Nepal, and the diaspora who are leading struggles to end violence against women.[30] And in the United States, we need to unearth the stories of the first of immigrant women who survived here under hostile conditions. These women are our role models. Among the post-1965 immigrants, women have taken the lead in identifying and addressing issues that concern our lives. Organizations focusing on domestic violence, communal harmony, gay and lesbian rights, are all being led by women. We, South Asian American women, are rising to the challenge and accepting the rich mantle of activism that our foremothers have laid out for us.

A Patchwork Shawl is an expression of this activism. It is an attempt to eliminate the imposed reticence that seems to fragment and hide our histories. It is an attempt to piece together our experiences, experiences that bridge two worlds, the one left behind and the one newly adopted. Of course, a simple definition of geographical borders cannot contain our consciousness; psychologically, we penetrate and transcend boundaries of time, space, and cultures. *A Patchwork Shawl* struggles with issues that are critical to us: identity, family, community, sexuality, violence, and being minorities within a minority. Our goal is not to force an ending but to claim the process. It is the struggle to negotiate these concerns in our own ways and define them in our own images that marks our warrior stance.

The theme of identity construction and reconstruction—identity that is ethnic, religious, gendered, sexual, and amalgamated—runs through the majority of chapters in this book. The questions of who we are and how we envision ourselves in this new context occupies us considerably. Grace Poore extends the crucial discussion on the language we use in delineating identity, the very vehicle of our negotiations. She explores the tensions inherent in building and avoiding political alliances in reaction to patriarchal forces in our diasporic environment. Naheed Hasnat, Surina Khan, Naheed Islam, and Lubna Chaudhry focus on the issues surrounding (re)construction of identities in our communities. In the process, they elaborate the complexities involved in consolidating new identities: articulations that constitute inclusions and oppositions, as well as exclusions and redefinitions. Ethnicity is a large part of this identity, yet this ethnicity is different from just belonging to one's nation of origin. Location in the United States also occupies a significant position in this identity, yet it is different from just being an American. Lubna Chaudhry aptly describes this identity as "hybrid," an identity that replaces intra- as well as extracommunity depictions with each creator's individualized imprint.

Equally powerful is the emergence of identities from our sexualities. In their essays, Naheed Islam and Surina Khan explore the construction of identities based on sexuality against the background of endemic repression in our communities. Their subjects are women who have routinely been excluded within our communities: women who love women—lesbians.

Much of the discord between the individual and our communities centers on the control of *all* sexualities, especially of women. The unblemished monolithic face that our communities seem intent on presenting to the outside rests to a great degree on universal heterosexuality. Dissenting voices are emphatically denied, and the resultant silence is vigilantly policed by the bourgeoisie. Nonetheless, nowhere else are our community leaders' powers of rejection more apparent than in the deliberate denial of homosexuality. Islam and Khan elaborate women's heroic refusal to be canceled for either sexuality or ethnicity. They assert that women's constructive resistance propels them to a higher and more complicated level of identity.

Concomitant to this identity (re)production is the awareness of the pushes and pulls exerted by the mainstays of our lives: family and community. Many of the chapters focus on understanding the relationship between our communities and our families. Manisha Roy takes this discussion into the home by inquiring into female intergenerational conflicts. Is a failure in communication or patriarchal repression responsible for driving a wedge between mothers and daughters in our communities? Sayantani, my daughter, and I have collaborated to write "Sex, Lies, and Women's Lives," an essay on the reshaping of young women's sexualities in our community. Under the guise of establishing natural culture and traditions, our immigrant society has been circumscribing and manipulating women's sexualities to reimpose control over them. Then, a fabricated culture is proffered to us as a barrier against (in)voluntary assimilation into the dominant mainstream. As mother-daughter pair, we pose strong challenges to the purported differences in generational sensibilities and national upbringing. We believe it is a violence that we must resist.

All the chapters carry a distinct consciousness of gendered repression and expose subterranean threats of psychological and physical homelessness that South Asian women endure continually. Rinita Mazumdar and Satya Krishnan and her colleagues push this issue further. They probe the underbelly of our cultural communities, where violence against women has become securely embedded. Their discussions focus on the extreme forms of this violence: sexual assault and intimate abuse.

I had the most difficulty placing the chapters on immigration and nation building on U.S. soil. This set of chapters establishes the fore- and backgrounds for all the others in this collection. In "The Habit of Ex-Nomination," Anannya Bhattacharjee challenges our immigrant leadership's exclusive claim to cultural proprietorship and authenticity, which effectively delegitimize women's experiences of violence within their homes. Her activism and writing, or writing as activism, struggle to make room for and amplify suppressed voices and (her)stories. Sunita Sunder Mukhi's chapter on the Indian immigrant communities' efforts to define nationhood through festival, songs, and dances and, more important, girls' and women's bodies and sexualities sheds further light on the fabrication of cultural selfhood that is in progress at this time. Their discussions contend that this wresting of truth, history, traditions, and cultural authenticity by the dominant does not play out in the lives of only certain women in our communities. In fact, all women are maimed by it.

Sonia Shah explores a topic that is overlooked much of the time in the explorations of our lives. With great insight, she analyzes South Asian immigrant women's work in the context of imperialism and labor exploitation, both internal and external to the community.

Certain other similarities tie this book together. The authors have over-whelmingly chosen the personal essay form for their narration. As a distinct style, personal essay seems to lend itself readily to the specific topics and general focus of this volume. Personal essays quite facilely mingle the cre-ative with the critical, the subjective with the objective, and the emotional with the analytical. For voices of the marginalized, the previously silenced, this is perhaps the most appropriate vehicle of expression. However, like any documentation of women's lives, *A Patchwork Shawl* is not complete. As a collection of essays, it does not represent all perspectives; neither does it pre-sume to speak for all South Asian women residing in the United States. In fact, it does not even represent all South Asian countries. At the simplest level, *A Patchwork Shawl* is a space where sixteen women of South Asian descent have decided to speak, allowing us glimpses into their lives and thoughts. It is only a beginning.

The question persists, "Who are we?" With each answer more ques-tions arise. At best, we can answer it only temporarily and re-ask the ques-tion periodically. It is our work in progress. We are daughters, mothers, lovers, sisters, granddaughters, academics, friends, workers, and, above all else, in-dividuals. We are also chroniclers. And this book is an attempt to record, as well as bring meaning to, our adventures in this country. It is an expression of our resistance, resistance to invisibility, "othering," and silence, resistance to being defined by others and being corraled into an artificial "culture" that renounces our diversity of experience and being. *A Patchwork Shawl* is our assertion: We are, we are!

Notes

1. S. D. Dasgupta and S. Warrier, "Stereotypes of Asian Indian Women," *In Visible Terms: Domestic Violence in the Asian Indian Context* (Bloomfield, N. J.: Manavi, 1995).
2. P. Saran, *The Asian Indian Experience in the United States* (Cambridge, Mass.: Schenkman, 1985), 97.
3. Kanta Chandra Gupta, *Committee on South Asian Women Bulletin* 5, nos. 1–2 (1987): 7.
4. J. M. Jensen, *Passage from India: Asian Indian Immigrants in North America* (New Haven, Conn.: Yale University Press, 1988).
5. B. Martin and C. T. Mohanty, "Feminist Politics: What's Home Got to Do with It?" in T. de Lauretis (ed.), *Feminist Studies, Critical Studies* (Bloomington: In-diana University Press, 1986), 191–212.
6. J. K. Puar, "Writing My Way 'Home': Traveling South Asian Bodies and Diasporic Journeys," *Socialist Review* 24, no. 4 (1994): 75–108.

7. P. C. Jain, "Five Patterns of Indian Emigration," in J. K. Motwani and J. Barot-Motwani (eds.), *Global Migration of Indians: Saga of Adventure, Enterprise, Identity and Integration* (New York: National Federation of Indian-American Associations, 1989).

8. The South Asians who were allowed to immigrate to the United States after the relaxation of immigration and naturalization policies in 1965 were highly educated and financially secure. Over 70 percent of South Asian women entered this country after 1970, sponsored by their husbands or close relatives. They consequently belonged to the middle and upper classes. According to the 1990 U.S. census, over 55 percent of South Asian women have at least a bachelor's degree, and 59 percent of this group are working women.

9. All names have been changed to protect people's identities.

10. Martin and Mohanty, 210.

11. G. Hongo, "Introduction: Culture Wars in Asian America," in G. Hongo (ed.), *Under Western Eyes: Personal Essays from Asian America* (New York: Anchor/Doubleday, 1995), 14.

12. D. Rasiah, "*Mississippi Masala* and Khush: Redefining Community," in Women of the South Asian Descent Collective (eds.), *Our Feet Walk the Sky: Women of the South Asian Diaspora* (San Francisco: Aunt Lute, 1993), 270.

13. L. Mani, "Gender, Class and Cultural Conflict: Indu Krishnan's Knowing Her Place," in *Our Feet Walk the Sky*, 34–35.

14. People who either entered this country as dependent children or were born to immigrant parents and brought up here are considered second generation.

15. P. Agarwal states, "The popular definition of a 'good Indian girl' is one who does not date, is shy and delicate and marries a man of her parents' choosing," *Passage from India: Post-1965 Indian Immigrants and Their Children—Conflicts, Concerns, and Solutions* (Palos Verdes, Calif.: Yuvati, 1991), 51.

16. S. DasGupta and S. D. Dasgupta, "Women in Exile: Gender Relations among Asian Indians in the United States," in S. Maira and R. Srikanth (eds.), *Contours of the Heart: South Asians Map North America* (New York: Asian American Writers' Workshop, 1996).

17. N. Islam, "In the Belly of the Multicultural Beast I Am Named South Asian," in *Our Feet Walk the Sky*, 244.

18. Ibid.

19. M. Gillespie, *Television, Ethnicity and Cultural Change* (London: Routledge, 1995).

20. S. D. Dasgupta and S. DasGupta, "Public Face, Private Space: Asian Indian Women and Sexuality," in N. B. Maglin and D. Perry (eds.), *"Bad Girls"/"Good Girls": Women, Sex, and Power in the Nineties* (New Brunswick, N.J.: Rutgers University Press, 1996), 226–43.

21. A. Bhattacharjee, "The Habit of Ex-Nomination: Nation, Woman, and the Indian Immigrant Bourgeoisie," *Public Culture* 5 (1992): 19–44.

22. Women of the South Asian Descent Collective; Maira and Srikanth; and R. Ratti, *A Lotus of Another Color: An Unfolding of the South Asian Gay and Lesbian Experience* (Boston: Alyson, 1993).

23. U. Narayan, "A Culture of One's Own: Situating Feminist Perspectives inside

Third World Cultures," *Committee on South Asian Women Bulletin* 9, nos. 1–4 (n.d.): 4.
24. Ibid.
25. Agarwal, 52.
26. R. Kumar, *The History of Doing: An Illustrated Account of Movements for Women's Rights and Feminism in India, 1800–1990* (New York: Verso, 1993).
27. *Mississippi Masala* (1992), a feature film directed by Mira Nair.
28. For more discussion on the film, see S. DasGupta, "Glass Shawls and Long Hair: A South Asian Woman Talks Sexual Politics," *Ms.* 3, no. 5 (1993): 76–77; and Rasiah.
29. B. Mukherjee, *Jasmine* (New York: Grove Weidenfeld, 1989).
30. Stree Shakti Sanghatana, *We Were Making History: Women and the Telangana Uprising* (London: Zed, 1989).

Who Am I?

RE-QUESTING IDENTITY

The Language of Identity

—

GRACE POORE

$\mathcal{T}$he term "woman/women of color " is widely accepted in the United States and Canada as a category to distinguish nonwhite women from women of European ethnicity. It implies the politicization of definition—where women whose legacy of oppression as a by-product of racism can assert their difference from the privileged norm of whiteness. In nearly the same way, other terms denoting identity have become a part of nonmainstream and, in some instances, also mainstream vocabulary: such as South Asian, Latina, woman with disability, undocumented resident.[1]

In this essay, I question the ongoing usefulness of terms, born out of struggles to assert ethnoracial identities, to those they are meant to empower because we (as minority and majority) have taken these terms so much for granted that we not only excuse co-optation of culture and the language of identity by white people of varying shades of political and cultural correctness, but we also overlook misappropriation of the struggle for language of identity by communities of color.

To illustrate my points, I will juxtapose different situations within the United States as well as draw analogies between situations in the United States and situations in Malaysia. In a country like Malaysia, where I was born and raised, the multiethnic makeup of society is organized according to cultural grouping. Nonanglicized names are the easiest markers of whether a Malaysian is Chinese, Malay, or South Asian. Our names are particular to our ethnicity: Wong Wai Sum is Chinese, Rani Parameswaran is South Asian, Zakiah Abdullah is Malay. Even with an anglicized first name, it is easy to identify a Malaysian's ethnicity and, usually, religious background by her family name: Jessica Wong, Alice Parameswaran, Phoebe Abdullah. Similarly, Malaysians can almost always identify each other by look: Chinese look Chinese, Malays look Malay, and South Asians—well, we do not look Chinese or Malay; we look South Asian.

Most Asians in Asia, or wherever in the diaspora we may be living, are not familiar with or choose not to use the term "South Asian." I became familiar with the term in the late 1980s and have found it useful for describing people from Bangladesh, Bhutan, India, Nepal, Myanmar, Pakistan, and Sri Lanka. In fact "South Asia" seemed more appropriate than "Indian subcontinent" because it shifts the geographic frame of reference from one country (India) to a whole region made up of ethnically, culturally, and linguistically diverse peoples. Yet I could not quite extend the usage of "South Asian" to Malaysians even if many of us shared the ancestral heritage of the region.

My partner, who is from Sri Lanka, has in the past teased me about calling myself a Malaysian Indian when it is only my mother's side of the family that is Indian, specifically Indian Tamil, while my father's side of the family is Sri Lankan Tamil. The particular irony of this misidentification is that on my birth certificate, I am only defined by my father's Ceylon Tamil heritage, but according to Malaysian census takers, I am only defined by my mother's (no longer Tamil, but generic) Indian heritage. Until 1990 therefore, I was happily calling myself a Malaysian Indian because that was all there was—the only box to check off on all official Malaysian documents: Malay, Chinese, Indian, Eurasian, Other.

Despite the Malaysian policy of collapsing all South Asians into one category, South Asians in Malaysia make sharp distinctions, often acrimoniously, among one another—a practice less motivated by identity politics and more by ethnic chauvinism. This chauvinism manifests itself in the mutual stereotyping that goes on among each of these communities about the other's inferiority (and therefore its own superiority) regarding character, educational achievement, work ethic, and upward mobility.

For instance, during a family visit three years ago, I listened to my brother-in-law, a lower-middle-class (Indian) Tamil, express great pleasure at the Sri Lankan government's intent to bomb Jaffna. He felt justified in this pleasure because he clung to a historic "Indian Tamil" grudge against the high and mighty "Jaffna Tamil" arrogance. My brother-in-law's vituperative relationship with Malaysians of Sri Lankan (also read Jaffna) Tamil heritage is based on collapsing the distinctions between Sri Lanka and Malaysia—and between two historically connected but also different communities, one in South Asia and one in diaspora. My brother-in-law is not an exception in Malaysia or among South Asians there. The old tensions which thrive on his side of the family disturb, but do not surprise, me. My Jaffna Tamil paternal grandmother, for example, was extremely vocal in her disdain for Indian Tamil people, including my mother, who she believed was inferior by virtue of caste and class. Ironically, my mother's family is from a higher caste than my grandmother's, but this was lost on my grandmother, whose views about Indian Tamils were "colored" by the status they were assigned as laborers in the plantation sectors.

Communalist tendencies among Malaysian South Asians are exacerbated by the different "immigration" histories of each community of South Asians who came to Malaysia. These histories determined the kinds of jobs people had, the respect they could demand, and the "power" they could exercise within the confines of British-instituted immigrant hierarchy. The vast majority of Indian Tamils who first came to Malaysia were brought as indentured labor by the British East India Company to work the rubber plantations of British-occupied Malaya. The later wave of Malayalee Indians, who came from the South Indian coastal state of Kerala, were better educated and brought by the British to serve as foremen and middle management on rubber plantations. The Tamil and Sinhala people from Sri Lanka (to date, still referred to by others and themselves as Ceylonese) were not only better educated but also came mainly as immigrants to take up jobs in the British-run civil service—the railways, post office, telecommunications, and electricity board, for example. The Punjabi community from India came as later immigrants in search of new opportunities, many of them farmers who also instituted loan schemes for the growing South Asian population. In time, the composition of Indians grew—Sindhis, Bengalis, Kannada people, and, after independence, a small community of Gurhka people from Nepal, whose men were conscripted by the British army.

Despite this cultural mix, the largest South Asian communities in Malaysia are the descendants of Malayalees, Punjabis, and Tamils from India, and the Jaffna Tamils from northern Sri Lanka. These communities make up the bulk of what is classified as Malaysian Indian. Given the science and practice of keeping inventories, it is not surprising that the British during their occupation, and the Malaysian bureaucrats who have followed since, chose expediency over accuracy in categorizing all those who came "from that part of the world" as Indian.

The relationships among diaspora communities is shaped and mediated by politicized struggle. So is the language of politicized kinship. It was not until I came to the United States and met South Asians from South Asia and those born in the United States that I became increasingly irritated when all South Asians were referred to as Indian because we looked, well, "indian." Suddenly, as a matter of preserving my identity, which hinged on preserving distinctions, I dropped the "Indian" in my introductions and became a Malaysian Tamil. Then my partner's ribbing prompted me to take back the hidden Sri Lankan part of my identity, so that now I am a South Asian of dual Tamil heritage born and raised in Malaysia. This is a mouthful, but at least it is accurate.

Like the term "Indian" the U.S. term "of color" has also become a catch-all expression. It lumps women of various cultures and ethnicities into one group, a consequence of which is that employers, funders, and university officials (to name a few obvious culprits) who prefer some colors over others can simply use the term "of color" as a smoke screen to exclude certain colored people who are on the wrong side of the culture line. What a great way for us to be co-opted into a system that makes us feel included. And what a cop-out on our part to feel we've managed to "colorize" an office, a panel, a department, a funder's agenda—when the concept of multi-ethnicity that should be embedded in the words "of color" is conveniently ignored.

The term "women of color" was never about demographics. It was always a political definition. It was always about agency. Over time, however, it has become a demographic indicator, a matter of constituency. Consequently, irrespective of whether we are in New England, the South, or the California coast, the term "of color" is used like an honorific title to signify "inclusion" when often all it does is indicate, "not all white." But which non-white women are being included, and how many from which community are being included? These questions are never resolved when I see "women of color encouraged to apply." Rather, experience has shown that the job-candidate search has often been aimed at finding one particular color—to balance out the white ratio, not complete the rainbow.

As with "Indian" in Malaysia, "of color" denies distinctions of heritage, immigration history, nationality, language, and cultural practices. It disaffirms the different complexities involved in claiming identities. It connotes sameness when in fact there is multiplicity. It imposes oneness when in fact the dynamics of hegemony also operate among "minority" communities. It implies solidarity where, often, there is division. As with "Indian" in Malaysia, it unregisters internal borders.

"Of color" is not the only suffix to grow out of race politics that is caught in the cross fire between inclusion and nationalism. The term "Asian," which should include South Asians, continues to privilege East or Southeast Asians, rendering South Asians as the nonexistent Asians among Asians and non-Asians alike. I have actually talked to East Asians who do not consider South Asians to "be" Asians because they have never recognized "that part of the world" to be part of Asia. Rather, they see South Asia and South Asians to be "off by themselves somewhere." On the other hand, the term "South Asian," which seemed like a perfect solution to encompass the multiplicity of South Asian communities has slowly been co-opted, frequently by Indians who have fallen prey to and reflect Indian hegemony even beyond the subcontinent. As a consequence, South Asians from Southeast Asia, the Caribbean, or Africa are excluded from and in turn exclude themselves from the gatherings, collaborative projects, and political alliances being formed by an increasingly visible and vocal South Asian community in movements for gay rights, women's rights, and college students' rights in the United States. These exclusions further limit the geopolitical perspectives of the South Asian diaspora in the United States to North America, North American Indian, or both.

Not long ago, a Canada-based South Asian from Singapore exclaimed, "I am so glad that you are from my part of the world!" and began speaking in Malay to reestablish a cultural connection that the North American–South Asian diaspora had not provided her. "I am not a South Asian," she said in despair, "I am a bloody Singaporean. I eat with chopsticks." Although I could understand what this young woman was going through, I also realized in that moment that in Singapore, with its Chinese majority and Chinese ethnic chauvinism, she would not have been treated as just Singaporean but as uncategorically Indian, just as in Malaysia, with its Malay majority and Malay nationalism, I am always treated as Indian. Yet, for both of us, the classification "Indian" back home meant something different from what it meant here, in North America. Back home, our being Indian was reason for discrimination. In North America, being Indian was to be assumed for another.

"Asian American" is another term that was born out of political consciousness and struggle. Within the context of identity struggles in the United States, this naming recognizes the rightful place in the United States of Asians who are American. It also challenges the assumption that many Americans make about Asians as "not being really from the United States" when the reality is that several generations of Asian people in the United States have been born and raised here or became naturalized citizens more than twenty years ago.

While U.S. acceptance of the identity "Asian American" is another victory in the struggle for setting the record straight in U.S. social history, the term, unfortunately, subsumes those of us who are Asian but not American. It imposes a false identity on those of us who have chosen deliberately not to become citizens of the United States for our own political reasons. When I pointed out to one Asian American that I was an Asian but not American who happened to be living in the United States, he retorted, "You are ghettoizing us." Only an Asian who is American could dare to diminish historical and cultural differences and claim my Asia as his. Only an American who is Asian could misappropriate the support I give to Asian-American struggles by refusing to recognize that my being who I am can co-exist with who he is. Only American chauvinism could conveniently glide over the reality that the United States is a superpower that exercises considerable exploitative economic and military power over many countries in Asia.

Cultural chauvinism is a precursor to "othering" our own and ourselves. It is the unspoken, unconscious justification for the East Asian/South Asian split in many parts of the world, the North American Indian/rest of South Asian diaspora split in the United States, the splits among and against people of mixed Asian heritage because of the Asia they do or do not have.

The assumption that all Asians in the United States want to be identified as Asian American negates our right to be in the United States without becoming American. It presumes our allegiance to Asian-American politics, which in some communities is so United States–centric that I've been appalled. Furthermore, dubbing all Asians in the United States as Asian American overlooks the reality that many Asian Americans know nothing about Asia, Asian history, and Asian cultures—making their ignorance about and stereotyping of people from Third World Asia as offensive as stereotyping by Euro-Americans and African Americans.

Not long ago, during a telephone conversation, I heard a new term that apparently has grown out of what I think is the tendency to "morph" identity politics into interchangeable "isms." The term was "woman of diversity." Talk about political chic! Whoever coined "woman of diversity" has "de-identified" the personal altogether. If "of color" turns our shades and identities into an indistinguishable brown, "of diversity" certainly completes the homogenization. The term could refer to a woman of different cultural heritage, a woman with a disability, a lesbian, an indigenous woman of the First Nation, a woman living with HIV/AIDS, or a woman living at the intersection of any number of these identities. Perhaps the intent of this term is to signal difference and acknowledge inclusion simultaneously. Yet all it does is erase difference, which in turn, makes inclusion redundant.

One of these days, there will be (perhaps it already exists) the term "post–woman of color" where "post" could be a statement about race, gender, and/or sexuality, so that "she" need not be woman-born woman or woman with non-Caucasian ethnicity. It has been pointed out to me that—since even before the antiessentialist debates, lesbians have been passing as heterosexual, women of color have been passing as white, and women have been passing as men—the concept of essential woman or, for that matter, lesbian of color is antiquated. Yet the fact remains that women are being raped, battered, and killed solely for being women, and lesbians of color are, as activist-organizer Diana Onley-Campbell observes, "the fringe of the fringe because of our color, our gender, and for many because of our economic class."

For me, language was never meant to be a culmination, only a movement toward transformative change. Yet the language and concepts of identity politics related to race have started to feel static. They appear to lag behind the realities of whom racism affects and how it affects different people differently. They prioritize racism (the racial bigotry by white people toward people of color, backed by institutional, political, and economic power) without confronting cross-racial hostility, racialism, and the violence of racialism.[2]

Take, for instance, the discourse of "claiming our (racial/cultural) identity." In a country like the United States, where capitalism intersects with so-called race awareness, exploiting third world cultures, and spiritualities pass for ethnic chic or multicultural liberalism. Somewhere along the process of asserting cultural pride, people of color have begun commodifying our own and other colored (particularly geographic Third World and indigenous) people's cultures. It is trendy to "credit-card" our way into someone else's spirituality and traditional health practices, with only a surface understanding of that spirituality or health tradition. It even seems permissible to misappropriate symbols and rituals out of context—"I like elephants" becomes the consumerist justification for buying a statue of Ganesh.

If we call white people's appropriation and commodification of our cultural legacies colonization, what do we call it when people of color commodify their own ancestral heritages? After all, people of color do have private import-export businesses in "native" artifacts. We do participate in corporate America's far-reaching multinational exploits. The reality is that U.S. people of color are also involved in the colonization of people in the geographical Third World—be it through economic ventures or military aggression (one cannot forget Vietnam and Iraq).

In the arts and academic arenas, multicultural liberalism comes in the form of funders, publishers, museum curators, educators, communications experts, and racism managers who are not only white men but also white feminists, not only white people but also people of color—men and women, heterosexual and lesbian. I have heard people of color argue that a white blitz is attempting to gain access to the resources and gain control of the discourse on oppression, including racism. I have certainly seen this scenario play itself out in conferences and at the workplace. But by participating in multicultural exchange at the level of tokenism or exhibitionism, we allow ourselves to become color rations; we willingly become Benetton's color-coded people, with all the ethnic accessories, while remaining "minority," on multiple levels.

As women of color in the United States, we are all, on many levels, expendable to a system (irrespective of whether we are undocumented residents or documented residents, whether we are U.S. born or visitors, whether we have a green card or citizenship). For those of us who look or sound foreign, we are even more suspect; we are "aliens." The current anti-immigrant backlash not only throws back in our faces the distinctive identities we have tried to create but also increases arbitrary racist responses—overwhelmingly, but not exclusively, by white people. Anyone not perceived to be "American made" has equal opportunity to be subjected to American xenophobia—be it from the racist/racialist bus driver, school teacher, police officer, immigration officer, college loans administrator, or supermarket check-out clerk. They feel they can now show us how our difference is a threat to their identity—their country, their flag—all this fed by congressional reforms that scapegoat the black, brown, and yellow peoples who come to the United States

As is often typical in situations where some groups of people viewed as suspect by a majority turn against one another to vie for favored status, I have heard some South Asian immigrants, with upper- and middle-class economic privilege, blame "those who can't speak English, have no education, and come in illegally" for giving "immigrants like us" a bad name. They blame welfare fraud on "Latina women with no job skills and African-American women with too many children." They blame high unemployment on lazy people of color—those others who are unlike them. The system has always ranked foreigners as "acceptable" and "unacceptable" by color, class, gender, and country of origin. This callousness is inevitable from a callous system. But when we who are the foreigners start ranking immigrants "like us" against immigrants "like them" and colored people "like us" against colored people "like that," we become dangerous to one another. At the end of the day, the distinctions we make will not protect our rights or our dignity from U.S. politicians and their constituencies who view foreign-sounding, foreign-looking people as "the problem" no matter now well-behaved we might be. At the end of the day, any community of color can end up being the wrong color, with or without citizenship.

I am not surprised that the splintering within communities of color, combined with a virulently conservative Congress and a cleverly choreographed right-wing backlash, has created a despair among many of the activists working on rights for people on the basis identity politics. This despair appears to have also claimed activists who are using cross-issue frameworks not limited to identity politics. A frequent complaint is: "Identity politics are getting in the way of forging a common agenda."

Identity politics are dangerous if they become the goal and not an organizing tool for social justice. Without constant vigilance, they are a process for rights-based organizing that can be co-opted and eventually corrupted. However, blaming the lack of a common agenda on multivocal politics begs the questions: How can we have a common agenda in the first place when significant numbers of people continue to be imagined out of community, strategies, and solutions? For whom would the common agenda be when differences in power and privilege among us have not been acknowledged and acted on in a consistent manner? What is it that is common among us? Who is the "us"? Who gets to talk?

We cannot form alliances by pretending that our differences do not exist. When alliances fail, it is not because there are different agendas but because groups with different identities clash over their different agendas—coalition politics fall apart when identity politics begin, but only when the politics being touted in the first place are infused not with desire for shared power but a "rattle-the-chains" approach to power: whoever rattles the loudest gets to hold the scepter temporarily.

In 1993, at the retreat of the Asian and Pacific Islander Lesbian and Bisexual Network (APLBN), out of 145 participants, seven were native Pacific Islanders. After the last day's plenary, a native woman from Hawaii confronted the network about paying lip service to the "P" in APLBN. She said that Asian members of the network used the terms "Asian" and "Pacific Islander" as if they were interchangeable, when in reality they are not. Her challenge to those of us who were not Pacific Islanders was: Make the network a space for both Asians and Pacific Islanders; otherwise take the "P" out. As a member of APLBN, I feel that the network should include Pacific Islander issues on our agenda whether or not we decide to keep the "P" in our name. There are several reasons for my position, but I will name two. First, Hawaii is a U.S. colony and several of the Pacific Islands have served as U.S. nuclear testing sites. Therefore, Asian-American members in the network have a responsibility to confront their government's actions in the Pacific Islands. Second, indigenous people's land rights are no longer an issue that only white people can be held responsible for. For instance, I have to ask what my responsibilities are toward Native Americans, on whose land I am currently residing. Likewise, Asian lesbians and bisexual women who vacation in Hawaii (as people from so many other cultures do) need to confront the reality that while hotels and tourist companies carry on a booming business on the islands, many native peoples of Hawaii are denied access to their own land, decent wages, adequate medical care, and housing. We also have to confront the reality that within the multitiered society that exists in Hawaii, native Hawaiians are on the bottom—below whites, non-Asian Americans, and Hawaiians of Asian and/or mixed Asian descent. In my opinion then, the goal of the APLB network to bridge the divide between the different Asian lesbians and bisexual women in the United States would be in keeping with bridging the divide between those who are Asians and those who are Pacific Islanders on the U.S. mainland and annexed islands.

During the confrontation by the Pacific Islanders, I remember wondering how many people present that day recalled a similar confrontation by South Asian lesbians four years earlier in 1989. The South Asians were tired of being excluded by East Asians in the network, just as the Pacific Islanders were tired of being erased by the Asians. They had demanded from the network a commitment to stop the East Asian tendency to marginalize South Asians within the network. In 1993, when the Pacific Islanders raised their concerns at the retreat, South Asian concerns had still not been dealt with. So there we were—playing musical chairs with whoever felt most marginalized at a particular gathering until one group exploded, the confronted parties cried and apologized, and business went back to usual.

I use this example to point out that the confrontations by one community of color can sometimes be experienced by people from other communities of color as little more than dramatic theater, an opportunity for cathartic release, where the protest or walkout is reduced to an end in itself. Often this is precisely the outcome when white people are confronted about racism. Perhaps because of this, I expect more from communities of color. I expect East Asians to better understand the myopia of narrow ethnic politics in a multiethnic setting. I expect African-American women to better grasp the parochialism of Afrocentrism in a women of color setting. I expect South Asians to shun racialism any time, all the time.

The language of identity, when shorn of its political implications, is counterproductive to community organizing because it ends up glossing over the intricacies of different struggles. It feeds into reductive politics. It stops us from dealing with the challenge of making present the absences in our midst—not only of diverse voices but also of diverse perspectives. Basically, it mires us in bad process.

To clean up this process, I recommend the following: Counter coalition politics that degenerate into majority rule. De-center those who claim to represent us by banking on their "minority" status as a justification for the abuse of their power and authority. Intervene in situations when "angrier, louder" women use verbal combat to bully other women into silence. Question activism that neutralizes confrontation with imposed harmony. Intervene when "quiet diplomacy" kills issues that are deemed less pivotal to the struggle. Instead of pandering to it, confront the guilt induced by anti-oppression politics. While fighting for the rights we do not have, we need to recognize the privilege we do have and use it to make a difference in the lives of others without that privilege. And for many of us who have no choice, keep on voicing and pushing for accountability even if we are one out of many, few out of a majority.

The struggle to come up with language often mediates other struggles for rights and justice—all the more reason that it reflect the spirit and uncompromising integrity of shared resistance.

Notes

1. An undocumented resident is someone without legal immigration status in the United States and is labeled "alien" or "illegal alien" by the state, media, statisticians, and policymakers. Unfortunately, many activists and so-called progressive individuals also resort to the terms "alien" and "illegal alien" for convenience, with little thought to the racist connotations of such categorizing. Although the term "undocumented resident" is meant to describe a person's immigration status, to become undocumented is in fact to take on and live out an identity that for many people involves discrimination, marginalization, and demonization.

2. I use "racialism" here to refer to the power and position that one community of color uses against another community(ies) of color. In many parts of the world, where there are no white people, the dynamics of racialism work in nearly the same way as racism does in the United States. Despite the ongoing legacy of racism in the United States, I think that racialism is also alive and well here in some parts of the country. Just because white people have the power to be racist

does not automatically mean that different communities of color therefore have no power to be racialist among one another—or should be excused for their bigotry, particularly when it causes and creates ethnic conflict and racialist hatred. Consequences of racialism include discrimination, callous treatment of others, and cross-racial violence. While holding white people accountable for their racism, we must hold each other accountable when there is racialism.

Being "Amreekan"

FRIED CHICKEN VERSUS CHICKEN TIKKA

NAHEED HASNAT

Praise belongs to God, Lord of the Worlds,
The Compassionate, the Merciful,
King of the Day of Judgment
'Tis Thee we worship and Thee we ask for help.
Guide us on the straight path.
The path of those whom Thou has favored,
Not the path of those who incur Thine anger
Nor those who go astray.
Quran, Surah 1:1

God, Don't Let It Be Some Stupid, Misguided Muslim

While I was watching the five o'clock news on April 19, 1995, my eyes tried to absorb the devastation the Oklahoma bombing had caused. The massive bomb, placed inside a rental truck, had blown half of the nine-story Murrah Federal Building into oblivion. One hundred and sixty people died that day, many of them young children. It was deemed the worst terrorist attack on U.S. soil. After I took in the devastation, the next thought that raced through my mind was, "God, don't let it be some stupid, misguided Muslim." The memory of the World Trade Center bombing was once again reawakened in me, as well as in the rest of the nation, as the media, in its pursuit to find the "truth," began to link the incident to an Islamic fundamentalist conspiracy. Muslim-Americans around the country held their breath, waiting fearfully for what might happen if the blame was laid at the feet of a Islamic terrorist group.

A nearly audible sigh of relief went though the Muslim-American *ummah* (community), when Timothy McVeigh was apprehended and charged with the bombing. The handing off of blame did not diminish the horror of the event, but to a community who had already been found at fault, it provided a sense of vindication. Unfortunately, a wave of anti-Muslim sentiment had already begun across the country, regardless of whether the culprits were Muslims or not. The media had once again awakened the fear and mistrust the West holds for Islam.

The majority of Muslims in the United States, and around the world, abhor violence and the use of terrorism. In the World Trade Center bombing, Muslims around the country condemned the actions of Sheikh Omar Abder Rahman and his followers. A few Islamic extremists, in their misguided fervor, believing themselves to be the vanguard of Islam, use terrorism to gain attention in order to push their agenda. The agenda usually has nothing to do with Islam, but with their own political goals. But as common sense tells us, we cannot judge an entire group by the actions of a few. It would be analogous to that of calling all the Irish terrorists because of the actions of the Irish Republican Army. The Muslim community was once again caught in the spotlight, as accusing fingers began to be pointed their way. This incident once again highlighted for me that even though I was born in this country, as a Muslim, I am still viewed with suspicion.

Islam versus the West

Time magazine recently ran a story entitled "The Growth of Islam: Should We Be Frightened?" Mainstream media are helping the spread of negative images of Islam by portraying Muslims as extremists bent on undermining the West. These images are absorbed by Americans who unquestioningly believe these portrayals to be true. In general, there is a great deal of ignorance in the United States about what Islam is. Americans frequently ask questions such as "What is the power of Islam?" "Why is it spreading?" and "What is the appeal of so inhumane a religion?"[1] Islam is identified with direct attacks on strategic U.S. interests, such as Lebanon, and more recently the bombing of the military installation in Saudi Arabia. Such incidents have led Americans to believe that Islam is a fundamentalist religion which threatens the interests of the United States.

Since the Crusades, Islam has been portrayed in the West as an inhumane religion which cuts off the hands of thieves, promotes terrorism, and treats women as second-class citizens. Western countries have long judged societies, in part, on the basis of how they treat their women. They specifically cite what they conceive to be the unequal treatment of women as an excuse to declare the inferiority of Muslims and Islam. Many popular and scholarly articles in the West portray Muslim women as one of two extremes: voluptuous objects of desire, surrounded by servants and slaves, or abject and submissive victims at the mercy of husbands and fathers.[2]

Over the past years, the backlash against the growing Muslim-American community in this country has increased. This has resulted in Muslims' having a guarded and apprehensive attitude toward non-Muslim Americans and mainstream Western society. In addition to the fear of physical violence and the spread of negative imagery by mainstream media, Muslims worry about the greater threat of the subversive influences of an American lifestyle. This trepidation is apparent in the South Asian Pakistani community, which is deeply afraid of losing the next generation to the corruptive influences of the West. The prevailing attitude is that one needs to keep away from Americans and their culture. The first generation of immigrants live the ideology that one may work with Americans, go to school with them, live next door to them, but should not socialize with them on too personal a level. As their children cross these carefully drawn boundaries, the parents are threatened by what they imagine to be the dire consequences of such associations.

The Oklahoma bombing brought to light the difficult road that lies ahead of me in not only finding my niche within mainstream American society as a Muslim-American but also carving out my position as a Muslim woman in the South Asian Pakistani community.

Catch-22

Such a catch-22! Your classmates do not think you are American enough, and your parents think you're too Westernized. At school you are the strange brown kid trying to fit in. At home, you are forgetting your cultural customs, beginning to like fried chicken more than chicken tikka, and choosing to speak English over Urdu. It was 1974, and my parents felt that they were losing their daughter, my older sister, to America. They were having an extremely difficult time trying to find a balance in raising their daughter in a country where they themselves felt alienated. As new immigrants, they were horrified to see the slow Americanization of their eight-year-old daughter, who was trying her hardest to fit into a new country, make friends, and just be normal.

Pakistani immigrants like my parents, who arrived here in the early

1960s, saw their stay here as temporary. The American government was inviting South Asian professionals to fill the increasing demand for skilled workers, and my parents expected to live here a few years, save some money, and move back to Pakistan. They did not attempt to assimilate into mainstream American society and maintained a distance from "Amreekans," whom they saw as part of a too liberal, promiscuous, and atheistic society. San Francisco in the 1960s was a very different place from Karachi, and they were horrified by the hippie movement, speeches about free love, rock and roll music, and the drug culture. When they saw my sister adopting American mannerisms and expressing a desire for American things, they saw her making a choice: America over Pakistan.

When I asked my sister about her experiences of migration, she recalled that she had arrived from Pakistan with a sense of wonder and a twinge of fear. One of her greatest challenges was to pick up English as quickly as possible so that she could fit in and communicate with the other children at school. As all kids do, she soaked it up like a sponge. Soon she began practicing her new skill at home, which my parents tried to discourage strongly, as they did not feel comfortable with the invasion of a foreign tongue into their home. Once you crossed the threshold of our house, all things American were to be left behind, including English. One of my parents' greatest fears was that she would lose her ability to speak Urdu. Not only did they consider Urdu to be a mode of communication, but to them, it also represented a vital link to culture, traditional values, and modes of respect, and to their homeland.

When my parents, in particular my father, began to see a reflection of American culture in my sister, he began to worry that she was losing touch with her religion and culture. The proverbial straw that broke the camel's back was when he overheard my sister saying "fuck you" to some boys from school who had been teasing her about belonging to a Native American tribe. Even at the age of eight, they felt she was becoming too independent and individualistic, separating herself from Pakistani culture. So they did what many South Asian couples did, and still do today. They sent her back to Pakistan to live with my grandparents. It was my father's decision to send my sister to Pakistan. My mother had not wanted her to go back, but her objections were overruled. As the head of our household, and the one on whom my sister's behaviors reflected, my father felt that he had to remove her from the corrupting influences of American society.

My sister still resents the fact that my parents had sent her back to Pakistan and did not take the responsibility to raise her here. Coming back to the United States in her late teenage years was an extremely difficult adjustment. We have met many other women who had the same experience and feel the same way. It is interesting to note that a half-dozen or so children we know who were sent back to their parents' native country, all are girls. Somehow, the task of raising girls under the umbrella of religion and culture was far more difficult for their parents than it was in raising boys. This is a double standard that continues today in our community. Boys are raised with a lighter hand than are girls and are allowed much more freedom.

I was not born until the early 1970s, and my father's work took us to Saudi Arabia, a conservative Muslim state, for a few years. I spent most of my formative years there, and because of its close proximity to India and Pakistan, we traveled there at least twice a year. I grew up with my Pakistani cousins, speaking Urdu and immersing myself in the traditions. Although I went to an American school, my parents did not feel a threat from the international community in Saudi Arabia, as they had in the United States. Living in the close confines of an expatriate community, my parents felt more confident about sheltering and protecting me from Western influences, which the Saudi government tried to filter strictly anyway. In the male-dominated, patriarchal society of Saudi Arabia, my father's role of protector and maintainer of the family honor was firmly established and remained unchallenged.

During my childhood, I never had reason to challenge my father's authority as, unwittingly, my sister had done, mainly because I grew up in a traditional environment and followed the role established for Pakistani women. I displayed all the characteristics of a good, obedient Pakistani daughter and did not try to assert a newfound sense of American individuality, as my sister had done. When I returned to America, my parents' old fears were reawakened. It is a pervasive fear the community has: America will corrupt their youth by tempting them away from traditional values and religious principles.

Woman by Nature, Muslim by Faith, American by Birth, and Pakistani by Heritage

Finding my identity has been an evolutionary process, one that I and other Muslim women like myself have undergone in an effort to define ourselves. Growing up in America in a generation where there were not many other Pakistani-Muslim women to serve as role models, I had to create a means whereby I could establish my own selfhood. I was faced with the dilemma of choosing only one identity by melting all others together or becoming a chameleon by changing my identity to suit the occasion. Entering college, those great years of introspection, I posed the ultimate question to myself: Exactly who was I? Was I an American first because I was born here? Was I a Muslim because I practiced the faith? Was I Pakistani because that is where my family came from? Or was I a woman, as God and DNA had determined me to be?

After much debate and deliberation, I came to the conclusion that I am first a woman by nature, then a Muslim by faith, an American by birth, and a Pakistani by heritage. But why this specific order? God made me a woman; thus I am. My gender defines the core of my being. It determines my physiology: curve of hips and breasts, monthly menstrual cycle, the ability to bear children, as well as hormonal and psychological makeup. Being female established how I was raised—with sugar and spice and everything nice. I was given dresses and fancy *shalwar kameez* (traditional Pakistani clothing) to wear, my hair was allowed to grow long, I was told to walk with grace, dragged into the kitchen to learn how to cook, and taught to be quiet, respectful, and deferential to elders.

However, my primary chosen source of identity comes from Islam. Many scholars would argue that one is Muslim even before the establishment of sex. I was born into a Muslim family and am therefore a Muslim by default. I followed the culturally prescribed Islam of my community. It was not until I was older and studied the religion on my own that I found pure Islam, one unadulterated by South Asian cultural influences. Islam is where I get my guidelines for living, codes of morality, and spiritual well-being. Ask any Muslim, and most will say that they are a Muslim first, for it supersedes any other root of identity. Following the path of Islam takes effort and discipline, for it is not an easy religion to practice. But to the believer it has high rewards, in this world, and in the hereafter.

Next I am an American, because the United States is where I was born and consider to be my home. This country, which began as a haven for immigrants, provides an environment that allows me the freedom and gives me the right to determine who I want to be. I did my duty as a citizen and voted yesterday, as it was a presidential election year. Standing in line at the voting booth, I noticed that even my most apathetic neighbor, who professed not to care about politics, had regained a little bit of patriotic fervor and was eagerly ticking off boxes. Out of self-interest, and for the sake of future generations, it is important to participate in the workings of this country, creating a place which will continue to provide a forum where one can say what one wants to do what one wants to, and practice whatever religion one wants to, without fear of persecution.

Last, I identify myself as a Pakistani. Although I am ethnically Pakistani and love my culture, language, and customs, I know that in the long run, as I continue to live in this country, this cultural identity will eventually fade. I often question how important Pakistan will be to my children and grandchildren. What if I marry a non-Pakistani? My only responsibility, according to Islam, is that I marry a good Muslim, whether he be Arab, African-American, Chinese, or Bosnian. My parents would have difficulty accepting the ethnic differences, but if they are the good, sincere Muslims they profess to be, they cannot quarrel with this basic tenet of Islam.

Many of my friends have married outside the Indo-Pakistani community, and although they share the pleasures of their cultures, they identify themselves as Muslim- American couples. Their children will identify themselves as Muslim Americans. This trend has been noted by researchers such as Marcia K. Hermansen, who notes that intercultural marriages between Arab and Pakistani-American children are occurring more frequently because young people committed to Islam feel that religion should be the main criterion for choosing a spouse rather than ethnic heritage.[3]

So, after all that, I conclude that I am a woman, Muslim, American, and Pakistani. I am an amalgamation of all of these. All identities flowing together to create a whole. At work, school, and on the street I am an American; at home in the community I am a Pakistani; overall I am a woman and a Muslim. It has never been difficult for me to play so many roles, for they are each a part of me and have a place in my life. There are points when there is conflict, when my opinions are too American and Western for the Pakistani community, or too conservative for mainstream American thought. But living in a country which allows me my opinion, I can decide what is right for me.

I and other Muslim-American Pakistani women, raised in America, face a tremendous challenge balancing religious, cultural, and Western values while choosing a path that is comfortable for us. I feel that I am fighting two battles: one dealing with religious and racial prejudices within mainstream American society and the other, at home and in my community, wrestling to keep my rights granted by Islam and denied by a patriarchal cultural system. According to the older generation in the Pakistani community, one is either a good Muslim girl or an "Amreekan." In reality, one can be both, by gaining strength from religion, culture, and the American democratic system.

Muslims as the First Feminists

When I assert my rights as a woman, I stand behind the tenets that were established for women under Islam. Muslims are perhaps the first feminists.[4] Many people, including Muslims themselves, may believe this statement to be an oxymoron. Muslims are feminists? Look at the way they treat their women! It is ironic that the prophet Muhammad, the founder of Islam, was among the world's greatest reformers when it came to the position of women in society. He supported women and, in doing so, was following the word of God, who said to men and women equally: "The self surrounding men, the self surrounding women, the believing men and the believing women, the obedient men, and the obedient women, the truthful men, and the truthful women, the enduring men and the enduring women, the submissive men and the submissive women, the almsgiving men and the almsgiving women, the fasting men and the fasting women, the continent men and the continent women, the Allah remembering men and the Allah remembering women—for them Allah has prepared forgiveness and a mighty reward" (Quran, Surah 33:35).

According to Islam, God sent down his word to both men and women equally, and both have the same duties and obligations of practicing Islam. Both are rewarded and punished in accordance with their deeds. The Prophet said, "All people are equal, as equal as the teeth of a comb. There is not claim of merit of an Arab over a non-Arab or of a white over a black person, or of a male over a female. Only God fearing people merit a preference with God."[5]

When the Prophet established Islam, he abolished such discriminatory practices as female infanticide, slavery, and levirate (marriage between a man and his brother's widow), while introducing concepts guaranteeing women the right to inherit and bequeath property, and the right to exercise full possession and control over their own wealth. At that time, this was virtually unheard of anywhere else in the world. Islam established that a woman is a completely independent personality and granted women rights and sought ways to protect them. Under Islam, women could make any contracts and bequests in her own name and could inherit in her position as mother, wife, sister, and daughter. In addition, they had the liberty to choose their own husbands. Today, our community leaders seek to follow in the Prophet's righteous path and extol his virtues and practices, yet they fail to honor the position and rights granted to women.

When I began the journey to find my identity, I discovered the legitimate rights given to me by Islam and the government of the United States, in contrast to the biased attitudes promulgated by patriarchy and my culture.

To gain an education and independence, I had to justify my actions to a Pakistani community where the elders still held to traditional cultural beliefs about women's subservience. Turning to Islam and quoting the Scriptures, I and other Muslim women pointed out that the first convert to Islam was a woman, Hadrat Khadijah, the Prophet's wife. She is often looked upon as a role model for Muslim women by both men and women. She was a businesswoman and headed her own thriving trading company. She was an intelligent, independent, determined woman and reported to be an excellent judge of character. She was, not surprisingly, highly influential in her community.

Islam versus Culture

Dr. Parveen Shaukat, a period historian, writes:

> The status of women during Muslim rule over the subcontinent, and later under British rule, was based mostly on custom and environment produced by the interaction of various cultural and religious groups. It did not, however, strictly adhere to religious principles. Islam had given woman a very respectable niche, had conferred upon her certain fundamental rights in matters relating to marriage, divorce, and inheritance. Her social dignity and the contributions she could make towards the betterment of life in society were recognized in unequivocal terms. In practice, however, over the Indo-Pakistani subcontinent, [as in] the rest of the Muslim world, women were degraded in social prestige and economic equality. They were mostly confined to domestic drudgery and, draped in Purdah, they were completely debarred from public life. Ideals of chastity and virtue were formulated in a manner that always favored men.[6]

In Pakistani society, the code of honor and shame has been a central issue in community dynamics. A family's honor is linked to the purity of its women, which means not only that the woman must retain her virginity before marriage and be faithful after but also that she ensure that no hint of scandal be cast upon the family through rumor. In order to keep women from being involved in questionable situations, those communities adopted sex segregation.

Veiling and seclusion illustrate the interaction of Quranic prescription and customary practices.[7] Both are customs adopted from the conquered Persian and Byzantine societies and are viewed as appropriate expressions of Quranic norms and values. The Quran does not require veiling or seclusion, it only proposes certain rules of modesty and appropriate behavior between the sexes. Veiling and seclusion were, in the beginning, intended to protect and honor women of the upper classes. Village and rural women were slower to adopt these customs, as they impeded their work in the fields. Over the centuries, veiling and the seclusion of women spread across all strata of society. Women became cut off from the outside world and no longer knew what their true position was as taught by Islam.

Islam advises men to act as protectors and providers of their families. South Asian cultural practices absorbed these ideas and created a system where men became the guardians of women. In addition, the idea that the only way to provide and care for women was to confine and segregate them pervaded those societies. Thus the roles defined for men and women in Islam were transformed into rigid, unwieldy positions created by culture. Women's sphere of influence became the home and children, and men's sphere of influence encompassed the outside world. Men held their position as heads of the household, which automatically extended their rule over women's sphere.

The pressures of a strong, culturally patriarchal system kept women from exercising their rights to education, inheritance, and work. These traditional hierarchies have been transplanted to America, though not to the extreme of total segregation and seclusion. The concept of keeping women out of the public eye as a way of preserving the family's honor is still enforced. Most families have strict limitations and rules governing the actions of the women in the household in regard to activities outside the home. This is not just a carry-over of traditional practices but it serves as a defense against the encroachment of Western influences on the community and its women.

Many men in the Pakistani immigrant community fear that women, especially of my generation, who have been exposed to American colleges and universities, are being brainwashed by American feminism. They blame the Western feminist movement with accelerating the breakdown in the social structure of American society. In their eyes, the free intermingling of the sexes causes the breakdown of traditional male-female relations and leads to promiscuity and other scandalous behavior. Although the Pakistani immigrant community has softened its stance on a woman's right to an education, there is still conflict about allowing girls to go to college. This is yet another way of keeping women from becoming too independent and corrupted by Western liberal thinking. Upon completing their degrees, these women are expected to return to traditional roles: getting married and staying home. When they choose a career, women are believed to be encroaching on male dominance and furthering the breakdown of traditional values. The ultimate fear is that this new-found independence will bring shame upon the family.

The men and women of my generation do not fit into the neat cultural roles of our parents' generation. Brought up and educated in the United States, we have been influenced by Western ideologies of gender roles and responsibilities. We also have had the opportunity to look at the unadulterated versions of Islam and learn about the truth that has been buried by a history of ignorant cultural practices. This has led women to question the roles assigned to them by Indo-Pakistani cultures through the misinterpretation of Islam.

The rights established by the American Constitution of owning property, pursuing an education, and being functioning members of the community had already been bestowed on us by Islam. Hadrat Khadijah, cited as role model for Muslim women, was an excellent mother and educator to her children. Concurrently, she ran a successful business and participated in community and religious affairs. To operate under the rights granted by Islam, Muslim women need to distinguish between women's role as defined by Islam versus the role created for them through cultural practices.

Unfortunately, many women are ignorant of their rights guaranteed by Islam. Most women cannot understand the original Arabic script of the Quran and have relied on the translations and interpretations of others, most of whom are men. They have taken as gospel what the religious leaders and scholars have told them through the centuries. Thus, to a large degree, the backward position of Muslim women today is due to the intentional or unintentional misinterpretations of Islam. Interpreters of the religious texts emphasize Quranic messages that reinforce Islam's patriarchal aspects while they minimize its clear injunctions regarding gender equality, justice, and education. Islam as a religion liberated women, and now the same religion is being used to oppress them. Fortunately, women have begun to question what they have been told for so long and are learning Arabic to explore the correct teachings of Islam. Prophet Mohammed's intent regarding women has been both misinterpreted and misapplied to the point that his sympathies for women's rights are no longer reflected in modern Muslim communities. The Prophet had made women integral to his plan for Muslim education and learning when he declared: "Acquisition of knowledge is obligatory for every Muslim, male or female."[8]

In fact, during the Prophet's time, women were encouraged to study the Quran and take part in religious discussion. True Islam does not impede women's progress, forbid them from being leaders, or prohibit them from working. The Prophet permitted his wife Zeinab to work after their marriage, as she made excellent leather saddles. When Benazir Bhutto became prime minister of Pakistan after winning the elections of November 1988, all who monopolized the right to speak in the name of Islam raised the cry of blasphemy: "Never—horrors!—has a Muslim state been governed by a woman!" The intriguing point is that Pakistani politicians resorted to Muslim tradition only after their failure in the elections. Pakistan is not the only Islamic state that has had a woman head of state. Bangladesh and Turkey also have female heads of state. Women can, and do, become leaders in Islamic nations, cutting through patriarchal traditions that have kept power and politics in the hands of men.

The greatest challenge I and others like me face is to persuade the older generation to rethink what they believe is the position of women in Islam. I am not a scholar of Islamic jurisprudence or philosophy, nor can I claim to make rulings based on Islam. My beliefs and opinions come from what I have researched and read. However, central to the argument of learned scholars and community leaders is respect and understanding for the tenets of Islam. Trying to change age-old ideologies is difficult, to say the least, as change is viewed as subversive. I am a young, female voice questioning age-old practices. Many see me as an American feminist fighting against Islam, whereas I am a Muslim claiming for the rights already granted to me.

Being an "Amreekan"

Being "Amreekan" means balancing religion, culture, and an American way of life. I am allowed to be a chameleon here and take the best of all the cultures and ideologies that went into making this country. America has given me the freedom to practice the rights given to me by Islam and curtailed by South Asian cultural practices. These freedoms are written into the Constitution, which institutes equality for *all* under the law. Part of the responsibility of having freedom of religion, speech, and movement is to promote a greater understanding of Islam and to try alleviate the misconception of Muslim women. I am happy to see more universities offering advanced degrees in Islamic studies and organizations and groups promoting understanding of Islam.

On one hand, Pakistani women are assimilating into American society and are taking advantage of the benefits it provides. On the other hand, they do not want to lose touch with their religion and culture. They cite examples of Muslim women, such as Hadrat Khadija and others, to unveil the status Islam gives women. Such women fought and prayed alongside men and were held in high repute for their knowledge and faith. Women in the South Asian community are uncovering their rights in Islam and finding their niche in both mainstream American society and the Pakistani Muslim community. Like myself, they believe that they can be American yet preserve their faith in Islam and maintain their cultural identity.

Notes

1. J. L. Esposito, *Islam in Asia: Religion, Politics, and Society* (Oxford: Oxford University Press, 1987), 11.
2. Y. Y. Haddad and A. T. Lummis, *Islamic Values in the United States: A Comparative Study* (New York: Oxford University Press, 1987), 1.
3. M. K. Hermansen, "Two-Way Acculturation: Muslim Women in America between Individual Choice (Liminality) and Community Affiliation (Communitas)"; see also Y. Y. Haddad, *The Muslims of America* (New York: Oxford University Press, 1991), 195.
4. J. Goodwin, *Price of Honor: Muslim Women Lift the Veil of Silence on the Islamic World* (New York: Little, Brown, 1994), 203.
5. M. Abdul-Rauf, *The Islamic View of Women and the Family* (New York: York, 1977), 121–22.
6. P. S. Ali, *Status of Women in the Muslim World* (Lahore, 1975), 59–60.
7. J. L. Esposito, *Islam: The Straight Path* (New York: Oxford University Press, 1991), 100.
8. A. R. Doi, *Women in Shariah* (London: Ta-Ha, 1989), 139.

"We Are Graceful Swans Who Can Also Be Crows"

Hybrid Identities of Pakistani Muslim Women

———

Lubna Chaudhry

$\mathcal{T}$his is the story of four young women: Nida, Aisha, Fariha, and Sabeen.[1] All four identified themselves as Pakistani, Muslim, and immigrant. When I met them in the spring of 1992 after I moved to Northern California, they had all been living in the United States for six, ten, or more years. With the exception of Aisha, they were born in Pakistan and immigrated to the United States directly from there.

In April 1992, Nida was in her mid-twenties and finishing up her pre-medical requirements. She lived in the Bay Area with her mother, daughter, and husband. She entered a private medical school in the fall of that year. When we started to interact, Aisha was almost nineteen and in her first year of college. She had moved from Southern California, where her parents were at that time, to live in the same university town as I did in April 1992. At that time, Fariha was around sixteen, attending high school, and living with her mother and siblings in a town in the Central Valley. Sabeen was fifteen and also lived in the Central Valley with her parents and brother. She had been out of school for four years. She had managed to elude school authorities because her family moved around a lot. At one point, she was sent to Pakistan to attend school, but her mother became ill, so she came back to the United States to take care of her.

When I first began to interview and observe the four women, I had some notion of figuring out how they were oppressed as women, as Pakistanis, and as Muslims. The more I got to know them, the more I realized how complex their lives were. There was no neat and simple way I could reduce their multifaceted everyday realities to tidy categories. Their experiences in different family, community, and institutional contexts, and their perceptions of these experiences, were interconnected in some ways and yet very distinctive in others.

Ultimately, I became more interested in analyzing how these young women forged new cultural identities, hybrid identities, in their bids to empower themselves in the community and in school. I was struck by how consistently these women were confronting power structures through everyday practices that could be seen as acts of creative resistance.[2] I wanted to understand more fully how their identities were socially reconstituted by their individual responses to cultural symbols, power relations, and material conditions that limited and shaped opportunities in particular social contexts.[3] I wanted to focus particularly on how, in reconstructing their ethnic identities, these women were bringing together very different traditions of thought.[4]

I grounded my analysis of the identity formation processes in women-of-color feminist theories. I was especially influenced by theories of differential oppositional consciousness.[5] These theories refer to the guerrilla strategies developed by women of color in response to oppressive conditions. Flexibility becomes a key to survival, as women of color self-consciously take up and discard various identities for various lengths of time and in different contexts as an oppositional tactic to power structures.

Here, I will describe the manner in which hybrid identities were deployed by Pakistani Muslim immigrant women to resist power relations in some contexts. The stories of Nida, Aisha, Fariha, and Sabeen enabled me to grasp more clearly the relationship between a multiplicity of identities and resistance to power relations. First, I will present an overview of the relationship between hybridity and resistance that emerged from these stories. Next, for each of the four young women, I will provide specific instances of how resistance was articulated through the maneuvering of hybridity.

The Nature of Hybridity:
Multiple Identities and Worldviews

The concept of hybridity encompasses the fluid state of having multiple, shifting identities which are constructed and differentially privileged in response to contextual demands for alienation and allegiance. It also subsumes the protean condition of possessing multiple systems of meaning. Such multiple worldviews synthesize modes of cognition drawn from traditions of thought or cultural systems generally perceived as distinct or disparate.

The four women saw being Pakistani and Muslim as their primary identities. Their conceptions of what these identities symbolized were, however, contingent upon experiences and encounters in the United States. Fresh interactions opened up the possibilities for different kinds of identification and distancing processes. Their identities and their conceptions of these identities shifted depending on the context and the power relations. In a given context, one identity became more salient than others. Thus, their identities in different times and places could be contradictory or inconsistent.

The four young women were born and raised in families who adhered to cultural values and traditions which supposedly have their origins in different parts of Pakistan. Yet given the history of conquest, multiple colonizations, and immigration through the centuries in that part of the world, the idea that there ever was a pure culture in any region of Pakistan is a myth. Pakistan itself is a legacy of colonialism, as India was partitioned by the British before they left. The identities and value systems of those who live in the country continue to be ruptured and hybridized by neocolonial processes. The four young women and their families already had hybrid cultural systems when they came to the United States. In order to survive and function in the United States, they had to extend and modify their systems of meaning in accordance with previously unknown power relations. Furthermore, at times they had to learn and enact behaviors that sometimes contradicted each other. The hybridization of cultural systems for Aisha, Nida, Sabeen, Fariha, and their families was not additive, in that their worldview, at a certain point in time, could not be neatly segmented into its Pakistani or American parts or traced back to its antecedents.

The hybridity of the four women, then, was dynamic—simultaneously an attribute and a phenomenon, always transforming to suit the needs of changing contextual realities. Identification processes, systems of meaning, memories of past experiences, and power relations intersected in complex ways to produce their particular situations. In numerous contexts specific types of hybridization processes were deemed mandatory by the workings of power structures. The women, for instance, had little choice in refusing their identities as immigrants when seeking health services or renewing their green cards. Still, in some contexts, the women had more choice about the deployment of their hybridity. In such instances, the young women could either conform to the demands of the power relations or resist them through adhering to a certain identity or a particular discourse. It is this exercise of agency in resisting power relations that interested me.

Although the four women identified themselves as Pakistani Muslim women, and were exposed to cultural influences in Pakistani families and U.S. society, each young woman's hybridity was distinctive, rooted in her life circumstances and experiences. Each of the four women was marginalized, silenced, and oppressed in different contexts as a woman, as a Muslim, as a Pakistani, as a perceived minority in the United States, or as a conglomerate of these identities, yet they varied in how they interpreted the same identity labels. Their interpretation of their identification as Pakistani, Muslim, and female, and their hybrid worldviews, were shaped by such factors as family income and status in U.S. society, their links with Pakistan, immigration history, regional and ethnic affiliation, religious sect, age, relationships with family members, peer-group influences, and community, as well as neighborhood affiliations. It followed that their use of their hybridity to enact resistance would also be circumscribed by their particular realities. The potential for resistance, then, emerged from the effects of the same power centers structuring the marginal existence of these women and forcing them to hybridize their worldviews and identities. Nida's hybridity and resistance, for instance, were delimited by her family's higher socioeconomic status, just as Sabeen's were defined by her working-class background. Although they both shared a marginality born of their Pakistani and Muslim origins, this marginality manifested itself differentially because of their different circumstances.

Through the manipulation of their hybridity, the four women, in different ways and in different contexts, articulated resistant practices. The resistance was sometimes a reaction to perceived threats to identities or values. When it was felt, for instance, that Muslims, either individually or as a group, were being attacked, verbally or otherwise, the women performed behaviors which they saw as being true to their Muslim heritage. At other times, the resistance was a strategy to satisfy needs or desires arising from hybrid realities which certain power centers might be attempting to suppress. Although different identities were sometimes privileged in different contexts, it was also very important to the women to be recognized as Pakistani Muslim young women in America, and not just Pakistani Muslim or American. They asserted their "Americanness" in contexts where it was overlooked and stressed their Muslim and Pakistani origins when these were negated. To varying degrees, they were very aware that their being Muslim and Pakistani was influenced by being in the United States. Many times the resistance was an attempt to carve out circumstances where threats were dispelled and needs were fulfilled. Hybridity was then deployed to validate hybridity itself.

Resistance took on a variety of forms. For example, the women, depending on their intent, engaged in acts of cultural translation.[6] They executed behaviors in contexts where they appeared anomalous as a challenge to power relations. These behaviors were drawn from their hybrid repertoire of diverse cultural practices. The cultural practices had a specific meaning within the context of either their personal histories or the history of a group with whom they identified. Another form of resistance was the skillful conformity to the demands of various contexts in order to serve a cause or objective which otherwise would be jeopardized.

Sabeen: Defying Relational Boundaries

Sabeen did not go to school in the United States after fourth grade, and her contact with the outside world was minimal. When I knew her, she spent most of her time in the one-bedroom apartment she shared with her parents and two brothers. In addition to instructing children about the Koran and teaching Urdu at the local Islamic center, she would occasionally go grocery shopping, visit me, or sneak out to see her friend Anna and Anna's mother, Mimi. Despite her limited exposure to U.S. society, she was the only one of the four young women who had an intense, close friendship with someone who identified herself as "just American." Sabeen's friendship with Anna, a white teenager, was an act of resistance on many different levels.

In fact, Sabeen was going against the patriarchal norms her father upheld, values which he claimed were integral to his honor as a member of the Pushtun clan, an ethnic group from the northwestern mountains of the Indian subcontinent. As the daughter of an upstanding Pushtun family, she could violate the family honor by befriending a woman who would be considered immoral by their clan. Women born and raised in the United States were suspect in general, especially non-Muslim women, and Anna did not hide her intimate connections with men. Sabeen incurred her father's wrath several times by allowing Anna to visit her (Sabeen's father sense of hospitality as a Pushtun prevented him from being outright rude to Anna) or by arranging to meet her in the grocery store. She also faced the possibility of very serious repercussions by secretly accompanying Anna to parties and other outdoor expeditions on a few occasions.

Sabeen's friendship with Anna crossed racial, ethnic, and cultural borders. Sabeen had never had a Caucasian friend before, and all of Anna's other friends were white. On the surface the two teenagers had very little in common. The power balance in the friendship could easily have tilted in Anna's favor. Not only was she white and an American by birth, but she was also the one in school. Sabeen, however, asserted her own terms, and despite occasional friction, their friendship survived because of a mutual empathy deriving to a large extent from shared class and gender affiliations. The fondness they both exhibited for slapstick comedy also helped.

Through the building and maintenance of an alliance along class and gender lines, the two teenagers went beyond the racial barriers enacted by power centers to support the status quo in capitalistic societies. These divisions operate by drawing attention away from the common issues of those who are at the bottom of the totem pole. Sabeen and Anna, however, while acknowledging their own limitations, displayed an overall willingness to explore each other's worldviews and learn about each other's realities. Their friendship, thus, challenged power structures that sanctioned "othering" processes which have historically been used to rationalize colonization and slavery of "other" races in different parts of the world.

Sabeen's approach to friendship and the manner in which she expressed that friendship, verbally and otherwise, could be perceived as cultural translation. She exhibited strong feelings toward Anna. Her involvement with Anna and the life of Anna's mother was intense. She displayed and expected a level of commitment from the friendship which was not typically associated with nonsexual relationships between teenage girls in Anna's circle of friends. The politics of emotions which characterized her friendship, according to mainstream patriarchal ideas in U.S. society, were reserved for the domain of romantic love between males and females.

Since she did not go to school for long and she did not work a lot outside the home, Sabeen had not been socialized into establishing the transient, working kind of relationships which are intrinsically bound up with the functioning of capitalist societies. Throughout her life Sabeen had been exposed to very strongly positive views about the value of friendships between people of the same sex. The better-known stories in her clan, which her father related to Sabeen and her brothers, were about men and boys dying for each other. Her mother, and during her childhood her relatives in Pakistan, had narrated to her tales about powerful connections between women or girls and the sacrifices these females made for each other. Sabeen found the script for friendship handed to her through these stories infinitely more appealing than her reading of the dynamics of female friendships in U.S. society. She felt that relationships with boys were given priority. She told me how she had spent years imagining a very close friendship with another girl. Her relationship with Anna gave her the chance to prove her mettle as someone who could love her friend.

In her friendship with Anna, Sabeen deployed modes of relationality that she had learned at home in the United States and in Pakistan through her interactions and experiences with her immediate, as well as extended, family. As a member of an ethnic culture which was segregated on the basis of gender, Sabeen had been socialized into a strong sense of solidarity with the other females in her life. Her refusal to continue her formal schooling reflected, at one level, her determination to ally herself with her mother's sphere. She was close to her father and loved her brothers, but her first loyalty was to her mother and other kinswomen. It was this loyalty, underpinned by the realization that as females they all needed to support one another in a world where men made most of the rules, which she extended to Anna and her mother.

Sabeen was very conscious of her friendship as being transgressive on these different counts. She admitted that at times she was herself surprised at her closeness with Anna. She had never thought she could be friends with a white girl, because all the white girls seemed arrogant, superficial, and uncaring, especially toward other females. Her impressions, based on television representations and observations in stores, were validated by her memories of the bitter experiences she had as a child in school. Both white boys and girls had mistreated her, but she had been more disappointed and hurt by the girls' behavior. Evidently, she had not expected anything better from the boys. Sabeen's responsiveness toward Anna's bid for friendship was, therefore, in itself a hybridization process. She was revising her worldview vis-à-vis white females even as she tentatively reciprocated Anna's friendliness. The hybridization of her system of meaning continued as her friendship with Anna evolved.

Sabeen's friendship with Anna created new identities for her. In keeping with the context, she was, by turns, a friend, a teenaged female, and a lower-class person. She learned she could sometimes identify with a white girl, with someone who did not share her primary identities as Pakistani, Muslim, and Pushtun.

In addition to providing the terrain for complex identification processes, the friendship proved to be instrumental in offering Sabeen the opportunity to reaffirm and reevaluate her identities as Pakistani, Muslim, and Pushtun. Interactions with Anna, Anna's family, and Anna's other friends were at times characterized by a different kind of hybridizing process—alienation or distancing processes which entailed sharp, and often poignant, realizations of her differences in worldview, experiences, and allegiances from her friend. Sabeen extended her repertoire of acceptable behaviors and experiences to be around Anna or to take care of her. She found, however, that certain values were integral to her sense of self, especially when she felt someone expected her to give them up.

In cultivating the friendship with Anna and then honoring the commitment to the friendship, Sabeen was satisfying her need for companionship with someone of her age, as well as her desire to have a meaningful relationship on her terms. The satisfaction of the desire entailed resisting multilayered power regimes. The friendship became an assertion of agency on Sabeen's part. This agency in its turn derived its impetus from Sabeen's interpretation of multiple systems of meaning and the resulting conception of what it meant for her to have a fulfilling life.

Fariha: Romancing Resistance

For Fariha, a romantic liaison, which led to an elopement, became the means to resist her mother's authority. It also became a recourse to demonstrate to her peers at school that she did not have to compromise on the values she held sacred in order to have a man in her life. Fariha's idea of romance stemmed from her viewing of films from the Indian subcontinent. Her ideas were further nurtured by her attempts to read translations of the love stories written by famous Punjabi Sufi poets. In many East Indian and Pakistani films and in most of the Sufi renditions of heterosexual love, passion between men and women is a subversive force capable of undermining the dominant order, for which the segregation of sexes served as a mechanism of control. Such love was untainted by earthly considerations, and its consummation involved a union at the spiritual level. The physical realm was secondary or completely insignificant.

Fariha's mother had high expectations of her. Fariha was her oldest child and daughter, and she saw Fariha as responsible for her younger siblings. She was the one who was supposed to set an example of good performance at school, as well as proper behavior in line with Islamic principles and Punjabi cultural traditions. She desperately wanted Fariha to excel at school and pave the way for the advancement of the family. She also believed she had to be strict with Fariha and protect her from the negative influences of U.S. society. Her husband had not been able to withstand the temptations and the pressures of living in a comparatively less morally structured culture. He had taken to alcohol and womanizing, eventually abandoning his wife and the children. Fariha's mother felt Fariha was even more vulnerable to external societal forces. She was, after all, at an impressionable age.

Fariha, on the other hand, felt pressured by her mother's expectations and frustrated because her mother did not seem to understand the dilemmas and demands of having to cope with more than one culture. She respected her mother's faith in education and agreed, to a large extent, with her attitudes about morality and codes of behavior. Yet even as she judged her peers for being immodest or too invested in the physical side of love, she envied them their freedom to spend more time with people of their own age and to experiment with flirtation and sexually charged situations. Moreover, she craved acceptance by the very same peers she sometimes viewed as immoral. Fariha thought she could obtain that acceptance if young men were interested in her or if she led a less restricted existence. On several occasions, her sheltered existence was the butt of unkind jokes and cutting comments.

Despite the pressures of her situation, Fariha could not bring herself to be involved with someone who did not share, or at least understand, her upbringing and value systems. When boys at her school, at different points in time, exhibited behaviors which she perceived as attempts at flirtation, even seduction, Fariha backed off in trepidation. It was not until she met Razzaq, a young man who had just arrived from Pakistan, that she felt comfortable enough to explore the possibility of a romantic relationship. Razzaq might not have shared Fariha's idealized notion of romantic love, but he was definitely familiar with the conceptions structuring her reality. Besides realizing her romantic fantasies, Fariha's relationship with Razzaq gave her an opportunity to be really close to someone. This closeness was probably only approximated by her connection to one of her aunts before she got married and went to live with her husband. Razzaq was her best friend, as well as someone who could take her away from the miseries she encountered at school and the restrictions she lived with at home.

Fariha's elopement with Razzaq was a bold gesture of defiance. When her mother found out about the romance, her outrage at her daughter's behavior seemed to push Fariha further towards rebellion. She later told me she had insisted on getting married right away because she had not wanted to besmirch her family's honor in any way. Any kind of love that violated honor was not pure and sincere. Her subsequent return to her mother and insistence on an annulment of her marriage were never really clarified. From hints and certain details she revealed during our conversations, my inference was that she had been insulted by Razzaq's attempts to have sexual intercourse even before they had spent time to get to know each other better. She also started to suspect that Razzaq might have married her because she had an American passport.

Within the context of Fariha's life and circumstances, romance became a way of simultaneously resisting and satisfying the demands of various power relations structuring her reality. As a teenager in American society, she felt compelled to assert her sexuality. However, Fariha shared her family's general negative attitude toward the open expression of physical desires. She also shared their mistrust of those who were perceived as too "American" and unable to relate to people at a deep spiritual and emotional level. Despite her internal conflicts, the belief system she had internalized in home and community contexts with respect to love and sexuality prevented her from following the example of her peers.

Fariha constructed her script for romance, to a certain degree, from alternatives offered to her by sources from her region of origin. However, this script was mediated by the immediacy of her American existence. Her take on love and passion reflected her hybrid positioning. Her meeting with Razzaq resulted in further hybridization processes. She initially identified with Razzaq as a Pakistani and as someone who shared her view on love. Such a view privileged emotional closeness. Her romance with Razzaq, therefore, allowed her to assert her agency in the face of the narratives of romance imposed on her by U.S. society and by family traditions. She could have the kind of love in her life that she wanted and remain true to her cultural traditions. Her peers might not believe in the existence of love which was founded on bonds other than the physical, and her mother might not have faith in marital arrangements which departed from traditional norms in that they were based on love before marriage. But she could show them, through her experiences, that she could bring these different worlds together!

Fariha's romance did not unfold in the manner that she had expected. Her resistance to power structures continued when she did not give in to Razzaq's demands. She opted for an annulment because he had disappointed her in certain ways. Again it was important to her that she live up to her own expectations, and she manipulated prescribed scripts to suit her situation. Her family ended up helping her get the annulment. Patriarchal notions which represented daughters as the receptacles of family honor were harnessed to override the obligations decreed by other kinds of patriarchal norms pertaining to the institution of marriage.

Aisha: Transplanting the *Hijab*

The *hijab*, in the initial stages of the spread of Islam, was a strategy adopted by women to protect themselves from unwanted advances.[7] Aisha's adoption of the *hijab* while attending a university in the United States was a strategic, creative response to what she perceived as the undue stress on sexuality in her present environment. It was also a proclamation of her affiliation with Muslims. She especially wanted to represent her identification with young Muslims at college in the United States who believed in the inevitability of an Islamic state where people would live peacefully according to Koranic injunctions. Such a belief was very much a by-product of the anti-Muslim sensibility evident in the Euro-American media and the global political scene.

Aisha's use of the *hijab* constituted an act of cultural translation. Aisha articulated a cultural practice in an incongruous context in such a manner that the practice retained its historicity and the articulation expressed an awareness of and challenge to dominant relations of power. By covering her hair she resisted prescribed norms of beauty in U.S. society, which objectified women. Aisha deeply resented not being appreciated for her intellect and qualities other than her physical attributes. She decided to don the *hijab* in order to discourage attention from the "wrong kind of men." In reality, the *hijab* proved to be an effective screening mechanism, and Aisha was not very happy about the number of suitors and admirers she lost! Although her rationale was anchored in her realization of the historic significance of the *hijab* for Muslim women, Aisha's reasoning was motivated by her own experiences in U.S. society. The subversive potential of the *hijab* for Aisha stemmed from her interpretation of her surroundings. She found parallels between Medina in a state of civil war and the aggressive emphasis on sexuality around her.[8] The *hijab* took on a new meaning in the context of her life and the power relations structuring it.

Aisha's choice to wear the *hijab* reflected an attempt to exhibit a specific kind of Muslim identity. Her family identified themselves as Muslim, but neither her mother nor her sister wore the *hijab*. In fact, her mother strongly discouraged her from covering her hair because she was worried that "educated and modern Muslim men" would not want to marry Aisha. She would be seen as "backward." For Aisha, the *hijab* as an option emerged from her participation in Muslim students' organizations on the various campuses she attended. Within the context of the on-campus activities of these organizations, the *hijab* was a symbol of the Muslim woman's allegiance to the collective empowerment of Muslims in general, and Muslim students on U.S.

campuses in particular. Aisha's decision to don the *hijab* was not just a declaration of loyalty to the causes of these organizations. Still, her interactions with other Muslim students she met in college and university did generate complex identification processes which were instrumental in her consideration of the *hijab* as an option. The donning of the *hijab* did seem to signify a crystallization of her Muslim identity as a form of politics. It was, therefore, not coincidental that she decided to incorporate an expression of her experiences and perspectives as a Muslim woman in her art and writing soon afterward.

Aisha's covering of her hair by the *hijab* could also be perceived as a subscription to patriarchal values generated by power centers within Muslim students' organizations in particular, and larger Muslim institutions in general. Aisha, however, did not regard the *hijab* as oppressive. She argued that pious Muslim men as well as pious Muslim women were supposed to cover their sexualized parts. Moreover, she felt the *hijab* liberated her from certain constraints that characterized interactions between Muslim men and women. She felt men were more comfortable with her, since she did not present herself as a sexual object. The one major concern she had with the *hijab* was that too many practicing, strict, Muslim young men decided she would be a suitable partner for them after just a few cursory meetings.

Aisha did seem to use her *hijab* strategically to gain respect from Muslim men. To a certain degree, the *hijab* ensured her more voice in Muslim organizations. Nonetheless, the *hijab* was politically useful to Aisha only because of her specific commitment to the causes of Muslim women, her oppositional consciousness, and her interest in negotiating with those who shared her religious and cultural affiliations.

However, Aisha did not wholly subscribe to the notion of purdah.[9] She wore the *hijab* but continued to interact with men, Muslim and non-Muslim. She occasionally went through fits of remorse because she felt she engaged in an inordinate amount of verbal flirtation. She admitted that she enjoyed flirtation a lot. She could not understand why men sent her marriage proposals without getting to know her better even when it was pointed out to her that it was customary to do so in Pakistan. The *hijab* guaranteed her a certain kind of safety, as well as a sense of belonging to a collectivity, but she invested it with a hybrid meaning which echoed her own hybridity.

In certain contexts as an act of cultural translation, in other contexts as an act of strategic conformity, the *hijab* represented Aisha's attempts to negotiate her multiple realities. The negotiation involved resisting dominant ideas of sexuality so as to develop and assert alternative conceptions. The negotiation also meant conforming to patriarchal prescriptions for proper behavior based on Islamic teachings in order to perform a Muslim identity. This performance, given the anti-Muslim sensibilities in U.S. society, assumed a political significance.

Nida: Negotiating Formal Education

In order to realize her dream of going to medical school, Nida had a baby at eighteen to appease her in-laws. Her marriage had taken place at seventeen. As soon as she graduated from high school, her parents became anxious about her going to college in a coeducational setting. They did not want her to follow American customs of dating. The Syed clan to which she belonged was generally endogamous. Their tradition dictated that marriages happen as soon as possible after the onset of puberty. Moreover, her father's health was bad, and he wanted to perform his duty as a parent in an expedient manner.

Nida's husband was himself a graduate student. He initially supported her educational aspirations wholeheartedly even in the face of opposition from some of his family members. Nida and her parents had made sure he would be supportive when he was chosen as a suitable partner for her. After Nida's marriage and the birth of her daughter, her mother ensured that Nida pursue her goals by helping out with domestic responsibilities and child care herself. She also provided resources in the form of appropriate babysitters brought to the United States from Pakistan.

Nida's position as the daughter of an upper-class, landed family in Pakistan, which strictly adhered to the traditions of its clan, was responsible, to a large degree, for her early marriage and her obligation to have a child just after the marriage. Nida's socioeconomic class in Pakistan, as well as in the United States, and her status as the daughter of landed gentry in Pakistan also paved the way for the continuation of her education after her marriage. She, however, did have to struggle against customs in the family which frowned upon a married woman's perceived neglect of her husband and child. Her access to higher education and her husband's at-times grudging acceptance of her endeavors had a lot to do with her being financially independent. The business her father had set up continued to generate an income for her even after his death. Her mother also had the time to help take care of Zaini, Nida's daughter, because she did not have to work outside the house.

During high school in the United States, Nida was encouraged by her teachers to aim for an advanced degree because of her diligence and intelligence as a student. After she had transferred to U.S. schools from her colonial-style institution in Pakistan, she did not encounter any academic difficulties. However, college was harder because she had to juggle her marriage and her education. She did not enjoy her overextended schedule, but took it in her stride by thinking of it as the American way of life. In her opinion, it was her determination to learn to function effectively in U.S. society by getting to know the rules for different settings that led to her success at different levels.

Although the privileges of her class positioning facilitated her success in the educational sphere, it was Nida who decided that a degree in medicine would provide her the means of self-actualization. She learned to adapt herself strategically to what was required of her in different contexts in U.S. society and her home. She, thus, resisted patriarchal norms within her clan which restricted her roles to that of wife and mother. She also resisted institutionalized sexism within U.S. society which forces women to make a choice between being a mother and having a career. Her worldview juxtaposed devotion to her family and commitment to her educational career, and therefore reflected her hybridity. This hybridity manifested itself externally in her ability to take on multiple identities in keeping with the demands of the multiple contexts.

Conclusion: The Point of Resistance

During the summer of 1994, I was visiting Fariha and her mother when Fariha said what ultimately became the title of this essay. Fariha and I were getting ready to see an art exhibition at a local Chicana/o center. Before we left, we dutifully went to the kitchen to take leave of her mother. After surveying our all-black "hip" and "cool" denim outfits, Fariha's mother shrugged her shoulders and uttered a well-known Urdu proverb: "When the crow imitates the walking style of a swan, it forgets even its own walk." Fariha laughed and said, "No, it is the other way around. We are graceful swans who can also be crows. We remember all the ways of walking."

Underlying the resistance exhibited by the four women here was a consciousness of the effects of power relations. This consciousness was born out of their hybridity, their capacity to slip in and out of cultural systems. Of course, with the exception of Aisha, they did not couch their consciousness in terms of the theoretical language about "centers of power" and "marginality" that I am employing in this chapter. Neither was their consciousness constant in all contexts, nor was it complete in that they were always aware of the influences of power regimes in their entirety.

Nevertheless, fragmentary or otherwise, the consciousness of oppressive power structures and their effects led them to articulate practices of resistance. The practices were assertions of their agency, their ability at least to attempt to construct their own realities and control their lives. The conceptions of what constituted resistance and agency were shaped by the array of discourses available to them in different contexts which still surrounded them or which they had internalized during the course of their lifetime. The articulation of resistance and assertion of agency were tied up with their hybrid identities and hybrid worldviews. These complex relationships could only be adequately understood if scrutinized from within the context of their lives.

Although Aisha deployed the *hijab* (an icon transplanted from the Middle East) in her enactment of resistance, the mode she employed was the one that most obviously could be recognized by Euro-American standards. Her resistance, in its utilization of a piece of clothing to perform identity and express a viewpoint, was reminiscent of the methods employed by youth subcultures in Western contexts. Moreover, she was an active participant in Muslim organizations that followed Western-derived norms of resistance.

The resistance exhibited by Nida, Fariha, and Sabeen did not fall under the rubric of organized politics in the sense in which it is understood in common parlance in the United States. Yet in their everyday lives they continued to conform to or defy power relations in accordance with their perceived needs and desires. In doing so, they highlighted the multiplicity in the effects of the centers of power, as well as the potential for everyday practices to challenge these centers. Although they were not engaged in supporting political agendas in the style accepted as bona fide resistance, they were hardly passive victims of the power structures around them.

The resistance displayed by the four young women, organized or otherwise, points to the existence of spaces on the margins where the effects of power structures are attenuated. The four young women, through engagement with collectivities, acts of cultural translation, as well as strategic conformity and defiance in different contexts, effectively executed resistance to oppressive power structures. Their stories clearly illustrate that through a strategic use of hybridity, multiple systems of thought can be deployed to subvert power relations.

Notes

1. All names have been changed to preserve anonymity.
2. My conception of everyday practices as creative resistance was developed through

a reading of M. de Certeau's *Practice of Everyday Life* (Berkeley: University of California Press, 1984).

3. M. P. Smith and B. Tarallo, "The Postmodern City and the Social Construction of Ethnicity in California," in M. Cross and M. Keith (eds.), *Racism, the City, and the State* (London: Routledge, 1993), 61–76, write about how cultural identities of new immigrants are socially reconstituted when they construct themselves as "social actors" who "respond to the material conditions, semiotic codes, and power relations shaping the opportunities and constraints of a historically specific time and place" (61).

4. S. Hall, "New Ethnicities," in J. Donald and A. Rattansi (eds.), *Race, Culture, and Difference* (New York: Sage, 1992), 252–59, refers to this reconstruction of diasporic identities as "new ethnicities." H. Bhabha, "The Third Space: Interview with Homi Bhabha," in J. Rutherford (ed.), *Identity* (London: Wishart, 1990), 206–21, writes of this cultural reconstitution as cultural hybridization, a process which involves the "yoking together of unlikely traditions of thought" (212). Those engaged in hybridization processes are hybrids.

5. According to C. Sandoval, "U.S. Third World Feminism: The Theory and Method of Oppositional Consciousness in the Postmodern World," *Genders* 10 (1991): 1–24, theories of "differential oppositional consciousness" refer to the "grace, flexibility, and strength" developed by women of color as a response to oppressive conditions, which enable them "to confidently commit to a well-defined structure of identity for one hour, day, week, month, year," and "to self-consciously transform that identity according to the requisites of another oppositional ideological tactic if readings of power formations require it" (15).

6. Bhabha sees hybridity and cultural translation as inextricably linked. Hybridity is the "third space which enables other positions to emerge, . . . sets up new structures of authority, new political initiatives, [and] a new area of negotiation of meaning and representation" (207). Hybrids, those in a state of hybridity, engage in acts of cultural translation whereby certain behaviors are executed in temporal and spatial realms which have been hitherto atypical contexts for those actions.

7. The Arabic word *hijab* refers to what is commonly called the Muslim veil in Western contexts. It is a scarf worn by some Muslim women to cover their hair.

8. F. Mernissi, *The Veil and the Male Elite: A Feminist Interpretation of Women's Rights in Islam* (New York: Addison-Wesley, 1991), traces the institutionalized adoption of the *hijab* by Muslim women to the early years in Islamic history, when there was a civil war in Medina, a city in Saudi Arabia. She argues that women had to don the *hijab* as a protective strategy because unsafe conditions were created by masculinist warring agendas. During the civil war, the street became a space where the raping of women was permitted, and one way women could avoid being persecuted was to cover themselves.

9. Purdah in a broad sense encompasses traditions in Islam which decree segregation of the sexes and the covering of sexualized body parts.

Sexual Exiles

SURINA KHAN

I don't know whether my grandmother is dead or alive. I can't remember the last time I saw her. It must have been at least ten years ago when I was in Pakistan for an extended visit. She was my only living grandparent, and her health was beginning to fail. Every once in a while I think she's probably dead and no one bothered to tell me.

I'm completely out of touch with my Pakistani life. As a kid, I remember being constantly reminded that I was different by my accent, my brown skin color, the smell of the food we ate, and my mother's traditional clothing. And so, I consciously Americanized myself—I spent my early childhood perfecting my American accent; my adolescence affirming my U.S. identity to others; and my late teens rejecting my Pakistani heritage. And now, at the age of twenty-nine, I'm feeling the void I created for myself.

I can hardly speak Urdu, my first language. I certainly can't read or write it. I have no idea how many cousins I have. I know my father comes from a large family—eleven brothers and sisters—but I don't know all their names. I've never read the Koran, and I don't have faith in Islam.

Sometimes I think of what my life would be like if my parents hadn't migrated from Pakistan to the United States. We moved to Connecticut in 1973 when I was five. At the time my uncle (my father's older brother) was running for prime minister against Zulfiqar Ali Bhutto. Although my parents were not politically active, their relation to my uncle put us in danger, and we left everything—our home, our heritage, our belongings. We left in the middle of a cold November night in a mustard-orange-colored van which my father drove through the huge black mountains of the Khyber Pass to Afghanistan, where we stayed for five days. When we finally arrived in the United States three months later—after living in Iran, Spain, and England—I was constantly reminded I was different by my accent, my brown skin color, and my mother's traditional clothing. I consciously became Americanized quickly, and when, in 1978, my parents thought we kids were becoming too Westernized, they sent us back to Pakistan, where I felt like an American on foreign soil.

Most of my family has since moved back to Pakistan, and up until eight years ago, when I came out, I went back somewhat regularly, but always with a little ambivalence. I never liked going back. It made me feel stifled. Constrained. People were always talking about getting married. It was either, "Oh, you're almost old enough to start thinking about finding a nice husband," or "When are you getting married?" Now I imagine they'd say (with disappointment), "You'll be an old maid."

Fortunately, my family is more liberal than most Pakistani society. By U.S. standards, that translates as conservative (my mother raised money for George Bush). In any case, I was brought up in a family that valued education, independence, integrity, and love. Unlike some of my cousins, I never worried about my parents arranging a marriage for me even though I saw several of my first cousins arranged into marriages, sometimes with one another. Once I went to a wedding where the bride and groom saw each other for the first time when someone passed them a mirror *after* their wedding ceremony and they both looked into it at the same time. That's when I started thinking my family was "modern." Unfortunately they live in a fundamentalist culture that won't tolerate me.

I can't even bring myself to go back for a visit. The last time I was back was eight years ago for my father's funeral. My mother asks me to come visit every time I talk to her. And I tell her I'm too busy, that I can't get away. Five years ago I finally answered her truthfully. I told her that I didn't like the idea of traveling to a country where lesbians get a hundred lashes in public. And more important, I didn't feel comfortable visiting Pakistan when she and I had not talked about anything important in my life since I had come out to her.

Pakistan has always been my parents answer to everything. When they found out my sisters were smoking pot in the late 1970s, they shipped all of us back. "You need to get in touch with the Pakistani culture," my mother would say. When my oldest sister got hooked on transcendental meditation and started walking around the house in a trance, my father packed her up and put her on a plane back to the homeland. She's been there ever since. Being the youngest of six, I wised up quickly. I waited to drop my bomb until after I had moved out of the house and was financially independent of my family. If I had come out while I was still living in my parents home, you can bet I'd have been on the next flight to Islamabad.

When I came out to my mother, she suggested I go back to Pakistan for a few months. "Just get away from it all. You need some time. Clear your head," she begged. But I knew better. And when I insisted I was queer and was going to move to Washington, D.C., to live with my then-girlfriend, Robin, my mother grasped at straws. "You and your lover better watch out! There's a large Pakistani community in D.C., and they'll find out about you. They'll break your legs, mutilate your face." That pretty much did it for me. My mother had just validated all my fears associated with Pakistan, and I cut off all ties with the community, including my family. Pakistan became synonymous with homophobia.

My mother disowned me when I didn't heed her advice. But a year later, when Robin and I broke up, she came back into my life. Wishful thinking on her part! Though I do have to give her credit, not only for nurturing the strength in me to live by my convictions with integrity and honesty but also for eventually trying to understand me. I'll never forget the day I took her to see a lawyer friend of mine. My mother was on the verge of settling a lawsuit started by my father before he died and was unhappy with her lawyer. I took her to see Maggie Cassella, a lawyer based in Hartford, Connecticut, where I was again living. "I presume this woman's a lesbian," my mother said in the car on the way to Maggie's office. "Yes, she is," I replied, thinking, Oh no, here it comes again. But my mother took me totally by surprise: "Well, the men aren't helping me, I might as well go to the dykes." I didn't think she even knew the word "dyke." Now, *that* was a moment.

Her changing attitude about my lesbian identity was instilling a desire in me to reclaim my Pakistani identity. The best way to do this, I decided, would be to seek out other Pakistani lesbians. I barely knew any Pakistani people aside from my family, and I certainly didn't know any, or even know *of* any, Pakistani lesbians. I was just naive enough to think I was the only one. Having rejected my culture from a young age, when I came out, I identified only as a lesbian. I knew other lesbians, but I didn't know any Pakistani lesbians, and so it didn't occur to me to identify myself as a Pakistani lesbian. And in my zeal to be all-American, I threw myself into the U.S. queer-rights movement—not realizing (unfortunately) that there is an active South Asian gay and lesbian community in the United States—and many of us are here because we're able to be queer and out in the Western world, where at least there is an active, visible, and comparatively safe queer liberation movement.

In Pakistan, for the most part, gay people are closeted, and the likes of a queer community as we know it in the United States is nonexistent. Pakistan is not a safe place to be out. In Pakistan, sex is an issue that is rarely discussed, and the discussion of homosexuality is literally unheard of. There is no language for it. The repercussions of this silence for us South Asian queers living in the Western world is enormous, often resulting in a community that is not only invisible but also isolated from one another and underrepresented in media, literature, film, and politics.

South Asian culture is rampant with homophobia—but a homophobia that is so silent that people literally don't know the language for homosexuality. In South Asia, homosexuality is viewed as a Western phenomenon even though images of gays and lesbians have been a part of the history of the subcontinent for thousands of years. In the temples of Khajuraho and Konarak in India there are images of women together and men together in intimate positions. One temple carving depicts two women sharing an intimate touch, while another shows four women engaged in sexual play. There are also references to homosexuality in the *Kama Sutra* on the varieties of sex. Babar, the founder of the Mughal dynasty in India, is said to have been gay, as was Abu Nawas, a famous Islamic poet. The fact is that homosexuality is as native to South Asia as is heterosexuality. But the culture puts a great deal of pressure on South Asian women, especially, to reject our sexual identity—causing us to reject South Asian culture and, if we have the means, to assimilate into Western culture, leaving little time or energy to network actively and learn from other South Asian queers in order to build a strong and vibrant and visible South Asian queer community.

Despite the odds, I started my search for queer people from South Asia—and I found them, all across America, Canada, and England. Connecting with this network and talking with other queer South Asians have begun to fill the void I'd been feeling. But just as it took me years to reject my Pakistani heritage, it will likely take me as long, if not longer, to reintegrate my culture into my life as it is now.

I may not be ready to go back to Pakistan, but I am ready to start examining the hostility I feel toward a part of myself I thought I had rejected long ago. Examining my hostility toward my culture has led me to other South Asian lesbians who have experienced a similar sense of hostility and isolation.

While many South Asian lesbians living in the United States are visible and out, many more continue to live their lives in the closet. Finding South Asian women to be interviewed for this essay was a much more difficult task than I anticipated, with half the women interviewed refusing to use their full names—some out of "respect" for their parents and others because they are not U.S. citizens, and as lesbian "aliens," they are afraid of being deported by the U.S. government, even though they are out and visible in their communities. As a result, most of the names of the women interviewed for this essay have been changed to protect their identity.

South Asian culture is extremely uncomfortable with lesbian lives, and many believe homosexuality is a Western phenomenon. "I tried to tell my father that there is a history of homosexuality in India, and he refused to believe me," says Fauzia, a filmmaker who was born in Calcutta, India, and migrated with her family to Connecticut in 1972, when she was four. "He is convinced that it is a Western creation," she adds.

For South Asian lesbians living in the Western world—we have one foot in a culture where people structure identities from sexuality and the other foot in a subcontinent culture where women are not seen as sexual beings. For Ayesha, who was born and raised in the United States, albeit in a very traditional Pakistani environment, her lesbian identity is something she has trouble with. "I don't feel comfortable with my lesbian identity," she says. "I'm very Pakistani even though I've tried to reject it. I was raised to be *not sexual*."

Saira, a lesbian activist, had her first lesbian relationship when she was thirteen. But it wasn't until she was in her twenties that she learned the language to define that relationship. As a young girl living in Calcutta, she was taught *not* to think of herself in sexual terms—a struggle many South Asian lesbians share.

For many upper-class or privileged South Asian lesbians, education gave us the language to understand homosexuality. "I had sexual relationships with women since I was twenty-two, but I saw myself as straight because I wasn't aware of such a thing as a lesbian identity," says Maya Devi, a university professor who is struggling with her status as an illegal immigrant. "I realized that I had an option after reading a lot about lesbian feminists and about gender oppression, and that's when I finally came out." Saira had a similar experience. "I didn't know I was a lesbian although I had my first relationship with another woman when I was thirteen," she says. "I didn't identify as a lesbian because I didn't know what a lesbian was. We're talking about India. Sexuality is not something that one identifies in India."

"I may not have known I was a lesbian when I lived in India," stated Saira, "but I knew I was different and I knew that I would not survive there," she adds, stressing that when she was seventeen, she "lobbied hard" for her parents to migrate to the United States, where she knew she would be able to educate herself in the Western tradition and ultimately acknowledge her difference.

An Isolated Community

The feeling of isolation for South Asian lesbians seems to be universal—both from the South Asian community of family and friends, who usually don't respond well to lesbian identities, and from the Western lesbian community, which has very little understanding of South Asian history and culture. Like any other ethnic or social group that surrounds itself with others who share commonalities, South Asian lesbians ultimately feel a need to seek out other South Asian lesbians to form ties and affirm their South Asian lesbian experience in hopes of forming a strong and active community. However, this is no easy task. "We're so invisible," says Poonam, who migrated to the United States when she was twenty to pursue her education. "Not only because many of us are in the closet, but we're so isolated from one another. I don't know how to get in touch with other lesbians from South Asia," she adds.

Many of us assimilate so completely into the dominant U.S. culture that we have a difficult time connecting with other South Asian lesbians, further perpetuating the invisibility of the South Asian lesbian community. Ironically, one of the most influential lesbians in the broader gay and lesbian political movement, Urvashi Vaid, who as executive director of the National Gay and Lesbian Task Force from 1989 to 1992 and author of *Virtual Equality: The Mainstreaming of the Lesbian and Gay Liberation Movement*, is perhaps one of the best-known lesbians in the United States—and she is also South Asian. Her integral role in gay and lesbian politics is probably partly due to her assimilation into U.S. culture. "For all intents and purposes, I'm extremely Americanized," says Vaid, who emigrated with her family from India to the United States at the age of eight in 1966. And like millions of immigrant children whose parents came to the United States for jobs and educational opportunities, she was part of a family that very much identified with its heritage and culture while she assimilated into the U.S. culture. "I grew up in a conventional household, where we spoke Hindi, Punjabi, and English," says Vaid. "We grew up as children with all these different values and dual standards by which we were measured. One is the standard of the culture that you're living in and the other is the standard of the culture your parents are living in."

For Fauzia it was only after she came out that she felt more connected to South Asian culture. "We downplayed the Indian culture, and there was this whole issue of assimilating," she says. "You couldn't be too Indian because you'd get made fun of." While growing up in Connecticut, Fauzia says she didn't know many other Indian people, until she moved to San Francisco in 1989, when she was introduced to other Indian lesbians and bisexual women through Shamakami, a South Asian lesbian, bisexual women's group. And while there are a number of South Asian newsletters and organizations in the United States, Canada, and England, including San Francisco–based Trikone, SALGA (South Asian Lesbian and Gay Association) in New York, MASALA in Boston, and Khush in Washington, D.C., it has only been in the last few years that women have had a visible and active presence in these organizations.

Some say the male dominance of these organizations was due in part to the social focus of the organizations. And since as South Asian lesbians, we face added obstacles in coming to terms with our sexual orientation—we have to liberate ourselves as lesbians not only in a straight society but also in a patriarchal and misogynist culture—our priorities are more political than social. "When we were doing political activism within the organization, we saw the women's membership at an all-time high," says one member of SALGA who chose not to be identified. "When the group took a more social focus, the women seemed to drop out." Initially these groups served, and still do to a large extent, as a social support group—a way for other South Asians to meet and share stories and overcome their isolation. Many of the groups meet in restaurants and plan social activities in comfortable settings—often Indian restaurants.

A Different Kind of Oppression

Many South Asian lesbians agree that white U.S. culture is more accepting of certain kinds of Asians. Many Asians don't feel the same kind of outrage about color that some Latina and African-American women feel. "As a South Asian woman with my class background and my level of education, I am accepted more readily," says Maya. "There is a tendency to exoticize me," she adds. "I'm foreign and I'm not black. That makes a big difference," she adds.

Urvashi Vaid agrees. "In my experience I have found that people are fascinated by India. There is an exotic element. They are curious," she says. "And although I have had experiences of racism in my life and in the work I have done in the gay and lesbian community, I don't think it's anywhere near the extent that some of my black lesbian and gay friends have."

And even with the obvious cultural differences—the accent, the food, the language, and the clothing—many South Asian lesbians don't relate to issues that other people of color with similar cultural differences feel. "When I first came out, I didn't think I had any issues as a woman of color," says Poonam. "People assume that all women of color have cultural experiences that are similar," she adds.

Maya agrees. "When I came out, I identified only as a dyke, and that started to change when I began understanding myself as a woman of color," she says. "I was a woman and I was a lesbian. Race had nothing to do with it." And it wasn't until she moved to the United States at the age of twenty-eight that she started identifying as a woman of color, because, as she says, "In India there is no such thing as a woman of color."

An Underrepresented Culture

As the South Asian lesbian community continues to become more visible, there are still very few representations of South Asian lesbian lives. In fact, in 1993 Alyson Publications published the very first South Asian gay and lesbian anthology, *A Lotus of Another Color*, in which gay men and lesbians from India, Pakistan, and other South Asian countries tell their coming-out stories. Still, many of the writers in the anthology did not use their real names, feeling a need to hide their identities. And editor Rakesh Ratti has mentioned that the response to a call for submissions was disappointing.

However, South Asian literature continues to emerge, but nowhere near in the same quantity as African American or Latina literature. Other representations of South Asian literature include *Bombay Talkie*, a novel written by Ameena Meer and published by Serpent's Tail (1994); *Out on Main Street*, a collection of short fiction by Shani Mootoo and published by Press Gang Publishers (1993); *Our Feet Walk the Sky*, a collection of South Asian women's writing, including several lesbian-oriented pieces, edited by the Women of South Asian Descent Collective and published by Aunt Lute Books (1993); and *In Translation*, a novel by Annemarie Jagose published by Victoria University Press (1994).

Very few images of gay and lesbian South Asians exist in the television and film industry. For lesbian filmmaker Pratibha Parmar, a Kenya-born Indian who grew up in England, representing positive images of South Asian lesbians and gay men in her films is very important. "All we consistently get are negative images of ourselves, images and stereotypes that are not true to ourselves," says Parmar, whose works include *Sari Red*, a short piece that couples a lyrical narrative with haunting images exploring lethal racism in England; *Memory Pictures*, a video about gay South Asian photographer Sunil Gupta; *Flesh and Paper*, a film about lesbian poet and writer Suniti Namjoshi; and *Khush*, a film about gay and lesbian South Asians.

Parmar says her experience of being Asian in England made her become involved in antiracist struggles and says her strength comes from "meeting younger South Asian lesbians and gays who say that it's very important for them to see what I'm doing and to be out saying the things that I say." Parmar continues to make films relevant to the lesbian and gay South Asian experience mainly because of her anger at how the mainstream media depicts South Asian women as "meek and mild victims of arranged marriages."

Creating Community

South Asian lesbians continue to discover the diversity within our communities and, in trying to live, continue to confront the contradiction of the many identities that make up the South Asian lesbian community. The creation of safe spaces and support groups has made a difference and will continue to do so. In a society where South Asians are either invisible or alien, South Asian queer organizations are charged with creating safe spaces. However, lesbians in North America, in an effort to establish more supportive communities and in response to the gender inequalities in organizations like Trikone and SALGA, have developed their own networks through women's groups like Shamakami and, before that, Anamika. For many South Asian lesbians these organizations and networks have transformed our social structure. Pratibha Parmar recalls that when she first came out in England in 1976, "there were very few South Asian lesbians and gays around. We would travel hundreds of miles to meet. Now we have Shakti, a very strong, over 1,000–member lesbian and gay group with a newsletter, regular meetings and socials."

As South Asian lesbians, we are faced with the challenge of coming out to a culture that threatens to reject us and in a society where the South Asian community has been, and still is to a large degree, invisible. Even with the encouraging signs of social and support groups for South Asian lesbians, as well as South Asian lesbian literature and images of South Asian lesbians in film and media, there is still a haunting sense of isolation for many lesbians who are out and active in their communities. "I still feel very isolated," says Poonam, "I can count on one hand the South Asian lesbians that I have met in the eight years since I've come out."

Meeting other South Asian lesbians is not a solution to the isolation we feel. I have met many South Asian lesbians in trying to reconnect with my Pakistani culture, yet I still feel disconnected from it. The years I spent assimilating myself into the dominant U.S. culture cannot be stripped away merely by involving myself in the lesbian and gay South Asian community. Perhaps in continuing to integrate my different identities, I will be able to embrace my Pakistani heritage. I cannot deny my U.S. identity, just as I cannot deny my Pakistani identity. I am an American. I am Pakistani. I am an immigrant. And I am a lesbian.

Naming Desire, Shaping Identity

TRACING THE EXPERIENCES OF INDIAN LESBIANS IN THE UNITED STATES

NAHEED ISLAM

I know not any word for myself
but Khush
and even that is a mocking translation
I cannot envision
living in India
persevering in my "American" Individualism
loving a woman
building a home with her
defying family, friends
ignoring disapproval, silence
and still speaking, still fighting
to prevent silence.
      A. V., "A Response to 'A Room of One's Own'," *Shamakami*

*T*he fact that there is no word for lesbian in Bengali, Hindi or Urdu is a linguistic clue to cultural and structural organization of sexuality in the respective societies.[1] It is a reflection of the absence of an identity constructed primarily around sexuality. Gay identity is a rather new Western construction problematized by issues of gender, class and race. Historically this identity has been constructed by middle-class gay white men. As a result, it has placed them at the center and marginalized lesbians, racial minorities, and "other classes." Even when the concept is expanded to include white women, the exclusion of other racial and cultural groups remains. Indian-American lesbian is a complex identity which attempts to combine gender, sexuality, and national, cultural, and ideological constructions of an individual within a cohesive category.

Indian lesbians in the United States find themselves caught in a complex web of social and political structures which they must traverse. They are faced with different structures or systems of reference within which they must operate and express themselves. They categorize their lives in binary terms: life with their families in India and the "independent" lives they have created for themselves in the United States. Here they have defined a part of their identity through their sexuality, but they are not always able to accept the mainstream American construction of lesbian identity or translate it into their lives. In this chapter I will examine the changes in sexual expression experienced by upper- and middle-class (primarily) Indian immigrant women as they move from their home country and build lives in the United States. I will be scrutinizing situations in which people cross boundaries of social and economic systems and construct their identities in innovative ways. I will propose that in order to understand an Indian, or "South Asian," American conception of homosexuality one must reconceptualize the term gay/lesbian identity by examining the context in which it is named.[2] Sexuality is expressed within historically and culturally specific contexts. Women in India, depending on their caste or class, age, kinship terms, and religion, express their sexuality in relation to their social and economic position. As they move within and out of these structures, those relationships change. Therefore, immigrant women construct transnational concepts of sexuality, identity, and community.

For this research project, I used a combination of interviews and analysis of secondary data. Five Indian immigrant, urban, and middle- and upper-class women were interviewed. By virtue of their class and educational privilege, all of these women had come to the United States by the age of eighteen to study. They all became politically active in the United States on different issues. They have all engaged in a struggle with the category lesbian as an identity.[3] The three secondary sources used to explore patterns of self-definitions and related issues are: (1) *Trikone*, a Bay Area gay and lesbian newsletter, (2) *Anamika*, a lesbian newsletter, and (3) a recently published anthology of South Asian writings, entitled *A Lotus of Another Color: An Unfolding of the South Asian Gay and Lesbian Experience*.[4] These narratives are by women from India, Bangladesh, and Pakistan. Throughout the chapter I will refer to both the interviews and secondary narratives as the "informants/participants" of this study. I will distinguish between the two forms of narratives by citing their origin.

My own position as an interviewer/researcher for this project was both positive and problematic. I am a Bangladeshi heterosexual woman asking Indian women about their homosexuality. Our common ground was our class background and shared experience of growing up in South Asia and then moving to the United States. Our cultural reference point was similar. But it was also problematic for both my formulation of the research questions and interpretation. I was aware of the possibility of imposing my heterosexual interpretation of events occurring within close gender-based communities. There were questions raised about my intentions in conducting such research and my "straight" privilege and heterosexual perspective/interpretation. This tension was never resolved; rather, it formed the premise of the project by providing the grounds on which we raised questions regarding the boundaries of sexual identity.

Woman Loving Woman

It seems to me that one of the things that appears to be of prime importance within the women's liberation movement and the gay liberation movements . . . is to create social/cultural situations. In other words, a lesbian culture, or a women's culture—women's music, dance and stuff like that. Well, I think that all that may be a result of the patriarchy and how that operates in your [Western] cultures— you don't have distinctly different women's culture. Of course, in Third World countries we have entirely different priorities because, perhaps, we already have a distinct and separate women's community and culture.[5]

Men and women in South Asia live in mostly sex-segregated communities. The degree of interaction between them depends on the class, caste, and religion of each region. There are sanctioned arenas where they can meet or associate. Religion also plays a part in formulating gender codes and social norms. For instance, Muslim women of the middle and upper classes are more segregated than lower-class Muslims. The Brahmins, the highest Hindus' caste, also practice sex segregation. Thus it is considered a sign of status when middle- and upper-class women do not have to work and can live in a sex-segregated community.

Emotional and physical intimacy between persons of the same sex are common within sex-specific communities. The schools, workplaces, and public institutions that the women in this study attended were primarily sex segregated. "I went to a girl's high school and I never bothered to think about men" was a common response from the interviewees. Friendships were predominantly with people of the same sex. Therefore, men and women actually shared limited spaces of interaction.[6] Separate worlds were formed where these women bonded and shared emotional and physical experiences: "The people around us are women, and they're the ones who give us emotional support, they'll feed us, they'll nurture us, they'll care for us, and so we have incredibly deep emotional ties with each other."[7]

For Uma, food, affection, and close body contact between women are primary sensual components of her female friendships. This does not imply that all women's relations are "homosexual"; rather the boundaries of intimacy are different from the hegemonic form in the United States.[8] Women have a space in their community to formulate different levels of intimacy: "Women's friendships in India weren't sexual but they were like love affairs. Drama, trauma, jealousy, intimacy, hugging, holding, touching, an involvement far more intense and complete than any I have experienced in a friendship or sexual relationship in America."[9]

What may be considered as signs of homosexuality in mainstream U.S. culture does not carry such meaning in India. People of the same sex hold hands in public. They put their arms around each other, and women comb each other's hair and share the same bed.[10] One cannot clearly demarcate friendships and sexual relations. Intense emotional and physical relationships are not necessarily named as lesbian desire or acts. There are varying degrees and forms of intimacy: the everyday emotional and physical closeness such as hugging, holding hands, sleeping in the same bed, and genital sex.

Adrienne Rich conceives of all women's relationships in a lesbian continuum. A broadening of the term "lesbian" includes all women's relationships as part of an erotic involvement.

> As the term lesbian has been held to limiting, clinical associations in its patriarchal definition, female friendship and comradeship have been set apart from the erotic, thus limiting the erotic itself. But as we deepen and broaden the range of what we define as lesbian existence, as we delineate a lesbian continuum, we begin to discover the erotic in female terms: as that which is unconfined to any single part of the body or solely to the body itself, as an energy not only diffuse, but, as Audre Lorde has described it, omnipresent in "the sharing of joy, whether physical, emotional, psychic," and in the sharing of work.[11]

For Rich the continuum is disrupted by coercive heterosexuality.

However, if all of women's relationships are in the lesbian continuum, then how is lesbian identity defined? How does the same physical and emotional relationship become defined differently within two systems? How do we draw the lines between friendship and sexual relationship? Who is a lesbian and what demarcates it? Erotic choice? Then what is erotic?

I will suggest here that the meaning of any behavior is different depending on the context in which it is performed. For women who are traveling between India and the United States, the context shifts; therefore, the meaning of their behavior also changes. Identity based on sexuality also has to be analyzed in terms of the complex web of social relationships and the context which frames them. Caroll Smith Rosenberg and Martha Vicinus explore some of these issues in their studies of women's friendships in nineteenth-century America and England. They contend that while at first women's close relationships were considered friendships, they were gradually defined as deviant and lesbian acts. The same relationship thus became redefined in the public eye and discourse.[12]

Naming Desire

I wish to argue that gay men and lesbians have not always existed. Instead they are a product of history, and have come into existence in a specific historical era. This emergence is associated with the emergence of capitalism—more specifically, its free labor system that has allowed large numbers of men and women in the late twentieth century to call themselves gay, to see themselves as a part of a community of similar men and women, and to organize politically on the basis of that identity.[13]

By placing the age of repression in the seventeenth century, after hundreds of years of open spaces and free expression, one adjusts it to coincide with the development of capitalism: it becomes an integral part of the bourgeois order.[14]

According to D'Emilio, sexuality was expressed freely until the advent of capitalism. D'Emilio and Foucault state that homosexuality may have existed for centuries, but an identity formulated around sexual orientation is a phenomenon of the industrial era. However, as the industrial centers stabilized, sexual identity became embedded into a postindustrial economy. Therefore, homosexuality and gay identity and community need to be viewed within their historical contexts.

Homosexual behavior has changed and been defined differently through time, depending on the context in which it is performed.[15] It has not occupied the lower rung in the hierarchy of sexual order in all societies, at all times. Rather, in certain cultural and historical junctures sexual heterarchy existed or exists.[16] According to D'Emilio's theory, this then dispels the myths of the "eternal homosexual" and the belief that "until Gay liberation, Lesbians and Gay men were always the victims of systematic, undifferentiated, terrible oppression."[17] The meaning of homosexual behavior and of gay identity is construed according to culture, social structure, and specific historical developments. Only with the advent and penetration of capitalism do we see sexual repression in the West and the emergence of a new technology of sex. Foucault states that through pedagogy, medicine, and economics, sex becomes not only a secular concern but a concern of the state as well.[18] Foucault does not make economic structure the essential factor but rather shows the changes in the forms of control over peoples' bodies as the technology of production and the production of knowledge changes.

Scholars like Giti Thadani have been trying to examine precolonial signs of homosexuality in India. Thadani has looked at erotic art and dated the existence of homosexuality to the precolonial era. She examines the conceptualization of homoeroticism in the Bhakti movement. Erotic devotion to the goddess was required and this is said to have helped create a space for the expression of homoerotic desire in and by women. Thadani states, "The modes of identification are essentially of interrelatedness and merging into the other."[19]

According to Thadani, this sense of interconnected females, *yoni*, was later replaced by the heterosexual paradigm. *Yoni* was the womb, symbolized by a triangle of female twins and the earth. The twins could also be seen as *jami*, or a female-female sexual connection. As Thadani reports, the conception of reproduction in *jami* was not based on a male-female couple: "So, for example, families do not have the names of biological fathers, but the names of gods; and a child could have one mother for pleasure, one for knowledge, one for art and so on. Sexuality was based on pleasure and on fertility, not on progenity (the process of passing over the children to the man). Phallic discourse only appeared with progenic sexuality. So the first notion of 'heterosexuality' appeared under the terminology of *a-jami*, that which is not *jami*, which is not paired, fused as it is in the notion of 'homosexuality.'"[20] Thadani traces the suppression of sexuality, specifically homosexuality, to the "Aryan" invasion. It is at that time that the heterarchy of sexual practices was said to have been broken by the dominance of patriarchy.

Thadani's work uncovers important documentation of the existence of homosexuality in precolonial India. It points to evidence of changes in the position of homosexuality in Indian history. But the search for a classic and ideal place for homosexuality without further historical context is problematic. Stages of change, different from the white American trajectory, led to the transformation of many expressions of sexuality, both heterosexual and homosexual, in India. Orthodox interpretations of Islam, the Brahminization of Hinduism, forms of nationalism in response to colonizations, changes in the family structure, as well as legal and economic actions taken by the British with the support of local elite, were all crucial to changing conceptions of masculinity, femininity, and sexuality. One must examine sexual practices within the locus of those historical moments.

Sex has historically been a part of Indian art, songs, jokes, folklore and other exchanges.[21] For example, the oldest Indian sexual literary classic is the *Kama Sutra*, written in 4th–5th century C.E. It is an erotic work which includes a chapter, "Auparishtaka," addressing male-male sex, and another called "Antapura" (women's quarters) describing woman-woman sex.[22] In the sixteenth century, Muslim rulers and Hindu aristocrats were entertained by harems of young boys in the royal courts.[23] Persian poetry and fiction used homoerotic references, and in Islamic Sufi literature, the relationship between man and God has been homoeroticized.[24] There have also been many complex changes in the context and expression of sexuality through these periods. This chapter will sketch some of these changes in order to show the relationship between gender class, nationalism, and sexuality.

The middle class responded to British colonization with suppression of folk-cultural forms of expressing sexuality.[25] The British were shocked by the songs and stories shared in women's communities and found them to be licentious and voluptuous. The songs, dances, doggerel, poems, proverbs, and dramatic performances enacted by working-class women, who had access to the outside world, for isolated middle-class women were sexually explicit, and many also engaged in humorous male bashing. This shared popular culture slowly disappeared from the lives of middle- and upper-class women as the men enforced Western forms of education and decorum within the household.

Class position affects women, their level of mobility, and their place within the family. Within the middle class and upper class, women are less likely to work and more likely to be "domesticated." According to Liddle and Joshi, "The notion of domesticity, then, is firmly rooted in the middle class, and is strongly supported by economic conditions which make it possible for women to be supported within the family by men."[26] Sexuality is bounded by marriage, especially for middle- and upper-class women, and cultural space for unmarried people is limited. While working-class women continued to share folk expressions of sexuality within their own community, they were used as signifiers of improper female behavior. The nationalist movements constrained female expressions of sexuality even further by making them symbols of tradition and "upholder of the moral order of the subjected race."[27] "The hardest struggle for me has been, in general, to be a sexual being as a woman, and particularly so growing up in India, where women (at least those from the middle class) were not supposed to be sexual at all. In India, homosexuality is closeted for sure, but hell, even heterosexual sex before marriage is a big deal."[28]

Owing to the assumptions of heterosexuality among women in sex-segregated communities, they could be sheltered from some of the scrutiny of their relationships: "Customs being as they are in India, it is not unusual to have a same sex friend, a *yaar* or a *saheli*, who becomes your soul mate, at least platonically. So our parents did not suspect that we had any sort of romantic involvement. Because of our budding adolescence and the usual context for adolescence being a heterosexual one, it was passed about that we must be whoring around with boys."[29]

Heterosexuality is also reinforced by the academic system. Many elites in India send their children to private schools run by Catholic priests and nuns. These institutions also teach children that intimacy between the same gender is inappropriate, and they inculcate heterosexual morality. "At home I had the luxury of having my own room, which allowed us a good deal of privacy. It is natural for friends to spend nights together, and we took advantage of this. Like many of my peers, I attended a Catholic school even though I was raised Hindu. I may have thought my feelings perfectly natural but my world, especially my school, had other ideas. Sex education was a part of the moral science curriculum at this school. I soon learned through these classes that the kind of feelings I was having were wrong, immoral."[30] Women are seen as the upholders of morality and tradition. Therefore, through family, religion, and educational and other institutions, women and their sexuality are surveiled and contained.

In any period when a given act is publicly viewed as deviant sexual behavior, it is heavily punished: "I received most of my education at an all-girls boarding school [in Bangladesh], which I did not mind at all. There was much intimacy between the girls at this school, but this intimacy was mostly emotional; few felt safe enough to take it to a sexual level. I certainly know that I couldn't afford to express my desires. One of my friends was found out; she was given shock treatment and told repeatedly that she was crazy. Today she is mentally disturbed."[31] While sex segregation allows for intense friendships and interactions between women, transgressing the allowed boundaries of intimacy can be dangerous.

In India industrialization is partial and urbanization has different effects on women, depending on their class position. As Liddle and Joshi point out, the "freedom" to form new communities is limited for middle- and upper-class women. Urbanization has had an impact on the family unit and has changed its structure. Women are either in extended families or in urban areas, in nuclear or joint families.[32] All the participants in this study belong to a small stratum of a South Asian urban, industrialized population that is caught in the transformation from extended to nuclear family structure. Changing economic and social circumstances allowed these women to come to the United States for personal and educational opportunities. The change in economic and social structures and exposure to Western media also contributed to the circumstances and desire for independence and individualism in this group of women. This desire formed part of the reason for these middle-class youths' dream of leaving for the United States: "I mean, there is no question about the social freedom in terms of going out and having affairs or relationships and not having any interference from family and not worrying about people looking at you and people gossiping about you."[33]

For the participants of this study, migration allowed them to be outside the locus of their families and particular forms of control over their sexuality for the first time. This transition had a major impact on their lives. The critical years of making public, social, contractual, and familial commitments toward heterosexuality are after one turns eighteen and is therefore considered of marriageable age. It is important to note that the women interviewed left India at the time this transition was expected of them. They knew that their expected life trajectory was toward a heterosexual marriage. Even for women who considered their female relationships to be primary, marriage appeared as the only option. As Meera states eloquently, context is crucial to one's options and possibilities. Migration can be a vehicle to transport oneself to a different social context.

> We were being raised with the idea that the only possible life for a
> woman included the presence of a husband. Thus Bijli and I explored
> our feeling for boys. I used to tell Bijli that we should find a pair of
> brothers to marry so that we could live in the same house and con-

tinue our relationship. It seemed the closest thing to what we viewed as normal. When I was eighteen, I went to England. . . . On this trip I got my first view of what it meant to live as a gay person. I would walk up a street and see all of these signs of a healthy and visible gay life. There were gay bars everywhere. It blew my mind! My God! I thought, people actually live together, even openly, and its o.k.! I was excited, and I wrote a passionate letter to Bijli. Forget the whole marriage idea, I told her. We can move to England and live together.[34]

Shaping Identity

While the United States gave them the space to explore "individual freedom," the participants in this study found it to be a double-edged sword. Freedom from family and tight-knit communities also meant isolation. They searched for another community abroad. However, they found that in the United States communities were not organized around the same relationships as in the spaces they had been in. In the United States each community was centered on a highlighted identity. The postindustrial society fosters increased fragmentation, yet the hegemonic conception of a unitary self is based on a model of a suburban, upper-class white individual whose markers are made invisible.

> Within the U.S. is a world that is well developed. There are shoes for the sophisticate who loves partying. There is wallpaper meant for kids who need a Disney environment and ought not to be able to permanently disfigure the walls. There are candyless aisles in the supermarkets and magazines that talk only to computer game hackers. There is a cereal for those who are prone to heartburn, who love raisins but not calories. There are "I miss you" cards from a pining lover to his butch ex. In this wondrous world of specializations, separate bars for straights and gays are no surprise. Our American free enterprise and overzealous marketing prowess by no means stops there. We have gay bars that the young gay white males frequent. There are the Asian ghettos and separate bars for both blacks and latinos.[35]

Kim has aptly described the world South Asian immigrant women in general (and other minorities) may face. It is a society in which both specialization and fragmentation and identity politics work in conjunction.

Identity politics have developed in the postindustrial reorganized society.

They came out of an attempt to build collective identity and political resistance among those who are marginalized under dominant political, economic, or cultural institutions. The black power movement, women's movement, Chicano power, and gay and lesbian liberation movement developed in the sixties and seventies. While some of these movements made radical calls for larger social change, the politics of identity in and of themselves are limiting. "One major limitation of identity politics and its representation in multiculturalism is that we are all born within a web of overlapping identities and group affiliations," but we are pressed to disconnect those linkages to focus on one.[36] "The logic of the discourse of identity assumes a stable subject, that is, we've assumed that there is something which we can call our identity which, in a rapidly shifting world, has the great advantage of staying still. It's a kind of fixed point of thought and being, a ground of action, a still point in the turning world. The logic of identity is the logic of something like a 'true self.' And the language of identity has often been related to the search for a kind of authenticity to one's experience."[37] But as Minh-ha states, "Despite our desperate, eternal attempts to separate, contain, and mend, categories always leak."[38] Immigrant women are faced with particular and multiple marked identities which they must negotiate in the United States.

The women in this study found themselves defined and defining themselves as lesbians within the American context. This "identity" was crafted amid the context of the complex web of their transnational experiences: "Because I like to sleep with women, I found that I was labeled as a lesbian, only a lesbian. And I was expected to be with other lesbian women. But where I lived there were only white lesbians and I had nothing to talk to them about. I do not just sleep with women, I am also Indian and wear shalwar kameez and like to watch Hindi films and all that you know, and find it really strange when they talk about roles and all that. I mean I just don't understand it. And then, of course, people always wonder if I am *really* a lesbian."[39]

Most of the women initially saw American lesbians as white and butch. They state that they could not relate to the lesbian identity and community. "I had no concept of what it meant to be homosexual or lesbian before I moved to Canada. The first time that I saw a couple of lesbians at a restaurant, I was there with the guy I was then living with and I spent the whole evening looking at the two women. That was when it began to click in my mind that people could love in this manner, that it could be more than just thoughts and fantasy. Yet I was frightened of the idea of lesbians; I thought that all lesbians were mannish, wore sensible shoes and were not very attractive."[40]

While their sexual relationships define them as lesbian, Mina and other South Asian lesbians find that "whites," "Americans," and androgynous aesthetics are considered the norm for "real" lesbians. They found themselves having to prove their political allegiance by prioritizing feminist and sexual politics and excluding antiracist and other political affiliations.

It appears from "coming out" narratives found both in the interviews and in the anthology *A Lotus of Another Color* that exposure to feminism and defining one's sexuality often went hand-in-hand. There were two patterns in the narratives women used to describe their coming out experiences: (1) they claimed they always knew they were lesbian, and (2) they found their sexual identity through feminist politics. As Nayan Shah concurs in his analysis, the second form of narrative was more prevalent in women. This trajectory is similar to one described by Barbara Ponse in her book *Identities in the Lesbian World*. Ponse states that the lesbian community considers identity as essential to one's being. Women within the community see themselves as always having been lesbian but merely having come to the "realization" through an acknowledgment of their inclinations, that is, in the coming-out process: "Soon after, I left India to study in the United States. When I got here I began the process of becoming a feminist. Suddenly I had a framework to explain a lot of the feelings and frustrations I had been experiencing for a long time."[41] "My first encounters and relationships with women were not the results of choice, but rather being overwhelmed by what appeared to be a startling awakening of sexual feelings."[42]

Both Khayal and Bannerji express a frustration with naming a desire they felt and not having the framework to articulate it. They tried to discover the answers by exploring feminism and their own sexuality: "Before I went to college, I had not thought of myself as gay or lesbian. When I look back on my life, I can see that I was always lesbian, though I didn't know it at the time. To me, it was just a matter of exposure and recognition. In college, I also learned the labels and the theory, and came to some understandings. I realized that, gee, I think I am gay."[43] This recognition or realization of the authentic self is widely documented. As participants in this study narrate and reconstruct their experiences, they present a linear trajectory of development. However, this narrative (memory) is mediated by their transnational experiences.

> Kamini's knowledge of lesbian relationships informs her reflections about the intimacy between women in India. Kamini is able to name friendships between women in India "romances" through a language of lesbian relationships learned in the United States. While sexual

experiences may have occurred in Bangladesh or Sri Lanka, the framework to understand and celebrate these experiences as gay and lesbian identities developed in white societies. These coming out narratives reveal a shared strategy of reframing the past with present knowledge. Many times these narratives attempt to show a linear progression or the origination of an identity. But often the straight lines tumble into spirals or tangle into webs.[44]

These women's narratives are a class-, race-, and gender-specific negotiation of the transnational experiences of crafting a lesbian identity. They construct notions of what it is to be "Indian" and "lesbian" and develop narratives of "discovering" authentic selves that are problematic. Other parts of their narrative add complexity to the process of shaping sexual identity.

As their sexuality became defined as lesbian, these South Asian women sought lesbian organizations and communities. White lesbians were the majority and defined these spaces, South Asians were marginalized and exoticized because of their "differences." They were marked by their race and racialized notions of their "culture."

> *Anu:* We have to deal with is our invisibility, which is a part of their racism. They usually don't see us as lesbians. . . . They can't see through the myth that women of color are male identified. Also the way we dress doesn't fit into the image of the stereotypical lesbian white women.
> *Pramila:* Women in saris and shalwar kameez would never be seen as a lesbian.
> *Anu: White women believe* . . . that sexism is a more fundamental problem than racism.[45]

While their differences marked them as "outsiders," it also made them invisible as lesbians (insiders). They found that issues crucial to them such as racism and imperialism were not necessarily concerns shared by white lesbians. Rather, race and racialized markers became a fundamental schism between them. The white/feminist/lesbian community proved to be inadequate in meeting the South Asian women's needs. These women were marginalized within American society, with its white dominant ideology and control over socioeconomic and political institutions.

> Like so many other lesbian and gay people, I felt that calling myself a lesbian amounted to reducing my whole being into my sexual pref-

erence, while in reality many other aspects of my personality remained unnoticed. For a period I fought defining myself as a lesbian. I drifted into the politically and culturally active lesbian community, started to see that self-acceptance and social acceptance were connected. As a lesbian of Indian origin with an active relationship to India and to my family, I was struck by the conformity to androgyny that appeared to be the norm of white lesbian beauty. Having grown up with a body and an aesthetic value system that was utterly different than this white androgyny, I struggled to accept my Indian woman's body against all heterosexist odds. My breasts, hips and long hair were not seen by everyone as symbols integral to my identity as an Indian woman; they were reinterpreted by white lesbians as manifestations of my being femme.[46]

Many of these narratives construct and resist essentialist and racialized notions of the United States, India, and "American lesbians." They illuminate the contradictions and problems embedded within these categories. Many Indian women found themselves unable to fit in the boundaries or definition of these specific identities. South Asian women describe their marginal location within many communities, either exoticized or put in the category of the devalued/invisible "other." They are a part of two frameworks of reference. As Tomas Almaguer finds in his research on Chicano men, this struggle is faced by other immigrants.

The sexual behavior and sexual identity of Chicano male homosexuals is principally shaped by two distinct sexual systems, each of which attaches different significance and meaning to homosexuality. Both the European-American and Mexican/Latin American systems have their own unique ensemble of sexual meanings, categories for sexual actors, and scripts that circumscribe sexual behavior. Each system also maps the human body in different ways by placing different values on homosexual erotic zones. The primary socialization of Chicanos into Mexican/Latin American cultural norms, combined with their simultaneous socialization into the dominant European-American culture, largely structures how they negotiate sexual identity questions and confers meaning to sexual behavior during adolescence and childhood. Chicano men who embrace a "gay" identity (based on the European-American sexual system) must reconcile this sexual identity with their primary socialization into a Latino culture that does not recognize such a construction: there is no cultural equivalent to the modern "gay man" in the Mexican/Latin American sexual system.[47]

As the women in this study recognize these problems, they struggle with the social and political realities that make it important for them to align themselves as lesbians in the U.S. context. These immigrant women express frustration at not feeling as if they fit or "belong" in either South Asia or the United States. Yet both systems simultaneously give meaning to their lives and are intertwined. They make the political move of refocusing their sense of self and identity in multiple ways.

> I stopped identifying myself as a lesbian. I still find women sexually and romantically attractive, but the label was very restrictive. It made sexuality the central component of my identity, which was too narrow an approach for me.[48]
>
> Of course I am a lesbian. Now by saying lesbian I am not saying I am just like American (read: white). We have to think about our family and I have my parents' friends and some relatives who are here. I have to move about in those circles too. I have to do many things that Americans will never understand. Some of them think I am not strong because I don't come out to them or because they say I am codependent because I do many things for my lover or friends. I want to still be able to go to S—'s house and catch up with the news from back home. Who can live alone?[49]

Joda Ban Gaya Hai (On Being a Pair)

The issue of individualism versus extended self is another reason for the conflicts the South Asian immigrant women in this study have with identity politics. Indian women living in South Asia are embedded in a woman's community, religion, age hierarchy, class, and place within the family. These roles work in conjunction with one another, and any given identity is accentuated, depending on the context. Women experience an extended sense of self rather than an individualistic one. Suad Joseph describes this concept of self as the production of relationally oriented selves called familial selves. This familial self is constructed around "emotional connectedness, interdependence, and permeable outer-ego boundaries."[50] Women's relations are clearly reflected by the language they use to describe them. Sometimes a distinction is made in the nature of their relationship as "*joda ban gaya hai*" (they/we have become a pair). In Indian women's conception of their sexual relationship to other women, a person is not a lesbian; two women are a pair or couple in relation to each other. They do not embody their sexual identity but rather experience sexuality with other women as an extension of the self (and not simply with another).

When the women in this study moved to the United States, they were suddenly removed from this social organization and worldview. There was a demand to present oneself as an individual signified by particular marked identities. Joseph states, "Western psychological theory, clinical practice, Western education, and much of Western popular culture has highly valorized the production of selves which are bounded, separate, and autonomous. In much of Western thinking, the 'individual' has passed from being an historical construct to a 'naturally' existing identity."[51] For these women, being removed from the family network and having the financial ability to live alone and independently create a space for a more individualized definition of the self. These immigrants who prefer female sexual relationships are defined as lesbian. While they find this conception of self and "choice" of identities to be problematic, the need for a community, and the structure and organization of the social world, shape the marking of a selective identity. Therefore, despite the problems, most of the women in the study did identify themselves as lesbians and some as lesbians of color. They emphasized their differences and struggled to incorporate them in a redefinition of the term. They created racialized lesbian communities with other lesbians and gay men of color. "South Asians" too are trying to develop their own "cohesive" community which takes into account their particular transnational experience. They have appropriated the Hindi and Urdu word *khush* to signify gay and lesbian. In the eighties and nineties *Trikone* emerged in the Bay Area as a gay and lesbian newsletter, *Anamika* and *Shamakami* as lesbian newsletters. *A Lotus of Another Color* is a product of this naming and this self-defining by a particular stratum of South Asian gays and lesbians in the United States.

This focus on a sexual identity proves problematic on many fronts. The participants articulate a dismantling of their expectations of the United States.

> I always thought of going to the States, God knows why, 'cause I was in a colonial mindset, city, urban elite, and all that. I had this dream, I remember I used to think that I will be independent in America and have an apartment . . . some kind of a grand dream I had which later, when I was in the States, I said, fuck, man, I was isolated and alone in my room. I would say, is this what I came here for?[52]

Many of the women thought that the United States would mean "freedom" and "unrepressed" expressions of desire. But they realized that the intimacy and access to women that were available to them in India were not so easily accessible here. Both United States and India presented differing sets of supports and barriers to craft their lives around. Living in the United States did not resolve issues they defined as "Indian," and going "back home" did not resolve the "American" issues. The two reference systems are intertwined and cannot be severed despite geographic distance. Therefore, transnational constructions of identity are created out of this process of interaction and negotiation.

Renegotiating Self, Home, and Identity

While the women in this study are no longer in the locus of their families, they are not completely released from those ties. Coming out to parents can be an alien or irrelevant concept for most of them. If this label dislodges them from their primary community, that is, women, they may be giving up their most intimate relations. They also do not want to risk losing the support of the family, which is the only stable community they have.

> If we are out as lesbians and gays in our communities, then we take the risk of being rejected by our families and communities. More than rejected, completely shunned and not allowed access to any of our cultural events or anything like that. For many of us, our families are very important, as they give us a base, a refuge, from racism and give us a sense of our own identity as Indian people. That's what I mean by internal exiles, whether we come out or not we are exiles within our communities. If we come out, we are more often than not exiled by the community. If we don't come out, we feel that sense of exile because we are unable to share a very important part of our lives with them.[53]

Anguish over split lives and an understanding of the different worlds their parents live in inform the decisions women have to make regarding coming out to family members. Some have come out and been accepted into the family. But conflicts over expressing sexuality openly are still difficult.

> Living at home as a South Asian lesbian daughter has been complex and sometimes contradictory process for both myself and my parents. Yet it is rewarding and moving to see my parents at lesbian and gay pride day. Their presence is an acknowledgment also of the

many lesbians and gay men they consider to be their friends. On the other hand, in some ways my gradual transition to open lesbianism reflects my caution regarding both real and perceived notions that being "obviously" lesbian might alienate me from my family. Hence, only after living away from my parents home was I able to integrate clearly and unashamedly a lesbian world view into my personal consciousness.[54]

Not all South Asians can negotiate homosexuality openly with their parents. Sometimes even when they do, they are expected to carry out heterosexual rituals of marriage. According to the cultural norms of South Asia, homosexuality does not negate marriage. Just because you are homosexual does not mean you can refuse to get married. Especially the men are frequently asked, So what has that got to do with marriage? One is seen as quite capable of carrying on both roles as a heterosexual husband and maintaining a homosexual lover on the side. For women the choices are more restricted. Women, like men, are under constant pressure to marry and conform to their gender roles. Their choices of remaining single are further constrained by the lack of economic power and social sanction about living alone. The following advertisement in *Trikone* shows the compulsions of marriage and obligations to families that Indian gays and lesbians feel. Some are experimenting with new strategies to cope with these pressures. "Twenty-four year old lesbian/bisexual woman is searching for a gay South Asian man settled in United States with whom to enact matrimonial rituals to dissuade harried parents from aging prematurely while drowning her in guilt. Friendly, supportive, seeking same. Is this a laugh or what?"[55]

Despite the brevity of the note, one can sense its poignancy. This struggle to please one's parents, continue to be involved in the larger South Asian community, and live a gay/lesbian life is difficult. Most of the interviewees go to India for regular visits, and some have considered moving there permanently. Returning to their home countries is sometimes neither an economically nor personally viable option. Economic independence and the ability for women to live alone and maintain the same lifestyle in their home countries are impossible.

Going "home" takes on a double meaning. The interviewees recount that when they first return to India, they distance themselves from their lives in the United States. They immerse themselves in the familiar surroundings and people. Then, slowly, one woman reported, "as the days pass and I catch up on the events that have marked the lives of my friends, rejoicing in their triumphs and commiserating with them in their sorrow, I find myself getting angry with their privilege. Privilege to confide in me. To rely on me emotionally without so much as a doubt, while I struggle with the gulf between us, wondering what would happen to our friendship if I were really to take them into my heart. My life in the United States begins to look more real."[56] Life in the United States is now home as well.

Through exposure to feminism, the gay and lesbian liberation movement, a racialized politics, the ability to live alone in an urban environment, economic independence, dislocation and distance from the family, they gave meaning to their emotional and sexual ties to other women as South Asian lesbianism. This political statement created both an affirmation of their sexual preference and a struggle to find a space within a lesbian community. This process also gave them a new home, family, community, and ways of negotiating self and identity.

The narratives and testimonies reflect an effort to draw a linear progression that led to the political lesbian of the present and pose the East and West as binary opposites. Sociopolitical, economic, and technological shifts within India are also changing the context of defining sexuality (particularly in urban centers) in those nations. Like the United States, South Asian nations have permeable and fluid boundaries that interact owing to international political, economic, and technological linkages. These women are participants in this interaction, moving in both directions and influencing and being influenced by social movements in their country of origin and the United States. Through multiple overlapping and contradictory experiences these women redefine their identities and give particular meaning to the term "South Asian lesbian." They find themselves both developing a sense of individualism and rejecting it as the only way of conceptualizing the self and its relationship to others. They straddle the transnational terrain of reference and negotiate race, class, culture, gender position, sexual preference, linguistic differences, and family ties within them to define their space.

Notes

This research project began in Professor Tomas Almaguer's graduate seminar class in 1989. His work as a teacher and scholar was an inspiration in times of struggle. I would also like to thank Arvind Kumar, Raihan Zamil, and Shamita Das Dasgupta for their support and encouragement in bringing this chapter out of its hibernation.

1. *Khush*, in the epigraph, is a literal translation of the word "gay" into Hindi/Urdu. It means happy.

2. "South Asian" is a new group identity developed within the United States for and by peoples of India, Pakistan, Bangladesh, Sri Lanka, Nepal, Bhutan, Burma, and Maldives. It usually refers to people from India and its old borders of Bangladesh and Pakistan, as well as Sri Lanka. Indians are the numerical majority, both in terms of population in the United States and composition of groups using this designation. Gay and lesbian groups tend to identify themselves as South Asian. Therefore, I use the term in this chapter to refer to the self-designation by these groups and individuals.

3. The sample for the interviews was chosen because of their engagement with the category "lesbian." These interviews give important clues to why some Indian and Bangladeshi immigrants whose sexual and emotional preference is woman-centered may choose not to label themselves as lesbians.

4. R. Ratti (ed.), *A Lotus of Another Color* (Boston: Alyson, 1993), allowed me to look at the different forms of narratives used to depict the past, construct the present, and describe "coming out" experiences.

5. Uma, "UMA," *Connexions* (Fall 1983): 6.

6. With urbanization there was an increase in the contact between middle- and upper-class men and women in the cities. Many changes have occurred within nuclear families, making women more dependant on men for social and emotional interaction, but extended families and other factors continue to shape the maintenance of sex segregation and gender roles.

7. Uma, 7.

8. In India people of the opposite sex are not allowed to hold hands in public. Men and women can show public physical affection and hold hands with others of their sex without censure. Therefore in these sex-segregated public spaces, there are different boundaries of intimacy than the United States.

9. Kamini, interview with author (1989).

10. This level of physical intimacy is not looked upon as homosexual behavior. But there is also an acknowledgment that another level of physical intimacy exists, such as genital sex. For men in cities, anonymous sex in public parks is clearly separated from emotional relationships. While for women the lines are much more blurred owing to the lack of available spaces where only physical acts/genital sex takes place.

11. A. Rich. "Compulsory Heterosexuality," in *Powers of Desire/The Politics of Sexuality* (New York: Monthly Review Press, 1983), 193.

12. C. Smith-Rosenberg, "The Female World of Love and Ritual: Relations between Women in Nineteenth Century America," *Signs* 1, no.1 (1975): 1–29; M. Vicinus, "Distance and Desire; English Boarding School Friendships," *Signs* 9, no. 4 (1984): 600–622.

13. J. D'Emilio, "Capitalism and Gay Identity," in *Powers of Desire/The Politics of Sexuality* (New York: Monthly Review Press, 1983), 102.

14. M. Foucault, *The History of Sexuality*, vol. 1 (New York: Vintage Books, 1978), 5.

15. E. Blackwood, *Anthropology and Homosexual Behavior* (New York: Haworth, 1986); M. Duberman, M. Vicinus, and G. Chauncey, *Hidden from History: Reclaiming the Gay and Lesbian Past* (New York: NAL, 1989); J. Katz, *Gay American History: Lesbian and Gay in the U.S.* (New York: Harper and Row, 1985);

C. Smith-Rosenberg, "The Female World of Love and Ritual"; T. Almaguer, "The Cartography of Homosexual Desire and Identity among Chicano Men," *Differences: A Journal of Feminist Cultural Studies* 3, no.2 (Summer 1991); and J. Weeks, *Sexuality and Its Discontents: Meaning, Myths and Modern Sexualities* (New York: Routledge and Kegan, 1985).

16. According to C. L. Crumley, "A Dialectical Critique of Hierarchy," in T. Patterson and C. Gailey (eds.), *Power Relations and State Formations* (Washington, D.C.: American Anthropological Association, 1987): "Structures are heterarchical when each element is either unranked relative to other elements or possesses the potential for being ranked in a number of different ways."

17. D'Emilio, "Capitalism and Gay Identity," 101.

18. Foucault, *History of Sexuality*, 53–91.

19. G. Thadani, "Shifting Cosmologies and the Paradigms of Sexuality in Indian Religion," paper presented at the International Gay and Lesbian Conference, Stockholm, June–July 1990.

20. Ibid.

21. India here refers to the pre-1947 nation state that is now divided into India, Bangladesh, and Pakistan.

22. "The *Kama Sutra* records that Auparishtaka is practiced by the following—male citizens who know each other well, among themselves; women, when they are amorous, do the acts of the mouth on the *yonis* (vaginas) of one another; some men do the same with women; male servants of some men carry on the mouth congress with their masters; eunuchs with males," ABVA, "Homosexuality in India: Culture and Heritage," in Ratti, *Lotus of Another Color*, 22.

23. Ibid., 31.

24. Ibid., 32.

25. S. Banerjee, "Marginalization of Women's Popular Culture in Nineteenth Century Bengal," in K. Sangari and S. Vaid (eds.), *Recasting Women in Colonial History* (New Delhi: Kali for Women, 1989).

26. J. Liddle and R. Joshi, *Daughters of Independence: Gender Caste and Class in India* (New Brunswick, N.J.: Rutgers University Press, 1986), 187.

27. S. Sen, "Motherhood and Mothercraft: Gender and Nationalism in Bengal," *Gender and History* 5, no. 2 (Summer 1993): 233.

28. K. Chaudhary, "The Scent of Roses," in Ratti, *Lotus of Another Color*, 149.

29. Meera, "Finding Community," in Ratti, *Lotus of Another Color*, 235.

30. Ibid., 234–35.

31. S. Islam, "The Toughest Journey," in Ratti, *Lotus of Another Color*, 281.

32. Liddle and Joshi, *Daughters of Independence*, 142–56.

33. Kamini, interview with author (1989).

34. Meera, "Finding Community," 236–37.

35. Kim, "They Aren't That Primitive Back Home," in Ratti, *Lotus of Another Color*, 94.

36. J. Escoffier, "The Limits of Multiculturalism," *Socialist Review*, nos. 3–4 (1991): 64.

37. S. Hall, "Ethnicity, Identity and Difference," *Radical America* 23, no. 4 (1989): 10.

38. T. Min-ha, *Woman Native Other* (Bloomington: Indiana University Press, 1989), 94.

39. Mina, interview with author (1989).

40. Maria, "Coming Home," in Ratti, *Lotus of Another Color*, 207.

41. Khayal, "Khayal," *Anamika* 1, no. 2 (1986): 9.

42. K. Bannerji, "No Apologies," in Ratti, *Lotus of Another Color*, 59.

43. Meera, "Working Together: An Interview with Urvashi Vaid," in Ratti, *Lotus of Another Color*, 105.

44. N. Shah, "Sexuality, Identity, and Its uses in History," in Ratti, *Lotus of Another Color*, 117.

45. "Lesbians of Color, Loving and Struggling: A Conversation between Three Lesbians of Color," *Firewood*, no. 16 (1983): 86–93.

46. K. Bannerji, "No Apologies," 60.

47. Almaguer, "Cartography of Homosexual Desire," 75.

48. K. Chaudhary, "Some Thoughts on Bisexuality," in Ratti, *Lotus of Another Color*, 55. Kamini is also speaking of her bisexuality here. Therefore her struggles are not only with conceptions of self and the racial politics of the lesbian community but also with the debate over one's position within the so-called lesbian continuum.

49. Nasreen, interview with author (1990).

50. S. Joseph, "Fashioning Selves: Fieldwork and Dynamics of Personhood," paper presented at the Gender and Global Issues Conference, U.C.–Davis, 1992. This notion of extended, familial self should not be idealized. Familial and connected relationships work within their own framework of power and control.

51. Ibid.

52. Kamini, interview with author.

53. Khush, "Fighting Back," in Ratti, *Lotus of Another Color*, 36.

54. K. Bannerji, "No Apologies," 62.

55. Personal ad in *Trikone* 4, no.3 (1989): 6.

56. Anu, "Notes from an Indian Diary," *Anamika* 1, no.2 (1986): 7.

Me and We
FAMILY AND COMMUNITY

Mothers and Daughters in Indian-American Families

A FAILED COMMUNICATION?

MANISHA ROY

*T*his chapter is born out of my thirty-seven years living in the West as an Indian woman and as a psychological anthropologist and psychotherapist. However, I am not a mother myself. Therefore, my observations are not directly personal. I came to the United States as a student before the first big wave of immigration in the late sixties and seventies from South Asia. My own research and years of university teaching and private practice have helped me to keep in close contact with the South Asian immigrant communities for over thirty years. Thus, my efforts to analyze and understand the issues related to the Indian immigrant population have evolved over the years.[1]

Now, I see every social problem, including the one in this chapter, to be an ever-evolving process of sociocultural change, no matter how minuscule the change may be. For example, the communication problem between Asian(-born)–American mothers and their Asian–American(-born) daughters changes with the ages and stages of their life cycles and, of course, with the arrival of a third generation. When social scientists discuss a particular problem, sometimes they tend to see it as a fixed point, not as an ever-changing, natural progression. Seen in the perspective of a dynamic progression, all problems take on a slightly different color. My observations and analyses in this chapter keep this perspective in mind.

In the three following sections, I first pose the problem of communication between mothers and daughters and look at its implications, with some sample cases from my own observations and research. Then I discuss the historical, cultural, religious, and other antecedents to the present situation. In the final segment, I discuss the possible solutions and resolutions. A brief commentary on the methodology of research concludes the chapter.

The Problem and Observations

I would like to define "communication" not only as verbal instructions and exchanges but also as all interactions, including unconscious ones, that pass, in this case, between two generations as part of the natural course of living together, and over many generations, as well. This natural course of living together as a family is extremely complex because in addition to deep instinctive connections, parental hopes, aspirations, and children's need for love, security, and approval, there are unconscious complexes which are projected onto both sides. This is the way it has been between parents and children in all cultures at all times. In the past, parents struggled with the generation gap as a given situation—a rite of passage when the children were growing up which became less problematic as the children themselves became parents; and the parents, grandparents. Some authoritarian parents tried to solve the problems of the generation gap by forcing their children to comply with their wishes, risking a lifelong communication gap or, worse still, a continuation of the same pattern for the next generation and perhaps the one after that. A few wise ones remembered their own adolescence and youth and tried to be more understanding, keeping in mind that parenting is a demanding role that requires sacrifices. By shifting the responsibility more to themselves, such parents stood a better chance of an improved relationship with their children.

Why is the generation gap conspicuous among immigrant parents and their American-born children or, more specifically, among South Asian immigrant mothers and daughters? This chapter explores that very question. But before we try to answer that question, let me present a few typical scenarios in Asian-Indian families.[2]

Case One

Anita arrived in the United States from Calcutta in 1973 at the age of thirty-two, two years after her marriage. Her husband, an engineer, wanted to get away from the scrutiny of his joint family because, against strong objections from his family, he had married a widow. A friend suggested emigration, which seemed the best possible escape from family pressures. Within six months after they arrived here, the husband managed to get a good job and a year later they had a daughter. The mother concentrated on bringing up their daughter as the ideal Bengali girl, with the following aspirations: she had to become fluent in Bengali and trained in singing Tagore's songs; to be obedient and gentle to attract compliments from the Indian community; to be educated at a famous American university such as Harvard, MIT, Princeton, or Stanford—names which would impress her relatives back home; and, finally, to marry a highly educated Bengali boy of honorable character.

From her earliest memories the daughter, Nilima, recalled feeling different and not as good as people around her—first the children in the neighborhood, then the kids at school: "I used to have secret fantasies of having long blonde hair tied with those rubber bands, with two large colorful balls at the end. I was embarrassed of the differences between my parents and others. I prayed and hoped that my mother would change and look like Mrs. Hopkins next door, with short hair and fashionable business suits." Of course, these fantasies were only for superficial changes. At home she loved being Indian and being the center of her mother's attention. She was glad that her mother did not work. When she was twelve, the list of her future aspirations were as follows:

- To be the best student in the Bengali community and attend a good university;
- To please her parents with her academic success and gain approval from her community;
- To be able to buy sexy and expensive clothes and have the "jocks" in her high school football team ask her out to the junior prom and senior ball; and
- To be popular in school and be kissed by a light-haired, tall, and popular boy in school.

However, as Nilima was ready to graduate from high school, it became painfully clear to her parents that her grades and SAT scores were not good enough for a Ivy League college. Their disappointment hurt Nilima deeply, and she started to avoid her mother, insisting on moving to the local college dorm, where she began dating different boys. The mother, meanwhile, felt totally helpless and could not figure out where she and her husband had gone wrong. Although they may be extremely unhappy about broken dreams for their only child, parents find it hard to discuss the problem with their closest friends. Speaking to a professional is out of the question. They keep up a facade of "everything is fine" while their friends respect their need to protect themselves from prying. However, whispers and gossip pass from family to family, and the situation becomes common knowledge without being discussed openly. The last I heard was that Nilima had dropped out of college and was working part-time somewhere. Her parents have moved to another state and have little contact with Nilima. She telephones them occasionally for a brief conversation. The mother is under psychiatric care for depression.

Case Two

Nina is one of two children of her college professor father and research assistant mother. Her mother works in a science lab in the same university where her husband is an associate professor. Her brother is two years older and her mother's favorite, while Nina is close to her father. Nina's aspiration is to be a professor just like her father, and her academic performance in high school has already shown promise. Her brother is also a good student.

By the time he reached puberty, though, the brother began to distance himself from the family and spent a lot of time in his room listening to rock music; he also wore baggy pants, baseball caps, and sneakers and spoke nothing but English. In this household there was never any pressure to speak an Indian language. The brother also started to object to his mother's attention and demonstrations of affection. He rejected his mother's culture and solved the problem of confusion by "going American" in language, friends, and thinking. As a result, at age fourteen, Nina suddenly found herself at the center of her mother's attention. Her mother began to confide in her, telling stories of her suffering with her in-laws back home and also about her husband's neglect since their move to the States.

At first, Nina did not want to believe her mother, but gradually she identified with her mother's plight and began to notice her father's faults in many areas. A classmate lent her some books with feminist overtones, and suddenly she began to pay attention to stories of the oppression of women at home and at work. Her alliance shifted entirely toward her mother now. Together they discussed sexual politics, if not their own sexuality, and attended rallies and protest meetings. Nina's Indian friends envied her close friendship with her mother. They became the model mother-daughter pair. Her father noticed this change also but thought it was natural for a growing girl to be close to her mother.

Soon the parents' marital problems became obvious to others in the community. There was gossip that Nina's father was seen with an American graduate student here and there. Her mother began to lean on Nina more and more. She had never cultivated friendships with other Indian women her age, partly because she looked down on them. Nina and her mother were each other's only allies, and by the time she went to college, Nina was determined not to marry but to devote her whole life to becoming a successful doctor— her mother's choice of career—and help oppressed women in the Indian community. Nina's Indian friends and their families began to avoid her because of her tendency to lecture them. Finally, her parents divorced, and the brother moved out of state and did not want anything to do with the family. At age thirty, Nina was unmarried and still trying to enter medical schools without success. Her mother had given up her job and lived with Nina.

Nina feels betrayed by her upbringing and envies other Indian young women who seem to be doing well and do not have to take care of their mothers. Nina's mother never told her anything about Indian traditions, yet Nina feels guilty even thinking about not taking care of her single mother. This confusion has led Nina to seek professional help, and after a couple of years of therapy she now knows that her mother has given her political consciousness, but no love and understanding, for what she really needed to be satisfied with life.

Case Three

Lotika immigrated to the United States with her engineer husband and two-year-old daughter in the seventies. She came from a middle-class Brahmin family where women were the custodians of family rituals and religious practices. Even though she went to college and had a master's degree in economics, Lotika was not interested in a career. No woman in her family had ever worked. In the United States, her husband waited a whole year before finding a job. They had to borrow thousands of dollars from acquaintances and friends they knew from back home. Even after the husband landed a decent job, Lotika was very careful with money and managed the household with efficiency and frugality. They had few friends with whom they spoke in their mother tongue and never ventured any connection with the outside world.

Their only daughter, Usha, was brought up totally Indian. Every morning

Lotika took her bath and, in a fresh silk sari, sat praying for an hour in front of her small statues of gods in the corner of her bedroom. Her daughter followed the mother in such practices and somehow maintained a double life—one as a good Hindu girl and the other as the immigrant Indian American. She knew that she felt more comfortable with her Hindu Indian self even though she had to playact being an Indian American most of her waking hours. If she tried to remain herself—her Indian self—she felt like an outcast. Boys looked at her suspiciously. She was determined not to feel ashamed of her Indian heritage, which gave her more security and comfort. As she grew older—she is now in her twenties—Usha was not sure she could pull off this compartmentalization for long.

Usha was unsure about how her future was going to turn out. No Asian-American man seemed interested in her even though she was good looking, good natured, and intelligent. She would perhaps have to marry a man from India who earned a good living and was dependable. She knew that she would be happier living more in her Indian self. Whatever happened, she hoped her upbringing had equipped her with a religious philosophy that would act as a safety net in times of trouble.

I could extend this section with many more cases showing the variation between the first and the third cases. These would demonstrate variations of the same theme, namely, the confused upbringing of the American-born daughters by their Indian-born mothers. There are also families where, despite all odds, the immigrant mothers seem to bring up self-assured and mature daughters who make a healthy adjustment to the host culture while retaining the strength and depth of their Indian heritage. In most cases, these mothers claim little credit for such an outcome. They merely say, "We are just lucky."

Analysis and Discussion

A few observations can be made even from the three brief examples sketched above. Immigrant parents, especially the mothers, seem unable to understand and appreciate their daughters' realities. The daughters have more access not only to American language, education, customs, and clothing but also to mainstream American values, including individualism, self-reliance, and competition. Unlike the Indian identity, which gathers its strength and validity from the approval of family and community, a child in the West is very much under the influence of her immediate peers, at least in her adolescence.[3]

A major area of confusion for an Indian adolescent daughter is her sexuality. The information and instruction come in mixed messages from her family and are totally different from what she receives from her peers. In Indian families sexuality in adolescent is not only suppressed and repressed but even feared as potentially dangerous. Rarely does a mother discuss the mystery and seriousness of sexual awakening with her daughter. Sex education is left to nature and precocious peers. It is a taboo which has been handed down for generations. It appears that, in India, artistic expression—including mythology, literature, and mass media—has compensated for such repressions. Sexuality is approached indirectly through symbolic and metaphoric language rather than as a human behavior needing open discussion, understanding, and acceptance. These repressions are justified with the unspoken agreement that such a potentially dangerous awakening of body and psyche must be controlled and deferred until after marriage. Because—another rationale—women have the responsibility to preserve the family honor, by extension, they have been assigned guardianship of community honor as well.[4] This sense of responsibility for upholding her community's honor is still a part of another deeply internalized ideal, namely, her "community persona." I shall return to this important point again.

In the United States, sexual awareness and its expression contribute a major part to the identity of an adolescent girl, who is torn between her Indian morality and the American behavioral norm. To make things worse, a growing Indian girl faces a totally altered sexual image as she moves from high school to college. On a university campus, which may be more international, she may be considered exotic and sexy. She holds on to this image, which is better than before, when she was left out by the blue-eyed blond sex models. She may even play this game of being the exotic sex object, which may lead to an increasingly damaged self-esteem. The alternative choice is total withdrawal from the sexual arena in order to be the good Indian girl. Similar confusions arise in other value areas of life—respect for elders versus democratic treatment of one another, obedience versus independence, and dependence versus self-reliance—to name a few opposites that Indian-American children have to wrestle with and juggle constantly.

What are the historical, religious, and cultural factors which often make Indian immigrant parents blind to their children's reality? This is a complex question to answer. When the parents immigrate to the United States, their reasons are clear in their minds: To avoid joint family responsibility (mostly for the newlywed wife), to enhance educational skills, to improve economic conditions, and to offer better educational opportunities to their children.

Hardly anyone delves deep inside to ponder what might be the cultural and emotional implications of these goals.

When an Indian couple is uprooted from the native culture (albeit voluntarily) and is transplanted into the new American lifestyle, the couple may not be aware of how the finer and less-visible roots of their traditions and culture have been severed. On the surface the move appears exciting and challenging, even freeing them from all the age-old fetters of traditions. The young married woman now has the freedom to be the mistress of her home, which she decorates with American objects. Having a comfortable home that a woman rules entirely on her own is a major factor in her sense of security until it is rudely broken when her children reach the teen years. Now, suddenly, emotional nourishment by the past (which includes evocative memories of childhood food, language, and many traditional values, no matter how old-fashioned) becomes her lifeline. She clings to it and insists that her daughter not forget the past—a past which is fixed in her own memory and, therefore, hardly realistic.

Her husband has similar experiences, although in different ways. His struggle in the outer world as a minority competing with white American males is not balanced by the attention he would have received from doting female relatives back home, where he was the "king" and could do nothing wrong. Indian men are brought up to look after their parents and families—an ideal that contributes strongly to their identity. In America, they have to sacrifice that age-old ego booster and willy-nilly devote their full attention to their nuclear family, similar to their American counterparts. An Indian man is not brought up to separate from his family and mother for his own individuation. In the United States, all the shared housework and the feeling of being a second-class citizen outside undermine his satisfaction at earning more money, owning a house, and having all the other amenities—the universal masculine goal of being the envied provider. Besides, his acquaintances are often blessed with the same good fortune, which takes away the ego's satisfaction at being conspicuously successful. In other words, when the children come of age, the parents' psychology has changed considerably from the early years of naive complacency. Parts of them wish they could go back to the old existence in India, with its security of joint family and relaxed lifestyle. Naturally, the India they left behind, which now seems to be the solution, gets reinvented and projected onto the children, who in their turn are becoming more and more American.

Another pervasive psychology of the minority needs mentioning. According to many Indians, everything American is better and more sophisticated, therefore, more desirable than in India—a perception shared not only by the children but also by many parents, if not consciously, at least unconsciously. Clinging to "Indianness" for their children, therefore, could easily be an overcompensation for this psychology of racial inferiority inherited from colonial days. In addition to all these factors, of course, is the universal tendency to project one's unrealized dreams onto one's children.

One of the most important internalized ideals, or *samskar*, an Indian immigrant mother carries within is that of her public persona—the socially condoned and culturally supported posture and behavior to be presented in public. These behaviors are well defined to please others and to uphold the traditional Indian ideals of a "good woman." She is maternal, accommodating, gentle, self-effacing, serving, kind, and chaste. In India, a woman is brought up to be a "good woman" for her family and for her community. These duties create a well-grounded persona which helps her not only to adjust to her world but bolsters her self-esteem also. These ideal roles and duties are not created in one lifetime, but over generations, and reside in the deeper unconscious. These powerful habits, however, may not be as useful in adapting to American culture, whose ideals and goals are different.

The mother who was sure of herself back home soon discovers that the self-nourishing feedback loop is somehow broken when her daughter keeps questioning or, worse, avoiding the mother's role model. The more this happens, the less they are able to communicate. To avoid the confusion from this dissonance between her trained persona and the demand of the host culture, the mother tries to remain within her Indian group and Indian self. The daughter, who lives most of her life within the American culture, has little choice but to remain in confusion even when she goes overboard with an American persona. She too has inherited some of the age-old *samskar*. It is very difficult, for instance, for an American-born daughter to hurt her parents by defying their wishes in career choice and marriage.

Psychologically speaking, when a daughter disagrees with her mother's values, she may at the same time give unconscious signals of the opposite because of her internalized *samskar* of being a "good Indian daughter." No matter how different from her mother, for better or for worse, the daughter also holds the image of her mother inside her unconscious. "The parents always remain dormant in the depth of the children's hearts," said the great Bengali poet Rabindranath Tagore.

A corollary to the "good Indian girl" *samskar* is the slogan "What will others say?" which is repeated like a mantra by many Indian mothers. Consider the following fictional conversation between a mother and her daughter of nineteen who is going to a party with her friends on a Saturday evening:

> *Mother:* Please try to come home before midnight. Our friends will ask, "Where is Seema?" I wish you could stay a bit longer to at least say hello to our friends—your uncles and aunties.
>
> *Daughter:* Your friends never come on time. I shall have to wait forever to say hello. You can do that for me, please.
>
> *Mother (annoyed):* Also, don't bring your American friend to the door when you come home. It's not necessary to declare that kind of stuff in front of everyone. Your father and I have to live in a society.
>
> *Daughter (angry):* In this country if a young man does not see his date to the door, it's a sign of irresponsibility. It's called escorting a woman safely to her home. For god's sake, Ma, wake up! You have lived here long enough.

The need for others' approval can be an overwhelming obstacle to any real understanding or awareness of the problem. Women are too busy worrying about what looks good in others' eyes instead of what feels good inside. This preoccupation ultimately prevents a woman from being honest with herself and facing the painful struggle toward consciousness. In this regard, the daughter is more aware of her confusion. And as she suffers from the guilt of displeasing her parents and betraying her heritage, the mother avoids her own confusion by blaming American culture or her ill luck for everything.

One other internalized ideal that Indian women are fortunate to possess is *shakti*, a Sanskrit word which means inner strength and power. It refers to the kind of primeval feminine energy which is active and dynamic and is represented in Hindu mythology by the goddess Durga, along with her dark aspect, Kali. The goddess is benevolent and malevolent at different times, depending on the need for protection, nurturance, and destruction of evil. All Indian Hindu women have been brought up not only to worship these icons but also to internalize part of this *shakti*. The courage in many Indian women in the past and recent history comes from their owning their *shakti* and using it when appropriate. All of us have known women in our families who embody such power. Many of these women have initiated major social reforms and political changes. What, then, has contributed to the loss of this quality among immigrant women?

Of course, there are exceptions to the observations I make, and as time passes and the third generation is born, I believe such confusions will lessen.

It is happening already. Some young Indian mothers are encouraging their children, especially daughters, to integrate the two cultures as much as possible. I know of bright young women who are returning to India to do their thesis research on Indian topics. Obviously, they are returning to their roots through the intellect. Until such natural integration comes about, what can be done to improve the failed communications?

Possible Solutions

From my observations and analysis of the problems of communication between immigrant Indian mothers and their American-born daughters, it should be fairly obvious that the initial steps to a possible solution must be taken by the older generation. Because they made the decision to immigrate in the first place, they must try to be honest about the situation. The only way the parents will be able to take this responsibility is to be humble and shift their attitudes and philosophy. If they want to maintain good relationships with their children, they have hardly any choice but to rise above the nostalgia and guilt of leaving their families and tradition behind and look forward to making the best of the current situation. This is hard work and requires humility, honesty, flexibility, and sacrifice. The parents must look deep beneath the surface conflicts for a better understanding of their children's dilemma and then be ready to sacrifice some of the old habits and *samskars*, which are not serving them any longer. Following are a number of initial questions an immigrant mother needs to ask herself and try to answer honestly. Even if she is unable to answer these questions, in the process of *living* the questions, she may develop her first awareness of the situation.

1. Why are we really here?
2. Why do we need to hold on to the India of the sixties and seventies, which does not even exist in India anymore?
3. Is it fair to ask my daughter to follow the ideals which I haven't fully followed myself in my own youth?
4. Am I overcompensating for my own guilt at leaving family and country behind? Am I asking my daughter to uphold Indian values because of this?
5. Do I unintentionally treat my son different than my daughter? If the answer is yes, why do I do this?
6. Do I blame my husband and American society for things not going my way?

7. Do I trust my daughter's instincts enough to let her make her own mistakes and learn from them?
8. How much of my efforts to influence my daughter reflect my own power struggle with my husband?
9. Can I really insist on being my daughter's role model?
10. Am I in denial and being defensive about my own dissatisfactions in life?

Although these questions seem pedestrian, just facing them honestly may be the first step for some mothers in breaking the vicious circle of blame and projection. Once they face these questions directly, they may learn to be more relaxed about instructions and control and let the daughter use her own instincts and tap her own resources—her own *shakti*. Perhaps the mother can help the daughter, reminding her of that inner strength, by owning her own *shakti*, not just following Indian customs and rituals blindly. Her daughter needs to understand and believe that she is fortunate to have come from an ancient culture and be brought up in a new one. She has the power to turn this unique combination to her advantage.

After all, the daughter's creativity has a better chance if she combines her two heritages. It is well known that Indian literature, art, and science made a creative leap after the encounter and clash with Western influences in the early eighteenth century. An individual Indian should be able to utilize this opportunity fully. An Indian writer who came to this country at the age of two once told me the following, "I am most creative when I use faintly familiar forms and images from somewhere in the Indian past and express them through American experience and language." Being the "other" in one's new land can be an advantage provided one can use imagination. Finally, through this process, the mother may learn again the simple and universal truth that the generation gap is natural and a healthy necessity for children to become mature adults.

This brings me to another observation—almost a truism—which may be useful to keep in mind when we analyze social and cultural problems and suggest remedies. The generation gap and lack of communication between mothers and daughters—except for a few fortunate ones—is not only universal but also natural because it is part of the bigger picture of human socialization and maturation, albeit appearing more acutely in specific cases. Isolating individual problems within a defined social group and analyzing them microscopically have been an old habit for social scientists. This kind of analysis can be designed to prove or disprove one's hypothesis but ultimately is of limited use as coping mechanism.

This knowledge of a universal truth shifts the gravity of the problem in a way that a solution seems possible. Because, in the final analysis, all human problems are part of an ongoing evolution of life and its creative manifestation. Keeping this perspective may also help in the specific analysis to shift and sift the factors in more balanced way.

Conclusion

In conclusion, I would like to make a few comments on the methodology of such investigations and observations. Further understanding of problems faced by Indian-American immigrants in recreating their families in the United States will be limited indeed if we continue to use monolithic approaches. If we use only political or sociological or historical or even cultural explanations in understanding complex human behavior, which are often contradictory if not downright paradoxical, we shall remain forever distant and, yes, objective. But feelings are lost and solutions remain distant as well. It is important to use several different approaches with various assumptions and information. One method of analysis alone cannot do justice to such complex experience, which, as I mentioned, is an ongoing process and will change as time goes on.

Take, for example, political explanation. It has become a common practice to blame sexual politics for all the difficulties experienced by women. While patriarchy definitely bears a large share of the responsibility, I believe, such finger-pointing explanations shift the emotional responsibility to only one half of the group. Women must take responsibility for their fate as much as possible. The brand of feminism that advocates raising group consciousness often fails because, after a woman's initial exposure to shared experience, the reckoning must begin with herself. In a culture where the prescribed public persona pushes a woman to become a community person and protects her from her own self, a group movement can be easily manipulated. Even on an individual level, a theory about a subject such as sexual politics can take away the emotional experience of personal responsibility by intellectualizing the problem. Even when isolating a factor as a "cause," handling it with more understanding and compassion may help arrive at better resolutions. Using unidimensional explanations has the additional problem of externalizing the problem totally without any input of a subjective viewpoint.

After all is said and done, I believe, mothers and daughters may find better ways to solve the problem of communication if they do not forget their love and affection for each other, which need not be understood but remembered and acknowledged. Mothers who have little problem communicating with their daughters and say "we are just lucky" act from that center of instinct that makes the act of letting go easier.

Notes

1. Manisha Roy, "Change in Joint-Family Systems in India" (*Man in India* 25, no. 4 [1965]); *Bengali Women* (Chicago: University of Chicago Press, [1975] 1993); "The Concept of 'Femininity' and 'Liberation' in the Context of Changing Sex Roles: Women in Modern India and America," in D. Raphael, ed., *Being Female* (The Hague: Mouton, 1975); "The Oedipus Complex and the Bengali Family in India: A Study of Father-Daughter Relations in Bengal," in T. R. Williams, ed., *Psychological Anthropology* (The Hague: Mouton, 1975); "Letters between Three Generations," in K. Payne, ed., *Between Ourselves: Letters between Mothers and Daughters* (London: Michael Joseph, 1983); and "The Relationship between Indian Men and Women: An American Experience," paper presented at the Strength in Unity conference, sponsored by the Indian American Forum for Political Education, Lowell, Mass., 1995.
2. The names and a few factual details have been changed to protect the privacy of individuals. I thank Bonu Ghosh of San Francisco for her help in gathering some of the data.
3. S. Kakar, *The Inner World: A Psychoanalytic Study of Childhood and Society in India* (Oxford: Oxford University Press, 1978).
4. P. Agarwal, *Indian Immigrants and Their Children: Conflicts, Concerns, and Solutions* (Palos Verdes, Calif.: Yuvati, 1991).

Sex, Lies, and Women's Lives

AN INTERGENERATIONAL DIALOGUE

—

SAYANTANI DASGUPTA AND SHAMITA DAS DASGUPTA

What's the Big Problem?

The past twenty-five years of living in America have been a story of relative success for Asian-Indian immigrants. After two decades of Asian Indians' settling in, the nineties are witnessing the graying of the post-1965 immigrants and the coming of age of their children. As the U.S.-raised second generation is being initiated into adulthood, the Indian-American community has become excessively preoccupied with a collective problem. Frequently, concern about this problem erupts into full-fledged panic. Although it is given different names, such as "youth issues," "the second generation problem," and "cultural preservation," the nature of the Indian-American community's problem is common to many cultures: sexual control of youth.

In this chapter, we, a mother-daughter team, have attempted to understand and address this predicament in our community. We believe that many of these difficulties arise from the Asian-Indian community's rejection of women's sexuality in general, and young women's sexuality in particular. This attitude has created fearsome myths that effectively silence and divide the women in our community. We have approached this topic from different points of view: as women of two generations who have grown up in the distinct cultures of India and the United States. In our discussion, we have interwoven our personal experiences with pertinent theoretical viewpoints on South Asian women's sexuality. We present our own experiences in the extracts set off from the text, with *D* indicating the daughter's sections and *M* the mother's.

D: A few months ago, after seeing the film *Bhaji on the Beach*, my mother approached me with concern. She described a scene in which a young, pregnant woman of Indian descent mourns her lack of family support and asked me, "Do I not support you, give you room to talk about your personal life?"

"No, you don't at all," I shot back, "You talk to everyone else's daughters about their personal problems, but you don't want to hear about mine."

"So I'm a bad mother, is that what you're trying to tell me?" she asked half-jokingly, adding flippantly, "Too bad. If you don't like it, you're old enough to change yourself. Change."

Sexuality. It's a word my mother and I use often, particularly since I went to college. We discuss sexuality as it affects the South Asian community: the lack of attention to sexuality in my mother's field of domestic violence counseling, the impact of sexual silence on my field of interest, HIV/AIDS prevention, the growing voices of the lesbian, gay, and bisexual South Asian activists—and the list goes on. Yet, even though my mother and I have always been extremely close, our discussions of sexuality remain in the realm of theory. Seldom have we discussed how the issue affects our lives personally as women.

While I have few complaints about the way I was raised, and emotional baggage that amounts to only a light carry-on, an examination of my mother's and my inability to discuss issues of sexuality on a personal level can be not only cathartic for us but also potentially illuminating regarding one of the most charged intergenerational issues of conflict in the Indian-American immigrant community. And so, in writing this article, I try and take my mother's advice, to change.

In the Indian immigrant community, issues surrounding sex and sexuality have become the primary area of intergenerational conflict. Indeed, the community looks upon the individual sexual behavior of its youth as potentially destructive to the integrity of the group. Of particular concern is the sexual behavior of community daughters.[1] Nowhere is this distress more apparent than in parental attitudes toward the dating behavior of young girls. Mani articulates this problem accurately, "The fear of dating that consumes many South Asian families is primarily a fear of women dating. Although many parents may worry about interracial marriage for what it might imply for them in old age, there is little attempt to control men's sexuality. Women, meanwhile, are quite frequently policed with the stick of tradition: it is women who are called on to preserve the ways of the old country."[2]

The task of inculcating young, second-generation girls in their role as keepers of culture consists of rejecting dating and accepting the traditional practice of arranged marriage by presenting the latter as essential to "Indian" ways. Thus, any move toward independent sexual choices, especially by young women, is labeled "Americanization" and is posed as synonymous with un-principled and immoral behavior. The responsibility of socializing commu-nity youth, especially daughters, in traditional ways, falls on the shoulders of first-generation women, the immigrant mothers.[3] These maternal monitor-ings and restrictions are taken by young women as indications of the inher-ently "backward" and "oppressive" nature of Indian culture. Thus, it is mothers who most often come into conflict with second-generation young women regarding sexuality. As daughters of the Asian-Indian community seek sexual and social independence, they are faced with an apparent choice be-tween personal liberation and cultural loyalty.

> *M:* During many of my lecture tours to college campuses, where I talk about activism within the Indian immigrant community, I meet with young women who talk to me about their problems with their parents, the Asian-Indian community, and, basically, the whole In-dian culture. Most of their discontent seem to revolve around the is-sue of sexuality: dating, marriage, and the choice of a partner. "I can't talk to my mother! She won't hear of me dating or having a boy-friend, even if it is not serious," is a common lament. Many have talked about the stress they undergo either by trying to remain obe-dient to their parents' dictates or by discarding them to adopt "Ameri-can" ways. Others have questioned the compatibility of activism with Indian traditions.
>
> After one of my talks on sexuality, one young woman actually exclaimed, "But you look just like my mother!" The subtext was that mothers, who are keepers of traditions, cannot talk about progres-sive activism on the subject of sexuality. I remember another young woman who once asked me if I let my daughter date. Hearing my answer, she commented disapprovingly, "I have grown up within my culture; it is very strong in our home. I would never do something like that!"

As a mother and daughter who have faced many of our own conflicts regarding the issue of sexuality, we want to locate and articulate the essential points of this intergenerational struggle. We speak only for ourselves and our own experiences as heterosexual women of Hindu, Asian-Indian descent. Rather than providing solutions, this chapter is intended as a springboard for future dialogues.

What Is Indian Culture, Anyway?

In the decade after the passing of the 1965 Immigration and Naturalization Act, selective immigration policies created a rather homogeneous white-collar Asian-Indian community in the United States. When Indian immigration to America started in the 1970s, it was the professionally educated, Victorian-morality-influenced middle class that was the first to arrive. As a result, in the two decades after the influx of immigration started, the Asian-Indian community quickly established itself professionally and economically.[4] In the last few years, it is even knocking on the U.S. political door, with people such as Kanak Dutta, Neil Dhillon, Ram Uppuluri, Peter Mathews, and Kumar Bharve running in state and federal elections. Along with efforts to secure a place for themselves in American society, these educated and affluent immigrants have diligently endeavored to maintain the values, traditions, and rituals of their homeland. Research on the Indian community's adaptation to America indicates that these immigrants have retained the values regarding home, family, child rearing, religion, and marriage that they brought over from their native country.[5] Lumped under the rubric of "Indian culture" and stripped of the dynamism, diversity, and local idiosyncrasies present in the native land, many of these values and customs have taken on a generic hue. As a result, a vigorous reinvention of a hybrid "Indian culture" has taken place in the United States. This new Indian culture fundamentally constitutes the ideological "familiar essentials" redesigned by the dominant male bourgeoisie.[6] The values of a close-knit, interdependent family, clearly differentiated gender roles, familial hierarchy, recognition of insiders (Indians) versus outsiders (all other Americans), regionolinguistic media, religious rituals, and so on all make up these familiar essentials. A focal point of this re-creation is the image of the Indian woman as pure, chaste, nurturant, and upholder of culture, rituals, and traditional family values.

> *M:* When I first started going to college in this country and became
> involved in feminist activities, my daughter was three years old. Many
> of my Indian friends, who had been extremely supportive of me as
> a young wife and mother, now issued dire warnings. "Educating your-

self is wonderful," they said, "but not when you have a family. Take one or two courses for fun. But anything more means you are neglecting your family duties!" Others waxed effusive about my husband's enormous patience in putting up with my willfulness. Many men teased my husband openly about starting a battered men's forum and told him that they would never allow their wives to associate with me.

As the immigrant generation grows older, their sons and daughters, popularly known as the second generation, have started to claim their rightful place within the community. These are the children who were either born and reared in the United States or they accompanied their immigrant parents at a tender age, thereby precluding any realistic recollection of India. With the second generation of Asian Indians coming of age, the task of passing on "culture" has become a priority with the original immigrants. Consequently, each language/caste-culture/religion-based Asian-Indian organization in the United States abounds in celebrations of culture whose purpose is not only to assuage immigrant nostalgia but also to inculcate the second generation. Every Asian-Indian convention and conference invariably includes a "youth forum" with the objective of acquainting the next generation with the traditional and "tried and true" beliefs of their parents. However, such blatant indoctrinations meet with pockets of resistance. Quite often, magazines and newspapers carry voices of the second generation challenging such parental advice regarding acculturation and defining their own selves autonomously.[7]

> *D:* I had the opportunity to combine what I had learned from main-stream American feminism with the progressive parts of my Indian heritage. Since I was never shown a simplistic, mono-political picture of Indian culture, I never felt compelled to swallow a conservative Indian identity, or to reject my heritage as wholly "traditional.". . .
> We are a generation who has not only had to juggle multiple cultural identities, but learn to understand the oppressive forces at work around us.[8]

Women's Space: Is There Room for Us to Be "Bad"?

Patriarchy has long located women's power in their sexuality, attributing the female body with mystery, fear, and loathing. To gain control over this power, patriarchal societies have developed intricate methods of domination, including edicts against female economic, social, and sexual independence. The control of women also occurs through socialization of sexual mores and codes through the mechanism of metaphor. Indeed, the two most pervasive images of women across cultures are those of the "goddess" and the "whore." The goddess is the chaste and life-giving mother who gently influences all by her moral superiority, supporting rather than questioning the prevalent order of society. On the other hand, the whore is the immoral temptress who lures men to their destruction with her abundant sexuality. She challenges the status quo and may have the power to overturn it completely. In colloquial terms, images of the whore and the goddess are manifested in "women-who-do" and "women-who-don't": bad girls and good girls.

In the West, Mary and Eve are the archetypes of the goddess and the whore. Although both of these oppositional concepts exist in the Asian-Indian context, they do not seem to have such clear-cut representations. In Hindu cosmology, the feminine force arises from Prakriti, the dynamic energy of the universe. Prakriti's power becomes benevolent in the form of Devi (the goddess) only after the feminine force is willingly relinquished to a male consort. The antithesis of the nurturant Devi is Shakti, the malevolent feminine principle. Shakti is dangerous because she retains full control over her own sexuality. Unlike the whore, Shakti's wanton sexuality does not preclude her from motherhood. While Devi is the all-forgiving mother, Shakti is the punishing mother who can give life and, of course, take it away.

Although Devi is the ideal model for Hindu womanhood, Shakti is not completely excluded, nor is she as deplorable as the licentious Eve. In reality, she is represented by the *virangana*, the warrior woman who is a fearless leader and savior of the downtrodden. Thus, within the Hindu tradition, there has remained a limited space for a woman who is independent and self-reliant. However, the autonomous woman is considered dangerous when she is individualistic and self-promoting. She is accepted only when she dedicates her life to bringing about collective social good. Throughout history, during the nationalist *bhakti* and other such movements, Indian women have utilized the model of the *virangana* to create a room of their own.

British rule, with its Victorian moral strictures, sliced away a large part of women's autonomy that came with the model of the *virangana*. The colonizers saw Shakti only as the tongue-lolling, blood-sucking barbarian, and thus, much of the space afforded by this image was eroded. The constraints that ensued for Indian women were decidedly class based. The middle class, the hub of the British government's bureaucratic machinery, strongly internalized Victorian moral prescriptions and severely restricted autonomous female sexuality. Owing to their relative distance from the colonial government, the lower and upper classes were to a certain degree exempt from these moral constrictions. In the postindependence era, class continued to define sexual borderlands.

However, even within the narrow confines of "good" moral behavior, where female sexuality was publicly denied and kept under strict supervision, women managed to negotiate a private space for themselves that allowed for sexual expression. In the *andar-mahal* (women's quarters), in the kitchen, or during the afternoon siesta time, grandmothers, aunts, sisters, daughters, daughters-in-law, and mothers shared personal experiences, discussed neighborhood gossip, exchanged sexual advice, created bawdy songs and dances, gave newlywed brides seduction and birth-control tips, and supported and affirmed one another's sexual selves. This was the invisible space that women had eked out for themselves within the patriarchal order.

> *M:* My most pleasant recollections about growing up in Calcutta are the warm afternoons and nights when the older women in my family talked together about intimate matters. During most of these "hen-sessions" I had to feign sleep or risk being sent out of the room. Quite early, I realized that the topics of discussion were not meant for my tender ears and knew better than to be fully honest. These women, ranging in age from early twenties to seventies, were just as diverse in their relationships: older cousins, my mother, aunts, grandmother, sister-in-law, and a few select neighbors. Not all of them were married either. I was always amazed at how easily these otherwise prim and proper ladies exchanged gory details of their sexual experiences and how much they giggled. Even widowed grandmothers shared stories of their first night of sexual pleasure. As I grew older, I was casually incorporated into the ranks of these women. After my marriage, I received a lot of sexual training from the women in this group while my mother looked on with an amiable expression. Once I moved into my husband's family, I joined a new circle made up of my husband's cousins, sisters-in-law, and aunts. Now when I go home on vacations, I find that the membership of these circles has changed, yet the tradition seems to have remained just as strong.

This women's space of the afternoon chat, where otherwise "Victorian" and "chaste" ladies are allowed to let down their hair and be "bad," is based upon the tradition of the *andar-mahal* and therefore remains in the "private" sphere. The existence of this space in India, but not within the Indian-

American immigrant community, leads to the speculation that this private space has been lost in the migration process. In other words, it is only the public face of the Asian-Indian womanhood that has been transported to America in all its fierce circumscription.

> *D:* Despite the fact that I look upon the aunties of my Indian- American community as my extended family, I would never be able to approach them to ask for personal or sexual advice. Anything I said would get around the community in a second, and that would be devastatingly embarrassing for my family. My mother always tells me, "We don't talk about personal things to outsiders." Yet the situation is strikingly different in India. As I've grown older, I've realized that those giggling afternoon conversations my mother, grandmother, and aunt used to exclude me from are actually about gossip, marriage, dating, even sex! Still, I don't feel comfortable revealing my personal life to my relatives in India. I really want to be able to ask my mother for frank, intimate advice, but I'm afraid she would be disapproving, or even disappointed in my "American" preoccupation with dating, men, and other such "frivolities." I wish I had such a circle of my own—older, "wiser" Indian women I could approach for advice without exposing my intimate secrets to "outsiders."

How Do We See Ourselves?

The majority of post-1965 immigrant women to the United States grew up in the years after India's independence. These educated middle-class women, today's immigrant mothers, came of age in a highly nationalistic, moralistic, and sexually restrictive atmosphere. Despite the existence of limited spaces for sexual expression such as that of the *andar-mahal*, strict separations of public and private necessitated that Indian women hide their sexual selves in all other arenas. In fact, young Indian women at that time were hardly supposed to have any sexual consciousness at all. In most cases, young girls' early sexual experiences were surreptitious touches from male relatives and molestations received in public situations. The shame of these filthy accostings lay absolutely with the victims themselves. Although such experiences may have been freely shared among peers, they were intergenerational taboo topics. These traumatizing harassments quickly taught young women to monitor their own behavior and movement and to dress so as not to attract male attention. Indeed, the common understanding was that those who were assaulted were surely "bad" girls who had participated in or somehow invited their own violation.

> *M:* When I was about ten years old, I had gone to a local *mela* [carnival] with my mother and a group of my close relatives. In the middle of munching roasted corn I was shocked out of my wits by a rude hand touching me intimately. Noticing my agitation, an elder cousin sympathetically consoled, "Terrible, isn't it? Now that you are growing older, you will get many of these!" My mother looked at me sadly but did not say a word. In a few years, I learned how to wrap my sari to cover both my shoulders, how to hold myself in a mixed crowd, and why I should never stay in a room alone with certain male cousins. I also got the distinct message from my mother that such matters were not to be spoken of aloud.

Although the middle class set clear boundaries around women's moral behavior, it was acknowledged that the other classes were outside these rules. While middle-class women were expected to be sexually naive, chaste, and monogamous, it was "common knowledge" that the lower classes were promiscuous as well as knowledgeable about sexual matters, and did not hesitate to abandon their spouses at will. Analogously, the upper classes were also suspected of engaging in licentious and dissolute behavior. Whether or not these suspicions were true, the fact remains that lower- and upper-class women were allowed more sexual autonomy than their middle-class counterparts. When middle-class daughters sought such liberties, parents thwarted them by indicating that these behaviors were class inappropriate.

Of course, no matter how many restrictions a young woman's parents imposed on her, romantic relations flowered in secret. Women met their paramours in theaters, restaurants, and public parks, all the while hiding such relationships from parents. Although individualistic romances were considered incompatible with filial duty, most of the young women who engaged in premarital dating did not view this as inherently "bad." Indeed, the worst compunctions women had about their relationships were about being disobedient.

> *M:* I grew up with a cousin who was a couple of years older than me. Even before finishing school, she had fallen in love with a young man who was later to become her husband. Although young and strictly brought up, this was definitely not her first love. On clandestine rendezvous with her boyfriend, I was her "front." We

conspired to tell the adults that we were going shopping so that she could go meet her boyfriend. Later, when she had declared her engagement to her future husband and the family furor over it had passed, she was given formal permission to go out with him. On each of these outings, I was her chaperone.

Although my parents did not caution me directly, their alarm at my cousin's example became clear. One day, while discussing marriage and other philosophies of life, my father gently commented on the shortsightedness of choosing a partner on one's own: "Family and parents are the most important parts of one's life. How can a person love another without parents' wisdom or blessings? After all, the feelings of love are created by one's family!" I knew at that instant where my loyalties must lie. I know that my marriage must be in accordance with my parents' wishes.

The majority of Indian women are not primary immigrants to the United States but have followed their husbands here. Away from a gender-stereotyped society and the restrictions of extended families, these young wives have confessed to a certain degree of freedom and independence.[9] Nevertheless, confronted by relative sexual explicitness, acceptance of premarital sexuality, and the practice of individual choice of partners in America, first-generation parents have become anxious about the preservation of their cultural way of life. This fear of cultural erasure has further led these immigrant parents to adhere more strongly to Indian traditions. Moreover, as the keepers of culture, the mothers are actually showing more conservatism than the fathers.[10] Thus, although they have moved toward autonomy themselves, immigrant mothers have become more restrictive toward their daughters.

The recent movie by British director Gurinder Chadha, *Bhaji on the Beach*, illustrates this point wonderfully.[11] Although the characters of this film reside in England, they are similar to their Indian counterparts in America. The three older women in *Bhaji*, Pushpa, Asha, and Bina, are intent on continuing the heritage of Indian culture. In this endeavor they become so "Indian" that a tourist from India finds them completely anachronistic. One of the women, Asha, is repeatedly haunted by a giant religious icon that wants to make sure that she is following the rightful Indian path in all her undertakings. However, this Indianness is confined only to controlling the sexual behaviors of younger women. Unable to sympathize with the plights of the younger generation of women, the older matrons relentlessly berate them for their forwardness with the opposite sex and their disregard for marital conventions. Their panicked tries at keeping the younger women within a my-thologized "Indian culture" actually drive the latter away.

For Indian-American young women coming of age in the United States, conflicting stereotypes are translated into contradictory self-images. While growing up, daughters of Asian-Indian immigrants are surrounded by televi-sion and advertising images of blond, blue-eyed beauty, a standard against which they can only come up short. Indian-American women, like most women of color, often admit to seeing themselves as "ugly" in their youth, emphasizing a preoccupation with their darker skin color. This white beauty standard serves to reinforce the Indian cultural concept that only fair-skinned women are beautiful, thus desirable for marriage. As explained by Mira Nair in her film *Mississippi Masala*, "A marriageable girl can either be poor and fair, or rich and dark, but not poor and dark."[12]

> *D:* Having grown up in an almost all-white Midwestern American suburb, a little brown girl in an ocean of blonde hair and blue eyes, I had a self-image and concept of personal beauty that had always been particularly low. In the mid-seventies, before dolls of color, the Cosby show, and Disney's token brown-skinned princess Jasmine, I, like every other little girl of color, had nothing to compare myself to but the unattainable: Charlie's Angels, Barbie, and the golden-curled girls of the Brady Bunch. I remember a perpetual feeling of self-loathing; wishing I could just be "like everyone else," wanting to melt into the floor whenever someone looked at me, being sure that all eyes were always watching me, and all tongues ridiculing. These feelings were not, of course, only based on the lack of role models and self-affirmation around me. I faced repeated and con-stant racial slurs at school, from "nigger" to "injun" to "Hindoo." I, as one of the few children of color, was the equal opportunity target.

The formation of Indian-American women's sexual self-concept is, how-ever, influenced not only by the white American beauty standard but also by the West's fascination with the "mysterious" East. This fascination is seen in mainstream-targeted movies such as *Mississippi Masala*, in which Indian-American women are depicted as the long-hair-swinging, glass-embroidered-shawl-wearing, cosmopolitan "ethnochic."[13] Indeed, during an August 1993 Indian-American conference, women participating in a gender workshop ex-plained that among the stereotypes affecting their lives, the image of being con-sidered simultaneously "ugly" and "exotic" was one of the most detrimental to their self-concept.[14] In fact, the exotic/ugly dichotomy is perhaps the diasporic manifestation of the Asian-Indian goddess-whore construct.

The contradictory beauty stereotypes of Indian-American women as both exotic and ugly are coupled to sexual stereotypes. Indeed, in white America's categorization of racial others as sexually deviant, the Asian-Indian immigrant community is caught in a dual metaphor as both asexual and hypersexual: "There is a general assumption in white society that sees Asians as somehow sexually repressed, living in oppressed environments, both within the home and the community. That somehow, Asian people are not sexually expressive, but are rather restricted in this area of human activity. But also in opposition to this concept lies the idea that somehow the darker the skin the more lascivious the person, that Asians (and Africans) are somehow eternally 'in heat.' After all, didn't the *Kama Sutra* come from India?"[15] In this context, the "exotic" Indian-American woman is associated with the *Kama Sutra*, primal sexual energy, and other images of hypersexuality. Simultaneously, the alien, "ugly" Indian-American woman is associated with chastity, sexual repression, and hyperintellectualism.

Regardless of which end of the exotic/ugly spectrum an Indian-American daughter aligns herself with, such unattainable, double-jeopardy beauty and sexual standards most often lead to negative sexual self-perception. Although such negative self-perception may begin in the schoolyard, its impact often manifests itself in postadolescent rebellions. In the words of Sreemoee Mukherjee, a twenty-three-year-old Rutgers University graduate, "Half the girls in college were leading double lives. They partied wildly and had boyfriends at school, but were also arranged to marry someone from India. We weren't in the mainstream in high school due to our parents' rules and regulations. In college, we want to be mainstream, to be what Hollywood shows college students should be. I think Indian guys and girls always had a complex about what America thinks we should look like . . . and how we look at ourselves is negative in comparison to other Americans."[16]

What's the Big Deal with Dating?

Although the passing of the cultural baton to the second generation includes religious and language training, and the promotion of popular media such as Hindi cinema, music, and dances, the critical point is instilling in them an acceptance of the tradition of arranged marriage. Several studies have reported the anxiety and rejection of "dating" exhibited by Asian-Indian immigrant parents.[17] Indeed, youth dating has become a conference mainstay among the diasporic community. Immigrant parents repeatedly voice their concern over their children's "nontraditional" behavior, while the children of immigrants complain about parental strictures regarding hot topics like dating and the prom.[18] Most often, the parental fear underlying these debates seems to be of miscegenation, that the out-group marriage of community children will lead to cultural dilution. In an *India Abroad* letter entitled "Intercultural marriage," an immigrant father contends, "If the Asian partner moves away from his/her parental culture to become a part of the so-called American melting pot, that is a big loss to . . . the relatively small but growing Asian community in the United States."[19]

However, fears of youth dating stem from not only immigrant resistance to miscegenation but also a fear of second-generation sexual activity. A survey among the South Asian community in Toronto found "a perception and fear that younger generations, under pressure from peers and Western values, would become sexually active at an earlier age."[20] The South Asian immigrant community's reaction to issues of sexuality, including second-generation dating, HIV/AIDS, and homosexuality within the community, is influenced by its construction of identity around familial social terms rather than individual or sexual ones. In the words of Himani Bannerji, a poet and community activist from Toronto, "People identify themselves not by individual behavior but by social relations. Identity is constructed in familial social terms . . . there is little space to talk about sex or sexuality. Being lovers is a non-institutionalized relation. These are societies that are constructed around marriages. When marriage happens, a family happens and a legitimate social space where sexuality and reproductive activity can take place happens."[21] Thus, sexuality is "individualized" and "privatized" within the Asian-Indian context.[22] It is taken to imply individual, rather than familial, choice of partners and thus defined as destructive to the familial construction of social identity. Bannerji explains, "As a whole, sexuality is not something that is talked about. Even mothers are reticent to discuss menstruation with daughters. [Sexuality] is something that is done, but never revealed to others. It is a very private practice."[23]

> *D:* Despite my closeness with my mother, I did not reveal my childhood ghosts to her until I was an adult. And so racist incidents or slurs were never discussed, feelings of inadequacy never shared and self-doubt never revealed. I shielded her whenever I could from my perceptions of reality, assuming that the truth would only hurt her. Even when I was able to recognize my childhood experiences as

racism and sexism, I could not share with my mother my feelings of inadequacy regarding my sexuality. I was so socialized that if a car full of white men hooted at me, I assumed they were making fun of me as an undesirable woman—while the same behavior from men of color was recognized as annoying catcalls. Somehow, I could not reconcile my sexual desirability in the face of a white beauty standard. This conflict was amplified by my inability to discuss it with my mother. It wasn't as if she ever directly prevented me from bringing up sexuality. Yet, for some reason, I believed that sexual curiosity, desire, and interest were somehow "weak," "too American," and antithetical to what my mother wanted of me: academic and intellectual achievement.

Fears regarding the sexual activity of immigrant youth have a distinctly gendered bias since it is community daughters who are expected to be the guardians of tradition not only through language, clothing, and food but also through "chaste" behavior and marriage to community men of their parents' choosing. In the words of a forty-seven-year-old immigrant mother, "Culturally, we are very different. It is very foreign for us to let our girls go out alone with boys."[24]

There is an additional burden placed upon the "bad" immigrant daughter that is not shared by her Indian counterpart. By associating itself with the asexual Asian image, the Indian-American community posits itself as "traditional," "moral," and antithetical to the "American influences of drugs, promiscuity, and rebelliousness."[25] The argument against autonomous sexual behavior takes on a nationalistic rationale, with letters to Indian community newspapers asserting, "Indian tradition is not consistent with dating. Should we not be proud of that tradition?"[26] Thus, intergender relationships, dating, and sexual behavior become coded as some sort of evil Western ritual. A 1992 *India Today* article asserts, "Growing up in a society where schools drive home the message of safe sex by distributing condoms to students, where dating is a rite of passage, the youngsters (in their teens and early 20's) mix freely with the opposite sex, party frequently and admit frankly to encounters of the intimate kind."[27]

Thus, autonomous sexual behavior is indicative of a certain level of assimilation into mainstream American culture. The "whore," therefore, is not only the bad girl but also the betrayer of the community who makes the group vulnerable to cultural dilution. By linking the burdens of sexual chastity and cultural tradition, and placing both on the Indian-American daughter's shoulders, the Indian immigrant community protects itself from mainstream threats of assimilation. Indeed, the control of the daughter's sexuality becomes the community's main antiracist resistance. In line with the Indian construction of woman as potentially "polluting," Indian-American women carry the heavy burden of being potential polluters and diluters of the immigrant hegemony.

How Can Mothers and Daughters Bridge the Generation Gap?

For the post-1965 Asian-Indian community in the United States, sex and sexuality have become an intergenerational, cross-cultural war zone. The battle lines are drawn, with immigrant mothers, Indian culture, morality, and tradition on one side, and U.S.-raised daughters, Westernization, autonomy, and modernity on the other. In a community struggling to maintain its sense of cultural self against assimilatory forces, the icon of the perfect, chaste Indian woman plays a central role. Indeed, the Indian-American hegemony names community daughters the keepers of Indian culture, while it places immigrant mothers in the role of teachers and monitors of culture. By putting two generations of women in these highly conflicting roles, the Indian immigrant hegemony has effectively driven a wedge between mothers and daughters, preventing, to an extent, the formation of collective female power in the Indian-American community.

> *D:* I talk to my mother about almost everything: from the intellectual heights of diasporic identity politics to the trivialities of who said what to whom at what party. However, despite having developed our politics together, frequently collaborating on projects, and being good friends, silence has reigned between us when it comes to the erstwhile taboo topic of sexuality. Even though I've often yearned to share with her my personal romantic feelings, conflicts, and questions, I am distinctly aware that to do so would only embarrass us both. And so, in my mind, my romantic life continues to be at odds with my family and culture. Since my parents are my only true link to India, not being able to include them in my romantic decision making also means not being able to fully incorporate my Indian self into my sexual self.

The transmigration of only the public face of Indian womanhood, the image of the Devi without her Shakti, has resulted in a lack of autonomous sexual space for women. Even the very private, limited arena of the

andar-mahal has been left in India, so that immigrant mothers are left upholding the patriarchal agenda and passing on only the repressive iconography of Indian womanhood to their U.S.-raised daughters. Indian-American
daughters, on the other hand, have limited access to "true" Asian-Indian culture and therefore depend primarily on their parents for links to their cultural identity. Parental accusations that autonomous sexual behavior is
tantamount to cultural betrayal therefore carry great weight with these young
women.

It is this idea of cultural betrayal and dilution that must be critically
examined if Indian-American mothers and daughters are to heal the gaps between them. The Indian culture that immigrant parents try desperately to cling
to is neither monolithic nor fragile. Rather, it is an ancient, flexible, diverse
tradition that has withstood and incorporated internationalism for centuries;
the long parade of traders, invaders, and pilgrims to India is more than enough
proof of this ability. By having confidence that Asian-Indian culture will not
die, only change and continue to reinvent itself, mothers and daughters of
the community can disable the patriarchy's primary weapon against them.

It is only through conscious communication and active dialogue that
we as mothers and daughters can begin to feel less threatened by the forces
around us. By recognizing imperialism, racism, and sexism and resisting them
as a collective, we can counteract the community hegemony's attempts to control women's individual sexuality in the name of culture.

Notes

1. P. Agarwal, *Passage from India: Post 1965 Indian Immigrants and Their Children, Conflicts, Concerns, and Solutions* (Palos Verdes, Calif.: Yuvati, 1991); S.
   D. Dasgupta, "The Gift of Utter Daring: Cultural Continuity in Asian Indian Communities," in S. Mazumdar and J. Vaid, eds., *Women, Communities and Cultures:
   South Asians in America* (forthcoming).
2. L. Mani, "Gender, Class, and Cultural Conflict: Indu Krishnan's Knowing Her
   Place, *SAMAR* no. 1 (Winter 1992): 13.
3. S. D. Dasgupta, "The Gift of Utter Daring."
4. Agarwal, *Passage from India*; also A. W. Helweg and U. M. Helweg, *An Immigrant Success Story: East Indians in America* (Philadelphia: University of Pennsylvania Press, 1990).
5. M. L. Kaul, "Adaptation of Recently Arrived Professional Immigrants from India in Four Selected Communities in Ohio," *Journal of Applied Social Sciences*
   7, no. 2 (1983): 131–45; J. C. Naidoo, "Contemporary South Asian Women in
   the Canadian Mosaic," *International Journal of Women's Studies* 8, no. 4 (1985):
   338–50, and "Value Conflicts for South Asian Women in Multicultural Canada,"
   in L. Ekstrand, ed., *Ethnic Minority and Immigrant Research* (Lisse: Swets and

Zeitlinger, 1986); P. Saran, *The Asian Indian Experience in the United States* (Cambridge, Mass.: Schenkman, 1985); G. R. Sodowsky and J. C. Carey, "Asian Indian Immigrants in America: Factors Related to Adjustment," *Journal of Multicultural Counseling and Development*, "Special Issue: Cross-Cultural Counseling: The International Context, Part 2," 15, no. 3 (1987): 129–41, and "Relationships between Acculturation-related Demographics and Cultural Attitudes of an Asian-Indian Immigrant Group," *Journal of Multicultural Counseling and Development* 16 (1988): 117–36; U. A. Segal, "Cultural Variables in Asian Indian Families," *Families in Society: The Journal of Contemporary Human Services* 72, no. 4 (1991): 233–41; and S. D. Dasgupta, "The Gift of Utter Daring."

6. A. Bhattacharjee, "The Habit of Ex-Nomination: Nation, Woman, and the Indian Immigrant Bourgeoisie," *Public Culture* 5, no. 1 (1992): 19–44, and reprinted in this book.

7. V. Tamaskar, "Attitudes towards Dating in the 80s," 69–70; D. Motwani, "Arranged Marriage and Dating," 71–72; and S. Motwani and N. Motwani, "Parent-Child Conflict around Food," 66—all in *Proceedings of the Conference on Family and Youth* (Cleveland: National Federation of Asian Indian Organizations in America, 1988); and "Indian American Youth in the Dock," *Little India* (August 1994): 60–61.

8. S. DasGupta, "Thoughts from a Feminist ABCD," *India Currents* 6, no. 12 (1993): 26.

9. Agarwal, *Passage from India*.

10. S. D. Dasgupta, "The Gift of Utter Daring."

11. G. Chadha, *Bhaji on the Beach* (film) (London: Umbi Films, 1994).

12. M. Nair, *Mississippi Masala* (film) (Mirabai Films, 1992).

13. S. DasGupta, "Glass Shawls and Long Hair: A South Asian Woman Talks Sexual Politics," *Ms.* 3, no. 5 (1993): 76–77.

14. S. DasGupta, "Asian Indian Gender Roles," workshop held at the National Asian Indian Sammelan, Dayton, Ohio, Aug. 13–14, 1993.

15. S. Khan, "Sexuality and the Asian Communities," in *HIV/AIDS and the Asian Communities: Seminar Report* (London: HIV/AIDS and the Asian Communities Seminar, 1990), 20.

16. S. DasGupta, "Who Are We Anyway? Indian Americans Forging New Identities," *Onward* 1 (1994): 17.

17. C. M. Siddique, "Structural Separation and Family Change: An Exploratory Study of the Immigrant Indian and Pakistani Community in Saskatoon, Canada," *International Review of Sociology* 7 (1977): 13–34; S. M. Sharma, "Assimilation of Indian Immigrant Adolescents in British Society," *Journal of Psychology* 118 (1984): 79–84; M. Stopes- Roe and R. Cochrane, "The Process of Assimilation in Asians in Britain: A Study of Hindu, Muslim, and Sikh Immigrants and Their Young Adults," *International Journal of Comparative Sociology* 28, nos. 1–2 (1987): 43–56; G. Kurian, "Intergeneration Integration, with Special Reference to Indian Families," *Indian Journal of Social Work* 47, no. 1 (1986): 39–49, and "Changing Attitudes toward Asian Immigration, with Special Reference to Canada," paper presented at the First Global Conference of People of Indian Origin, New York, August 1989; and S. D. Dasgupta, "The Gift of Utter Daring."

18. S. DasGupta, "Thoughts from a Feminist ABCD."

19. B. N. Ghosh, "Intercultural Marriage," *India Abroad*, Sept. 11, 1992, p. 36.

20. South Asian AIDS Coalition, *Community Needs Assessment* (Toronto: South Asian AIDS Coalition, 1989), 2.

21. G. Saxena and I. Rashid, *Bolo! Bolo! Talking about Silence: AIDS and Gay Sexuality* (film) (Toronto: V Tape, 1991).

22. Anu, "Sexuality, Lesbianism, and South Asian Feminism," *Anamika* 1 (1987): 6–7.

23. Saxena and Rashid, *Bolo! Bolo!*

24. Agarwal, *Passage from India*, 49.

25. N. Shah, *The Ethnic Strife: A Study of Asian Indian Women in the United States* (New York: Pinkerton and Thomas, 1993), 58.

26. "We Don't Have to Date," *India Abroad*, May 22, 1992, p. 3.

27. A. K. Jha, "Campus Dating: Whitewashing Blues," *India Today*, October 31, 1992, p. 48h.

Marital Rape

Some Ethical and Cultural Considerations

———

Rinita Mazumdar

$\mathcal{T}$he concept of and debates in the Western world surrounding rape and its various forms—stranger rape, marital rape, acquaintance or date rape—have occupied much of modern feminist discourse. The determination of acts that constitute rape and their consequent penalties have been integral parts of this discussion. In every society it has been simpler to ascertain and legally sanction stranger rape than acquaintance or marital rape, as the perpetrator and victim are considered to be outside each other's realm of sexual interaction. With date and marital rapes, however, the definition and delineation of the parameters of rape usually are extremely difficult to fix, as both the perpetrator and victim are potential or current sexual partners.

As a South Asian feminist living in the United States, I have participated vigorously, through interaction and research, in the lively arguments around rape. Hence, my familiarity with the Euro-American perspectives of rape places me in an "epistemologically advantageous" position to analyze this phenomenon among Asian Indians in the United States.[1] I contend that unequivocal recognition of both marital and date rape is necessary before these can be legally condemned in society. Furthermore, identification of rape within the institution of marriage is essential to the understanding of domestic abuse and spousal violence against women.

In this chapter I will discuss the applicability of the concept of marital rape to the Asian-Indian context. Although I will focus on my immigrant community in the United States, I will refer quite extensively to the concept of marital rape as it exists in India itself. To comprehend the Asian-Indian immigrant's perspective on marital rape, we have to trace its roots to the soil where it originated. It is useful to note here that Indian immigrants do not lose their traditions and early socialization when they migrate to the new world. Rather, they transport their belief systems from their natal culture to the United States and rigidly adhere to these in an effort to preserve their heritage. In fact, Asian-Indian immigrant communications are deeply invested in creating an "authentic" and monolithic culture by glorifying traditional Hindu mores and codes. To ward off pressures of assimilation and maintain cultural distinction, the immigrants seem to conform strictly to this re-created culture in the United States. In contrast, free of similar tensions, the Indians in the native country deal with a culture that is dynamic, diverse, and multi-faceted. However, this cultural diversity in India may also be in jeopardy owing to the recent aggressive assaults of Hindu fanatics who seem to emphasize a uniform perspective on a mythical Hindu culture.

Nonetheless, India is a multiethnic, multicultural, multireligious, multicaste, and multiclass nation. Just as there are Hindus, Sikhs, Zoroastrians, Christians, and several other religious groups living together, so also are there various ethnolinguistic subgroups such as Punjabis, Bengalis, Tamils, and Marathis existing side by side. Despite this vast diversity, the Hindu culture has strongly influenced all others, as Hinduism is the dominant religion in India. Hence, I will scrutinize certain Hindu discourses and assert that these ideologies have affected the concept of marital rape in all other Indian cultures. I realize that analyzing merely the cultural and ideological aspect of the ethical permissibility of marital rape within any society leaves out important socioeconomic reasons why women accept sexual abuse from their partners. While such structural problems should be considered in any analysis such as this one, at present these remain outside the scope of this chapter.

My analysis below focuses on how violations of a woman's body are typically sanctioned within the marital institution. The first part of this discussion will present instances from life and literature that elucidate the ethical approval of marital rape in Indian culture. Later, I will assert that the internalization of such values generally prevents Asian-Indian immigrant women in the United States from speaking out against spousal sexual abuse. That is, cultural values which make rape within marriage "ethically permissible" are so deeply entrenched in the South Asian ethos that it effectively silences the immigrant woman from the region.

I submit here that, for the most part, marital rape has received "ethical permissibility" in the Hindu culture. I use the term "permissibility" here as it is commonly used in standard ethical theories denoting "right action by the individual." Permissibility in ethics can be predicated of *individual and kinds of actions*. For example, in the sentence "You are permitted to take off your seat belts now," permissibility is predicated of an individual's action. Here the actor or agent is permitted to act, and her action is justified as the right action in relation to norms or principles such as hazards to one's own life or to the life of others. These norms assume that life is valuable, and hence, the above justification makes sense. Permissibility, thus defined, carries with it the notion of sanction or justification: sanction, for example, of taking off one's seat belt. In the Hindu South-Asian culture, the violations of a woman's body within the marital institution is similarly sanctioned or permitted, the actions then justified by certain cultural norms.

One of the fundamental differences between "Hinduism" and other religions, particularly the Semitic ones, is that Hinduism is not an institutional religion. It has no strict, formal written codes of laws but is more a way of life. Thus, judging its influence on the vast population of the Indian subcontinent can be an extremely complex task. When Islam, Jainism, Buddhism, and Christianity were introduced into India, these religions primarily attracted Hindus from the "lower castes" and the "untouchables." Although the majority of the population converted to escape oppressive facets of Hinduism, many of its basic tenets survived. In many parts of India, for instance, Muslims and Christians practice the caste system and the taking and giving of dowry, a custom predominantly associated with Hindus.[2] Hindu rituals have endured even within folkways of other Indian cultures. Muslims in southern parts of West Bengal, for example, follow the Hindu religious custom of blowing a conch at twilight. Furthermore, Hinduism is not contained within India only. Nepal, Bangladesh, Sri Lanka, and Pakistan all have substantial Hindu populations, as do other Pacific Rim countries. Thus, Hindu codes and mores are confined not just to segments of the Indian population belonging to the same religion but to Hindus in other countries, as well as non-Hindus influenced by Hinduism.

The examples presented in this analysis are instances of marital rape. The first one is from fiction; nonetheless, it is a strong historical document. The second case is a mixture of fact and fiction, again a historical document, and the third is my personal observation while working with a women's organization in India.

The first case that I present here is from the novel *Pratham Pratishruti*, set in the first decade of this century, by the award-winning Bengali writer Ashapurna Devi.[3] The story centers on the evolution of a young rural woman, Satyavati, into a valiant feminist. In the story, Bhamini, a friend of Satyavati, relates the circumstances of her twelve-year-old sister's death. The sister's husband, an older widower, forced her to have sex with him repeatedly on the wedding night. Unable to bear this abuse, the tortured bride escapes by hiding in their ancestral home. Nevertheless, the husband relentlessly seeks her out and when she refuses to submit to him, beats her with a rolling pin, saying that one who refuses the sexual demands of a husband deserves to die. The girl dies three weeks later, suspiciously, under "unknown circumstances." On hearing this story, Satyavati, the heroine of the novel, wants to take the husband to the police for murdering the young bride. But Bhamini refuses, as she wants to prevent any unnecessary family scandal. After all, Bhamini argues, her sister, as the youngest child in the family, was greatly pampered. Was not her death really her parents' fault, as they did not teach her "proper ways of behaving towards the sexual advances of a husband"? While recognizing the husband as "cruel," the statement absolves him of any criminal action, for a husband is permitted to punish a wife for refusing to submit to his sexual demands and that punishment may include death. In other words, the husband acted well within his rights. It is, therefore, a justified action and death.

In a true story set in the 1950s, another celebrated Bengali novelist, Samaresh Majumdar, describes a similar incident in his two-part novel, *Sat Kahan*.[4] In this case, the sixteen-year-old bride is from a lower-middle-class family. Her parents accept the first proposal for marriage to marry her off quickly. The bride encounters her husband for the first time on the wedding night, when the groom forces her to undress, surprising the young girl, who is quite ignorant about sex. She rejects his advances by pushing him away. He tries to force himself on her, but fails. He then confesses that his father's motivation in arranging this marriage was to force the bride to produce an heir to their vast property as fast as possible. In case the groom fails to get results, the father would take over and impregnate the bride himself. (It is not clear from the text whether the groom or the father had sex with the young girl.) Next day, a servant helps the distraught bride to run away to her home. There, the doctor who is called in to examine her declares that she had been sexually assaulted and may suffer mentally for the rest of her life. The physician, however, shows no surprise or outrage at his patient's condition. Thereafter, the girl develops a loathing for all sexual activities, as well as her own body. Nonetheless, she was lucky, as her parents took her back. If they had not done so, her only refuge would have been an urban brothel. They did not, however, complain or see anything wrong with the sexual advances of the husband toward the young bride or that the father of the groom was preparing to do so; for the bride's parents, the in-laws were acting well within their rights. In fact, that is not the reason they took her back; they did so because the groom died on the wedding night, and by custom a widow is returned to her father's home.

The third case is the one I have personally experienced in the early eighties while working in a women's organization in Calcutta, India. Many poor women came to this agency to be vocationally trained in bookbinding and batik. I remember one woman particularly vividly, Kamala.[5] She was a tall woman of twenty from a suburb of Calcutta and was the second of seven children. While she was an apprentice at the organization, her relatives advised her parents to arrange her marriage. Kamala had no choice in this matter and was married off by her parents. She was also forced to leave the organization. Approximately seven days after the wedding, I remember Kamala coming back to the organization in a very distressed state. Her husband had forced her to have sex with him seventeen times over four days. When she sought refuge with her parents, they rejected her plea by stating that they had exhausted her share of the family finances on her wedding. Now she would become a "burden" on them. While she remained at the organization, her physical appearance and incoherent language suggested the need for psychiatric care.

All three incidents, fictional and real, are instances of forcible rape within the institution of marriage. Each situation involves a young woman who is uninformed in sexual matters and an older, more experienced man. As soon as the marriages take place, the husbands exhibit a sense of entitlement regarding their wives' bodies, as well as a total disregard for their physical and mental well-being. Consequences of the husbands' behavior for the women range from death to mental illness, yet the relatives and professionals are reluctant to blame the men. Moreover, there is always a clear recognition that the husbands are well within their rights.

To conclude whether any of these incidents of "forced sex" fit the definition of "rape," especially "marital rape," we need to consider a few formal definitions. One dictionary defines "rape" as, "carnal knowledge of a female against her will; the act of snatching or carrying off by force; to ravish or violate." Thus, we can characterize the actions of the male spouse in the above cases by stating that *the husband forces his wife to have sex*. In other words, the husband, by virtue of being married to his wife, feels entitled to force her to have sex. We can perfectly understand that kind of action as rape. However, Bhamini's reaction in *Pratham Pratishruti*, the doctor's reaction in *Sat Kahan*, and the parents' reaction in Kamala's case all show that many Indians do not consider these incidents as rape even though they fulfill our definition of it. In other words, such actions on the part of husbands are "permissible" in this particular society. The reasoning behind this acceptance of forcible sexual intercourse within marriage can be fully understood by analyzing the justifications hidden in the three cases:

- Entering into a marital contract obligates the female spouse to perform all duties that her husband judges right. For example, Bhamini's sister should have carried out her husband's wishes, however repugnant they were to her. Therefore, her noncompliance justifies her death.
- Entering into a marital contract obligates a woman to produce children; hence, actions performed to achieve this goal are justified. For example, in Majumdar's story, the bride is considered a receptacle for semen, a breeder, regardless of her relationship to the giver of semen.
- Marriage involves the transfer of a burden (the woman) from the parents (former owner) to the groom (present owner). By virtue of this transfer, the groom is entitled to every right over the bride, as the former owner surrenders all rights and retains no obligations. The refusal of Kamala's parents to assist her exemplifies this attitude clearly.

The above rationalizations involve a notion of *obligation* on the part of the bride. It is from this notion of obligation, I contend, that the justification for rape is derived in the South Asian context. The actions of the male spouses are justified in relation to certain norms and principles which exist in canonized forms in Sanskrit texts.[6] These norms and principles, in turn, assume certain significance in society.

To understand the value placed on women's roles and their bodies, let us examine the following three principles from the *Manu Samhita*, or *The Treatises of Manu*, written by an eighth century social theorist and codifier of laws:[7]

1. Of the eight forms of marriages, demonic (*rakshasha*) form is one. *Rakshasha* marriage involves raping a woman, thereby making her one's own.
2. Women are properties of fathers, husbands, and sons at different stages of their lives.
3. Wives are primarily to bear sons.

Although people in India no longer live explicitly by the laws of *Manu Samhita*, it has generated potent values which justify rape within the marital institution. For example, principles (1), (2), and (3) doubly justify marital rape. Marriage in any of the nine forms is a socially (and ethically) sanctioned institution that partners can enter into. Thus, individual *S* can marry individual *P* in any of nine ways prescribed by the laws of *Manu*. Now, the act of raping *P* by *S* is also a socially and ethically permissible action, for it falls under those nine accepted forms of marriage. Principles (2) and (3) generate values which give rise to arguments that women are property and their function is producing heirs. Marriage gives a husband the right to his wife's body. Thus, postmarital rape of a wife by a husband can be doubly justified for the following reasons: (1) The husband has a right to the wife's body by virtue of being married to her and (2) rape is an intrinsically permissible action. In addition, these principles generate notions of rights, duties, and obligations which give external and internal sanctions, or ethical permissibility, for rape within marriage.

Let us consider the nature of these external sanctions. If the marriage contract is equivalent to a promissory note from the father of the bride to the bridegroom, then the one who is giving away the bride, by the very act of giving, guarantees the new owner that he is permitted to do anything he wishes with her.[8] Thus, because a woman is denied all autonomy, her status as property within the marital relationship is formalized by this transfer. This, unequivocally, gives the husband the right to rape. Furthermore, the sexual act is viewed in marriage as teleological, that is, for the purpose of procreation only. While the sexual act itself between marital partners is viewed teleologically, for the female partner sex is regarded also as a *function*. In fact, her status as "property" inevitably leads to her function as breeder. To elaborate, it can be stated that all our properties have different functions for us. For example, a table has a definite function: I can keep my books on it. By the same logic, since a woman is a property, she can produce heirs.

In *Pratham Pratishruti*, Bhamini uses this "property" argument. In Majumdar's story, the groom's actions can only be justified by using the teleological view and the "function" argument. In addition, the above principles generate notions of rights and duties. As Barcalow, an eminent ethicist points out, rights are not conferred on an individual by any legal system but are derived from a system of moral principles.[9] Thus, although people in India today do not directly live by the legal codes established by *Manu*, the moral principles still exist and exert their influence. More specifically, they confer upon the male spouse a right over the body of his wife. Those who have bestowed the property to him are consequently *obligated* to see that the woman conforms to this moral edict by socializing her in fitting values and norms. Bhamini's words testify to the truth of such obligation.

In addition to the external sanctions, the three principles elaborated above have generated internal sanctions which, perhaps, are far more potent. This inculcation of values comes from a religion that is predominantly ritual based and is practiced at home mainly by women. It teaches women that if they stay within accepted roles, they will be venerated in life and beyond. This socialization is reinforced by the images of powerful mythological heroines such as Sita, Sati, and Savitri.

These three women, Sita, Sati, and Savitri, are exalted in society because of their steadfast devotion to their husbands. While Sita gave up her kingdom and wealth to spend fourteen years in poverty with her exiled husband, Sati sacrificed her own life because she could not bear the insults her father inflicted upon her husband. Savitri, on the other hand, with her piety, brought back her dead husband to life. These female archetypes are role models for most Hindu woman. Thus, a "good woman" in the Hindu culture is defined as one who smilingly joins her deceased husband on his funeral pyre. She fasts and worships Siva and, hence, is "blessed" with a good husband. Furthermore, once she achieves her ultimate goal of securing a husband, she embarks on the cyclic journey of births and rebirths through at least seven reincarnations with the same husband. A good woman carries her sick husband to the door of his mistress. If a woman does *all* this, her place in heaven is assured.

Simone de Beauvoir's statement about a woman in *The Second Sex* is appropriate here: "She is defined and differentiated with reference to man and not with reference to her; she is the incidental, the inessential as opposed to the essential. He is the Subject, he is the Absolute—she is the Other." Also, "Indeed along with the ethical urge of each individual to affirm his subjective existence, there is also the temptation to forgo liberty and become a thing, . . . When man makes of woman the *Other*, he may, then, expect her to manifest deep-seated tendencies toward complicity. Thus, woman may fail to lay claim to the status of subject because she lacks definite resources, because she feels the necessary bond that ties her to man regardless of reciprocity, and because she is often very well pleased with the role as the *Other*."[10]

From the perspective of the function argument that I have elucidated, a wife is viewed within the marital contract as a functional entity whose actions are deterministic, that is, follow causal laws. For example, the function of a copying machine (producing copies) can be described by strict physical (or deterministic) causal laws or cause-effect relationships. Its actions, however, are not intentional. Humans, as opposed to machines, have intentions or purpose. We intend to produce copies by using a copy machine. However, by virtue of the function argument, the female body is viewed by society as a machine which the male uses intentionally for procreation and pleasure. Thus, the male is the subject that intentionally uses the functional, strictly deterministic female object. Not only does she become a body to the man, but she herself also internalizes these values and thinks of herself only as a body. Although she becomes a body, she has no control over it owing to her status as property. In fact, she is never the body's owner at all. Jean Kilbourne maintains that this objectification and lack of ownership may lead women to loathe their own bodies.[11] This is evidenced in Majumdar's *Sat Kahan.*

The internalization and promotion of values regarding this wife role have far-reaching implications. This ethos, developed and consolidated in the motherland, does not necessarily lose its influence in the new world of immigrants. In fact, South Asian activists against domestic violence assert that an interesting behavior has emerged in the post-1965 Asian-Indian immigrant community. One activist, Shamita Das Dasgupta, observes that in her experience of working with South Asian victims of domestic violence, she has found that there are many women who are willing to talk about physical abuse; however, no one is willing to talk of sexual violence or rape within marriage.[12] "It thus seems irrational," Dasgupta states, "to suppose that while all other domestic violence occurs within the South Asian immigrant families in the United States, sexual violence or rape never happens." It is this *silence* of victims on issues of rape that makes the topic critical in society. She further writes, "South Asian communities of today are notorious for the oppressive silence they maintain around the topic of sexuality. As a group, we tend not to encourage open discussions about sexuality, let alone open sexual expressions. Even scholarly work on South Asian sexuality and sexual behavior is extremely rare. So much so that without the ancient books such as *Kama Sutra* and *Kokashashtra*, we can count books and articles written on the subject on one hand. Although this calculated avoidance seems to be pretty much gender blind, women have surely suffered more from this kind of repression due to their already limited position in society." Dasgupta also maintains,

> I have worked with Manavi since its inception in 1985. The majority of South Asian women's organization in the United States have been formed after our group came into existence and like us, they

seem to be concentrating on the issues of violence against women. However, within the area of women's abuse, most of our work centers around physical battery or domestic violence. Although many of us do not clearly specify the problems we focus on, the outreach material we develop, our training programs, our educational workshops, all zero in on domestic abuse. I have yet to hear of a South Asian group that has been formed around sexual abuse of women. Such reluctance on the part of the activists to acknowledge sexual violence as a crucial problem within our communities, further silences women who are socialized to regard sexual issues as the absolutely taboo topic. Ultimately, separating issues of violence into battery, sexual abuse, poverty, unemployment, etc., is artificial and unrealistic. It is naive to believe that a woman who is being battered is not simultaneously experiencing sexual abuse or vice versa. Violence does not come in neat packages for our administrative convenience. To support the argument we only have to look at women's realities. However, the system of funding, state coalitions, battered women's and rape crisis movements, as well as academic research in this country force us to delineate our organizing into either domestic violence or sexual assault work. Consequently, in conjunction with our inhibitions around issues of sexuality, acceptance of this artificial dichotomy has led to an unbalanced development of our activities.[13]

One of the reasons for this silence is that women in the immigrant culture carry with them the values that they inherited in their natal country. In another study Dasgupta and Warrier rightly observe, "The most important factor in these women's lives seemed to be the childhood indoctrination in the ideals of 'good' wife and mother that includes sacrifice of personal freedom and autonomy. Although the majority of women worked as professionals, economic independence did not seem to provide them with a sense of empowerment. Furthermore, they felt responsible for the reputation of their families in India, were eager not to compromise their families' honor with a divorce, and operated under the added pressures of preserving traditions and presenting an 'unblemished' image of the community to the U.S. mainstream."[14]

The image of Arundhati has very appropriately been evoked in this study conducted by Dasgupta and Warrier. Arundhati was the wife of Vashishtha, the learned sage. She was highly meritorious and had learned all the Vedas and other scriptures, in addition to being an extremely devoted wife. Despite her erudition, she was blessed by the gods and made a place for herself among the seven auspicious stars in the heaven only for her devotion to her husband. The case is similar to the twelve women that Dasgupta and Warrier interviewed. The women were professionals, yet they too had internalized the traditional values of a "good wife." Dasgupta and Warrier write, "Belief in the preeminence of marriage in a woman's life permeated the homes of all participants. . . . Each woman in this sample stated that they had unconsciously internalized the belief that a wife is secondary to her husband."[15] In addition, these women were under the pressure of upholding the traditional cultural values in a foreign country.

Experienced activists attest that many immigrant South Asian families, while reporting other forms of violence, will not report sexual violence. It is my contention that a significant reason for this behavior is the internalization of the values of the good wife, which entails unquestioning acceptance of the function of a wife as a breeder and her position as her spouse's property. This acceptance is not without its harmful consequences: injury to self-assertion and self-possession, autonomy, and integrity. Whether this damage is consciously recognized or not, it does occur. Robin West comments on the process of this subconscious impairment:

> A woman utterly lacking in self-assertiveness, self-possession, a sense of autonomy, or integrity will not experience the activities in which she engages that reinforce or constitute those qualities as *harmful*, because she, to that degree, lacks a self-asserting, self-possessed self who *could* experience those activities as a threat to her selfhood. But the fact that she does not experience these activities as harms certainly does not mean that they are not harmful. Indeed, that they are not felt as harmful is a consequence of the harm they have already caused. This phenomenon, of course, renders the "rationality" of these transactions tremendously and even tragically misleading. Although these women may be making rational calculations in the context of the particular decision facing them, they are by making those calculations, sustaining deeper and to some degree unfelt harms that undermine the very qualities that constitute the capacity for rationality being exercised.[16]

The discussion on the permissibility of marital rape within the South Asian culture would not be complete without an exploration of the solution to the problem. As the discussion indicates, rape within marriage is not just a historical fact; it is still a part of our society. Perhaps the challenge has to be taken up by domestic violence activists. Sexual and domestic violence can no longer be logically separated into watertight categories. They are integrally tied to each other, especially in a culture that assumes that spousal duties for women include sexual submission. Changing societal attitudes is not an easy task, especially within our culture, which still upholds many of its traditional values. Nonetheless, it can and must be done. The assignment is made even harder by the public face of the South Asian community as a model minority in the United States. For the members of the community, it is difficult to accept that the *private* life of such an exemplary group could be blemished.[17] In such a situation the onus of change rests with the activists. Dasgupta claims that working on domestic violence within the immigrant South Asian community was at first very difficult, simply because these issues are generally considered too private and too personal. Thus, women did not feel comfortable talking about them. The situation, as Dasgupta points out, has changed over the past ten years. Women are more willing to speak out on domestic violence. The same, however, is not true with issues of sexual violence.[18]

In most South Asian cultures, sexual issues are considered taboo. While most women are socialized not to discuss these issues, they are taught to internalize blame for sexual abuse. Dasgupta brings out a very interesting point about language in this context. She remarks that the activists, generally belonging to a particular social class, learn the language of sexuality only in terms of the language of the colonizer and not the colonized. Hence they can speak of sexual matters only in English. Thus, while the majority of the activists within the South Asian communities are fluent in two or more Indian languages, they have no discourse when it comes to speaking of sexual violence. Furthermore, Dasgupta maintains, the social class of the activists prevent them from talking about sexual issues in "colloquial or vernacular terms." As a result, a great language barrier has developed over the years in the area of domestic violence. Dasgupta writes, "Even in our work with domestic abuse victims, we tend to avoid bringing up the topic of sexuality because of our uncomfortability with language, class based sensibility, or lack of necessary information. We assume that if a woman (even if she is [a] victim of domestic violence) has not brought up issues of sexuality, they do not exist for her. Yet, it is imperative that we initiate such discussions with each woman and explore them thoroughly. Our neglect of this area effectively silences women who are not just abused within marriage or partnership relations, but may be victims of assault by strangers or intra-family relationships."[19]

I realize that I am analyzing the values and incidents of violent sexual encounters that have already been discussed from a Western-educated feminist's point of view. It is from this perspective that I label certain experiences as "marital rape." In light of my belief that marriage is a social contract between rationally self-interested individuals who have free will and who, by entering into a contract, promise not to violate each other's bodies, the previously described cases can be defined as nothing but forcible rapes. This thinking is in the tradition of social contract theories of the Enlightenment promoted by philosophers like Locke, Rousseau, and more recently by Rawls. According to this tradition, rationally self-interested individuals enter into contract with one another to give up part of their rights in order to enjoy certain privileges. Nonetheless, even as a part of a group—and in case of marriage it is usually a group of two—they remain *individuals*. Hence, the categories that I am using here to study marital rape are external to the traditions of South Asia. Thus, one may question the legitimacy my study and the whole issue of making cultural categories transcendent.

This leads to a very important point in the study of South Asia and its entire history. As a South Asian diasporic individual, I am trying to analyze cultural values of South Asia from a Western perspective and yet keep a balanced approach to history. For example, in discussing the values that are culturally entrenched in South Asian Hindu society, there is always the danger that we are, in our texts, making society a monolithic culture. In addition, the history of the South Asian people, a colonized people, has been written by the colonizer. Hence, to consider culturally ensconced values and principles derived from *Manu* may be questionable itself. I will offer some alternative explanations for the production of those values. The values generated by *Manu Samhita* and discussed above should not be treated as the only ones perpetuated by the ancient Indus Valley people. There are many other values and traditions that strengthen women's status in society. These are the values that need to be affirmed within the South Asian immigrant community. As South Asian women, we should be looking for segments of our culture that uphold women's status.

In fact, to peruse South Asian cultures from the vantage point of Western historiography is not to do full justice to the tradition which originally had no notion of vaginal chastity. The anarchistic culture of Indus Valley did not have a rigid concept of paternity or the "virgin bride." However, the laxity of this culture started changing once the centralized power systems of the Gupta and Maurya dynasties were established in the wake of Alexander's invasion of India. Such centralization of power was completely antithetical to the psyche of the people more used to living in local groups. With the rise of the centralized power system, the popular folk cultures were suppressed, and ready-made values, promoted by the centralized force of this vast kingdom, were forced upon the people.[20] These were the values regarding women's role in marriage: "wife for sons" and "wife as property." It should be noted that *Manu Samhita* was a product of this time and, hence, was established as the canon of law.

The effects of this historical document have not disappeared from South Asian society, nor from the immigrant culture in the United States. Dasgupta remarks,

> Not only are the traditional patriarchal power imbalances still strong and thriving, they may be gaining strength in the immigrant community in the guise of "maintaining culture." This conflation of "culture" and women-abuse is dangerous to the health of our community. Undoubtedly, adhering to one's traditions can be a way of resisting the powerful assimilatory forces that permeate the mainstream of American society. However, it is imperative that women's subjugation be separated from the content of our "culture." To this purpose, only a continuous and lively internal critique can help us disentangle the parts of our culture that empower us from the more disenfranchising forces. In fact, Hindu traditions provide women with role models that are powerful and dynamic. For instance, the concept of "Shakti," femininity in control of her own sexuality, and its real life translation, "Virangana" (the warrior woman), is a pervasive image that is widely accepted in society. . . . Indian history is also redolent with courageous and active women leaders.
>
> . . . These are the role models that the Asian Indian immigrants need to present to the daughters of their community. We believe that such a socialization process will empower women and free them from the obligation of accepting violence against them whenever it occurs.[21]

In this chapter I have mostly analyzed the Hindu discourse, but, as I noted earlier, the inherent ideas and ideologies have spread beyond the intellectual realms of any particular religion or population. When contrasted to Western cultures, South Asian cultures do appear to have many themes and motifs in common. The permissibility of marital rape may be such a phenomenon. This ideology may effectively silence women of diverse religious and regional communities in the diaspora. Reports of various South Asian activist organizations in the United States working on domestic violence attest to its importance.

As I noted, there are various socioeconomic, as well as structural, reasons behind a woman's decision to remain within an abusive relationship. Many immigrant women, for example, have to remain within abusive relationship because they are financially dependent on their husbands. Ideology, however, cannot be dismissed from this list of barriers confronting women. Dasgupta and Warrier's study, where the image of Arundhati has been successfully evoked, testifies to the importance of ideology. All the cases studied by these researchers included well-educated women who had the capacity to support themselves; nonetheless, they stayed on in abusive relationships to preserve "cultural images."

Furthermore, ideology affects not only the victim but the abuser and society as well, which then perceives this violence as expected and acceptable. I am aware that a skeptic might say that education will give information and choices, but it will not provide an antidote to the values which sanction or justify rape within marriage. However, it must be recognized that these ancient values are deeply entrenched in our culture, where a woman is primarily a not-self, or in existentialist term an *en soi*. Some may suggest that a feminist revolution is the only answer to reverse the values. That, of course, is a topic for a separate paper and I leave that for further research.

Notes

1. A subaltern has "epistemological advantage" because she participates in the knowledge of both the subaltern and the hegemonic groups.
2. In fact, the recent "politically correct" term *dalit*, or the downtrodden, encompasses not only the untouchables and oppressed among the Hindus but also the ones converted to Islam and Christianity a generation or two ago. Although there are several references to dowry in the Quran (see the translation by A. Ali [Princeton: Princeton University Press, 1950]), it is not considered a common practice among Muslims. Muslim husbands are obligated to provide their wives with *mehr* (property that is her alone) at the time of the wedding.
3. A. Devi, *Pratham Pratishruti* (First promise) (Calcutta: Ananda, 1968).
4. S. Majumdar, *Sat Kahan* (A long story) (Calcutta: Ananda, 1984).
5. The name has been changed to protect her identity.
6. Almost all traditional texts of Hindu discourse are in Sanskrit. One exception is the Vedas, which are written in Prakrit.
7. *The Laws of Manu*, tr. and ed. G. Buhler (New York: Dover, 1969), 100.
8. "I hereby promise to give you $100" entails "I must give you $100."
9. E. Barcalow, *Moral Philosophy* (Belmont, Calif.: Wadsworth, 1994), 184.
10. S. de Beauvoir, *The Second Sex*, tr. and ed. H. M. Parshley (New York: Knopf, 1968), 83.
11. J. Kilbourne, *Killing Us Softly* (film) (Cambridge, Mass.: Cambridge Documentary Film Center, 1979). Kilbourne narrates the film.

12. Personal communication from S. D. Dasgupta, who works with victims of domestic violence in South Asian immigrant families.

13. S. D. Dasgupta, "Sexuality: The Unexamined Factor in Domestic Violence Work," *Manavi Newsletter* 6, no. 1 (1994): 3.

14. S. D. Dasgupta and S. Warrier, "In the Footsteps of 'Arundhati': Asian Indian Women's Experience of Domestic Violence in the United States," *Violence against Women* 2, no. 3 (1996): 238–59.

15. Ibid.

16. R. West, "The Harms of Consensual Sex," *American Philosophical Association Newsletter* 94, no. 2 (1994): 53.

17. Dasgupta and Warrier, "In the Footsteps of 'Arundhati.'"

18. Dasgupta, "Sexuality," 4.

19. Ibid.

20. Personal communication from Soumitra Bose.

21. Dasgupta and Warrier, "In the Footsteps of 'Arundhati.'"

Lifting the Veil of Secrecy

DOMESTIC VIOLENCE AGAINST SOUTH ASIAN WOMEN IN THE UNITED STATES

—

SATYA P. KRISHNAN, MALAHAT BAIG-AMIN, LOUISA GILBERT,
NABILA EL-BASSEL, AND ANNE WATERS

*I would always be in fear. Even though I worked, I had to be
home at a certain time. Even if I was five minutes late or if there
was a traffic jam or something, I could not tell him that. I was in
fear all the time. I was in fear that I would lose my mind if I go
home late. I constantly made plans to be home on time.*
An interviewee's comments

𝒯he image of a woman being abused
by those who claim to love and honor her is horrifying. However, such abuse
is one that many of us have heard of or, perhaps, experienced in our own
lives. Domestic violence has been a part of our living landscape since the
beginning of time and is still a significant component of many women's lives.
Despite their abusive domestic circumstances, many women strive to work
quietly, raise children, care for their families, and try to establish a "normal"
existence in society.

Owing to the efforts of many dedicated community activists, the prevalence of domestic violence among South Asian women in the United States
is no longer a secret. The efforts of these advocates have been crucial in bringing acknowledgment, recognition, and understanding to the issues surrounding domestic violence in South Asian immigrant communities. As the number
of immigrants to the United States increases, the endeavors of these activists
have begun to shed light on a neglected public health issue in a singularly

underserved group, the South Asian American community.[1] Our interests in the issues of domestic violence among South Asian women stem from our research interests in immigrant women's health issues in general and our commitment to violence against women.

Despite the advocacy and activism of South Asian women's groups such as Manavi, Apna Ghar, and Sakhi for South Asian Women, often these communities have denied the very existence of domestic violence and, when forced to acknowledge it, they then have ignored it. This denial has perpetuated a pervasive myth that domestic violence does not exist in these communities, or, if it does, it needs to be addressed quietly in the contexts of family and community. This lack of acknowledgment and understanding of domestic violence among South Asian communities has to change if the issues are to be addressed effectively and adequately. In this chapter, we attempt to discuss domestic violence, specifically partner violence against South Asian women in the United States by examining women's experiences as articulated in their own words. Their stories bear testimony to their resilience and abilities to contend with difficulties. We hope that this discussion and our homage to these women's strength can serve to bring domestic violence to the forefront of South Asian communities' conscience.

Violence in Intimate Relationships: Issues in the Larger Society

Women often experience their greatest risk of violence not from acquaintances and strangers but from their intimate male partners.[2] Domestic violence is one of the most significant causes of injury to women, affecting about two million women in the United States every year. Today, domestic violence is being referred to as a "national epidemic" by physicians, public health experts, and politicians and is slowly becoming a part of the public consciousness in the United States.[3] Domestic violence, specifically intentional physical or nonphysical harm, or both, perpetrated by an intimate partner against a woman is pervasive and often an unrecognized cause of chronic physical and mental health problems.[4] These chronic health problems include such physical traumas as multiple contusions, fractures, bruises, bites, as well as burns on the face, head, abdomen, or genitals. In addition to direct injuries, victims may also suffer from chronic stress-related disorders such as gastric distress, lower back and pelvic pain, headaches, insomnia, and hyperventilation.[5] A variety of psychological and mental health symptoms such as anxiety disorders and panic attacks, depression, sense of helplessness and declining coping skills, self-blame, as well as lowered self-esteem may further accompany these physical impairments.[6]

Domestic Violence in South Asian Communities

The recent recognition of domestic violence in the United States and around the world as an extensive and long-existing phenomenon is largely due to the global efforts of battered women themselves. It is undeniable that the activities of community-based agencies and women's organizations have brought increasing policy, media, and research attention to intimate violence.[7] As the issues of domestic violence move from the private to the public arena in the larger community, a similar trend is reflected among South Asians in the United States.[8] Two factors appear to influence this shift: (1) the emergence and investment of South Asian women's groups and community-based organizations such as Manavi, Apna Ghar, and Sakhi for South Asian women and (2) the increased willingness of South Asian battered women to tell their stories to formal support systems.

In fact, South Asian community organizations and women's groups have played a pivotal role in bringing recognition to domestic violence within their communities. While they serve as safe havens for individual battered women, these agencies simultaneously aim to bring about social change by focusing attention on domestic violence itself. Generally, individual care comes in the form of counseling and emotional support, as well as intervention during emergencies. Social change, on the other hand, is attempted through publicizing particular issues of South Asian women in abusive relationships, training social and health-care workers, and influencing as well as improving legislation regarding domestic violence. Consequently, the visibility of women's groups and community-based organizations, and the willingness of South Asian women to talk about their experiences of violence, have begun to construct a clearer and more realistic picture of women's lives in South Asian immigrant communities.

Of the immigrants living in the United States, 2.8 percent are Asian, and the 1990 census indicates that a million are South Asians—Bangladeshi, Indian, Pakistani, Nepali, and Sri Lankan.[9] One estimate suggests that the incidence of domestic violence in these communities is about 20 to 25 percent.[10] However, this may be an underestimation because domestic violence cases in these communities often are underreported owing to underutilization of existing social and health services.[11] Issues such as immigration status, language barriers, lack of knowledge about helping services and organizations, social and cultural barriers, fear and isolation, as well as concerns of safety for themselves and their children, are often responsible for this underutilization. This constellation of issues can have a profound effect on how South Asian women respond to violence in intimate relationships. These issues, real and perceived, add to the vulnerability of battered South Asian women and influence the way they address violence in their personal lives.

Despite the prevalence of domestic violence among South Asian women living in the United States, little systematic understanding and documentation of the problem exists.[12] A lack of comprehension of the cultural and social factors that define domestic violence, difficulties in reaching out to victims, and the continued reluctance of many women to seek help all contribute to perpetuating intimate violence in our communities. However, current changing conditions within South Asian communities suggest the need for research approaches that can systematically record the scope and particularities of that violence. Such research will also provide better understanding of the factors and correlates of intimate violence, so that culturally appropriate and effective prevention and intervention strategies can be designed.

In this chapter, we hope to lift the veil of secrecy shrouding domestic violence by offering realistic views of South Asian women's experiences, concerns, needs, solutions, and hopes through the words, thoughts, ideas, and courage of the women themselves.

Domestic Violence Research and Focus Groups

In our work, we have used focus groups extensively to explore, discuss, and elaborate on a variety of issues concerning domestic violence among South Asian women living in the United States. A focus group discussion, very simply, is a qualitative method of gathering information from a group of eight to fifteen people who have at least one interest in common.[13] We chose to use focus groups over other methods because of its comfortable, safe, and sharing format. We observed that while participants told their own stories in these groups, they also heard from other women in similar circumstances and developed a sense of kinship and support for one another.

We conducted several focus groups in Chicago and in New York City, where the local South Asian women's organizations assisted us in contacting and recruiting participants for groups. Between five and ten South Asian (Indian, Pakistani, and Bangladeshi) women participated in each of the discussion groups. Some of the issues explored during the group sessions included:

- Personal, family, and community definitions and perceptions of domestic violence and its consequences;
- The type, context, and circumstances in which violence occurred;
- Effects and consequences of this violence on the women themselves and their children, and on other aspects of women's lives;
- Personal, family, and community norms, attitudes, perceptions, and acceptance of domestic violence;
- The issues of social support, both formal and informal, and the types of coping strategies used;
- Factors that perpetuate domestic violence in women's lives and those that alleviate the problem;
- Barriers to care- and help-seeking behaviors and the women's suggestions for change; and
- Whether migration has affected women's domestic violence experiences.

The focus group discussions were led by two facilitators who helped to moderate the discussions among participants. For South Asian women who were still in abusive situations, these discussion sessions proved to be "safe havens" where they felt comfortable about articulating their experiences of domestic violence and discussing a variety of other related issues. Furthermore, these discussions also appeared to be "therapeutic" and "empowering," as the participants themselves indicated that they welcomed the opportunity to talk about their lives and the violence and meet others in situations similar to theirs.

South Asian Women Define Domestic Violence

The recent interest in domestic violence has fueled a debate about what constitutes the phenomenon. Experts, politicians, activists, advocates, and academics have suggested varying definitions, including those rooted in feminist perspectives, those from the family preservation point of view, and others from the ecological standpoint. An important missing ingredient in this ongoing argument is the viewpoint of battered women, in this case, South Asian women in abusive relationships. Although their definitions may differ from those of the professionals, the South Asian women participating in our focus groups knew intuitively what was "not right" or what was "wrong" in their domestic lives. Meena, a young Indian women who recently moved to the United States, had a very simple definition of domestic violence and declared, "Beating is domestic violence."[14]

While Meena focused on the physical aspects of domestic violence, Kismat, a Pakistani mother of four, emphasized the psychological aspects of such abuse. She focused on the constant lack of respect from her spouse, which constituted domestic violence to her. This lack of respect often translated into jealousy and suspicion and led to various types of abuse and violence, including physical beatings. She said, "[Domestic violence] is when husbands do not give respect to their wives and are always suspicious. The persons who live with each other must have respect for each other."

Definitions of spousal violence offered by the women participating in the focus groups were not limited to physical or overt forms of abuse only. Their notion of ill treatment included emotional and verbal abuse, as well as subtle mistreatments such as standing around to overhear conversations with friends and family members. Munni, an Indian woman living in the Chicago area for a number of years, provided quite a comprehensive definition of domestic violence: "Emotional abuse is domestic violence. And verbal abuse, being suspicious, beating, and not supporting financially is domestic violence. Sometimes men think that they should treat women like a pair of shoes."

These interpretations of domestic violence indicate that the South Asian women in the focus groups understood intuitively that their experiences of physical, emotional, and psychological abuse were not normative. They were also able to distinguish among various types of domestic violence such as physical, psychological, emotional, verbal, and sexual. This distinction affected the consequences of abuse, as well as the demands on the women's coping skills. Clearly, these women recognized abuse in their relationships, even when it was perpetrated in subtle and quiet ways.

Although the women were quite willing to discuss their overall situations, cultural as well as community influences were obvious in the emphasis they placed on certain types of abuse and their reluctance to discuss others. For example, many of the focus group participants felt that verbal, psychological, and emotional abuse were more pervasive and therefore critical in their lives but felt that, unlike physical abuse, these were harder to document and explain. Furthermore, all women were significantly more reticent about broaching the subject of sexual abuse.

Another culture-specific aspect was that the women did not necessarily blame themselves for the violence in their domestic relationships but considered it more a consequence of "bad fate." This ability to contextualize domestic violence in terms of bad fate gave the participants the patience, tolerance, and dignity they needed to cope with it. Sheba, an Indian mother of two grown-up children, explained: "I don't think it was my fault at all. This was my fate. I just thought that this was part of my life. You know, no one's life is perfect. There's one thing or another in everyone's life. And I just look at this [domestic violence] as something that I had to tolerate."

Obedient Daughters, Faithful Wives, and Caring Mothers: Sexual Abuse in Conjugal Relationships

All of the participating women were very reluctant to acknowledge, include, and discuss sexual abuse as an integral part of domestic violence. Sexual abuse was by far the hardest topic to introduce in the discussions, and the women even refused to elaborate on the reasons for this discomfort. One can only speculate about their rationale in terms of the women's lack of ease with issues of sex, sexuality, and self-disclosure. Although they perceived the focus groups to be "safe" and "nonjudgmental," the majority of women were conscious of the constraints of their social norms. They were socialized to be "obedient daughters," "faithful wives," and "caring mothers," and these social norms required conformity to certain behavioral standards: subservience, propriety, and putting others' needs ahead of their own. These expectations ruled out any discussion regarding sex, pleasure, and personal enjoyment. The fact that they had moved into the public arena with their stories of domestic violence was already a great departure from tradition, and to discuss sexual abuse, another taboo issue, would have further taxed their coping skills.

Decision to Stay: Insights into a Process

Recent research indicates that women's length of stay in violent relationships varies with ethnicity, assimilation to the dominant culture and acculturation levels, attitudes, and norms about family, marriage, sex roles, and domestic violence, as well as other sociodemographic characteristics. In light of these studies, we tried to examine the factors that affect South Asian women's motivations to remain in violent relationships. Thus, the women participating in the focus groups spent a substantial amount of time exploring why each stayed in their abusive situations. Their discussions indicated a decision-making process that was personal, yet complex. The following were some considerations extracted from the women's testimonies regarding the process itself:

1. Evaluation of the pros and cons of their domestic circumstances;
2. Perceived choices and options available to them;
3. Concern for their children's safety and future;
4. Immigration status and financial stability;
5. Value placed on opinions and concerns of family members and community;
6. A sense of self-blame, guilt, and personal responsibility; and
7. Perceptions of societal norms and expectations of them.

Contrary to popular belief, the decisions these women made were neither irrational nor arbitrary. Most women based their decisions on a clear rationale. For example, Hala, a young Muslim woman, assessed her situation and found no relevant and viable solutions to her problem. In addition, she believed that she was expected to "tolerate" the violence she was experiencing. Thus, she based her decision to stay with her abusive spouse on these perceptions: "I guess that's the way its supposed to be. Women, they take it. They don't fight back, you know, like women here [American women in the United States] do. Asian women, however much educated they are, they don't fight back. That's the way I was—just be quiet, or walk out, or get out of the house, or go to the other room. Roja, another focus group participant, declared unceremoniously, "In my case, it was financial dependence."

The issue of economic dependency as a salient reason for continuing in a violent relationship was a theme that emerged often. Many of the participants were partially or totally dependent on their spouses for their finances, as well as other resources. Some perceived this dependency to be stronger than it may have been in actuality. Social isolation and lack of information about formal service provisions also contributed to exaggerating this problem of dependency. For some women in the focus groups, marriage had provided them with financial resources, a decent home, class privileges, respectability, and legitimacy in their community and families that they did not have before. In essence, the women had received respectability, a higher social class, and material comforts in exchange for private mistreatments. This exchange was a strategic choice that some participants indicated they made consciously, for themselves and for their children, for a limited length of time or for a lifetime.

For some participants, social norms, family traditions and marriage, and acceptance of men as authorities in the family were adequate reasons for maintaining their abusive relationships. Jila, a focus group participant, succinctly stated her reason for not leaving her violent husband: "Because we feel respect for our parents [and] we should try to keep good relations with our husbands—no matter what." Kamini, another woman in the groups, expressed similar sentiments: "For me, it's like everyone should be together, sit together, and there should be love amongst everyone. And it is a good impression for the children. This is what is in my faith and in my culture. Divorce in our family is very difficult. If you have children, you have to stay together for their sake. Children need to have both mother and father."

Barriers to Leaving:
A Glimpse into South Asian Women's Worlds

For most people, it is extremely difficult to comprehend why a woman continues to endure and cope with violence in her home. In our group discussions, South Asian women provided glimpses into a process of decision making that is often poorly understood and judged harshly. Despite the fear and uncertainty that most of these women face daily they seem to find a way to examine their own lives, available options, and their own capabilities in terms of complexities engendered by living in a "foreign" country. This rather calm and rational scrutiny in the midst of an otherwise chaotic life seemingly helped the group participants find reasons for continuing in their violent relationships and coming to terms with it.

Many of the barriers to leaving that these women experienced were not individual at all. Rather, women based their decisions to stay on factors such as family and cultural values. The following discussion clarifies some of the barriers these women commonly face.

Values and Norms-Related Factors

1. Societal, community, and family norms;
2. Community and family expectations; and
3. Patriarchy and prescribed gender roles.

The effects of these factors are illustrated in Munni's account of the circumstances of her marriage and conjugal life: "When I got married, my father said to my husband, 'My respect and honor is in your hands. Please take care of my daughter.' From then on he was my husband. It was my job to take care of him. For my family honor, family respect, and to maintain [this] respect, we have to just put up with it [violence]. Because of the family!" This is even more clear in Nilufer's statement "My husband forced me to have more children for citizenship purposes. I am sure that what he really wanted was to have sons. He hates daughters. I couldn't even tell you how much. Back in Pakistan, it is understood that girls are no good, and you shouldn't have them." Along with the perceived relevance of patriarchy in families, Nilufer's understanding and acceptance of gender positions is evident in this statement.

Support factors

1. Lack of social support;
2. Lack of structural support and material resources; and
3. Lack of knowledge of available formal support networks and systems.

The focus group discussions centered on three support factors. Suman, an Indian single mother living in New York with a young daughter, discussed the lack of social support she experienced: "I have no relatives. I have nobody, just me and my daughter now. It is hard, very hard." Savitri, a mother of three children, discussed the lack of structural support and material resources in terms of the availability of affordable baby-sitting and public transportation. She felt that a scarcity of both had prevented her from developing necessary skills to become self-sufficient and independent. "I have a baby-sitting problem. The daycare that is on our side is very expensive. Taking the public transport to another place itself costs five dollars," she lamented.

The lack of knowledge about available formal assistance programs can often prove to be an important reason why some South Asian women choose to continue in their violent domestic relationships. Roja, who had recently moved to Chicago from India, expressed her dilemma and her reasons for staying in her violent relationship: "And this is a new culture [the United States], language problem, no money, and with children. Where to go? And moreover, no relatives. There is nowhere to go. And there is no way to get out."

During discussions about support factors, focus group participants indicated the magnitude of their sense of isolation when they were attempting to address problems surrounding abuse in their lives. Suman declared, "Its quite difficult to make the adjustment and adapt to the new culture and it takes quite a bit of time. There are difficulties and problems. Especially when there is no one to turn to."

Individual Factors
These individual factors emerged from the focus group discussions:

1. Fear for safety for themselves and their children;
2. Fear for their future and possible deportation;
3. Inability to handle and cope with the stress of living alone in the United States;
4. Lack of job skills, language skills, and other life skills;
5. Desire to stay in the relationship or inability to accept and address the violence in their lives; and
6. Fear for the children's future.

Leela, a woman living in Chicago, focused on some of the personal factors that formed barriers for her: "My English speaking isn't very good. So getting a job and working is not a possibility yet. So I cannot get the things I need without the English. In addition I do not have a green card." Roja, another woman in Chicago, indicated racism as a factor contributing to her abusive situation: "My life now is for my children. That's why I need to work and support them. I had to swallow my hopes. I have to put all my hopes in my children. There are many tensions from the outside. He [the husband] wants what he had back home [in terms of a job]. A woman accepts whatever she can get, because we want to survive and support the family. Although the men have the education, they cannot find a suitable job or sometimes they do not want to work. So there is frustration outside and inside the home for all of us."

Why Leave Now?
Why South Asian Women Walk out of Their Marriages

Despite the hopelessness and lack of support they experienced, some of the South Asian women took the "uncharacteristic" and "unlikely" step of leaving their abusive relationships for good. Many indicated that they were seriously considering this option. Others stated that they were trying hard to cope with their present, violence-filled circumstances and hoping to "make them [their marriages] work."

Those who walked away from their abusive relationships indicated that they did so not because of one defining moment, or a single violent episode, but because of the sum total of their experiences. They had reached the end of their tolerance and recognized that they could seek and receive support and assistance from formal systems. Those who had walked away from their violent relationships, however, also acknowledged that it had been excruciatingly difficult and painful to start living on their own. They indicated that the support they received from local South Asian women's organizations and culturally sensitive domestic violence shelters were crucial in their decision making and follow-through processes. Also significant in their decision making was the support they received from informal kin and friendship networks such as friends, family members, neighbors, and co-workers. For those who were continuing in their present abusive circumstances, having a job and interacting with their colleagues at work, talking to supportive siblings, family members, and friends, the support and understanding of their children, and their own unwavering religious faith had all helped them to continue to cope. These factors gave them hope for a better future and life.

Hopes for the Future: Living in Peace and Tranquillity

Despite difficult circumstances and lives filled with violence and fear, the participating South Asian women expressed hopes and expectations for a better future. Those who had left their violent lives encouraged others to consider this option and offered to help in any way possible. Madhu, an Indian woman who participated in one of the focus groups in Chicago, voiced this optimism: "My hopes are that I want to study [and] I am doing a job in the library now. It's a good position, but I want to move ahead. So that's why I want to study more. I don't want a restaurant or a store job." Kismat, a Pakistani woman and a mother of four, expressed her desires in terms of her children. She remarked, "My life is with my children. I want to see my children have a good life with a good education, have good jobs. This is my biggest wish and hope." Sheba, who had started a life on her own, had this advice for other participants: "You need to make yourself good and show that you don't have less of anything. You can raise your children without him. And better than him. And you can be happy. You need to begin to say this to yourself and foster these kinds of thoughts."

During these discussions, the participants indicated that it was important to address domestic violence through simple and tangible strategies that were empowering and meaningful to women. They suggested that these strategies need to focus first and foremost on providing life skills, job skills, and language skills so that women could slowly find the peace and tranquillity that had eluded them for so long. Their suggestions included providing the following services: English classes, transportation, baby-sitting services, advice about legal issues and immigration laws, job training such as computer classes, some seed money to start their lives again, and support groups where they can talk with others and help others.

Their focus was simple, narrow, and targeted toward themselves. They felt that with these kinds of tangible assistance and services, they could emerge from behind the veil of secrecy, talk about their lives in public, not feel responsible for the violence in their lives, and, like other people, live a life of dignity and peace. During this part of the discussion, they seemed less concerned about the acceptance of domestic violence in their communities, about the history of domestic violence in their own lives, and about the norms and rules of their families and communities. The participants felt they could handle those issues once they were firmly on their feet and were free from violence. They wanted to tell their stories to the public and find ways of helping others in their communities who were still in violent relationships. Interestingly, the women stated that for the first time in their lives, they were being selfish and thinking only about themselves and their children and not about their families or traditions and norms. They wished to create a small, violence-free safe haven for themselves and their children. They wanted a chance once again to prove their worth, regain their dignity, and play a constructive role in their children's growth and lives. Lily, one of the focus group participants, summarized the hopes that many of the participants shared about their own futures and that of other women: "It is very important to send the word out to all girls and young ladies who are out there and who are getting married. It is very important to let them know that any tension that you feel from your husband, it is very important to get away then, and try not to put up with this. There can be a better life, you know."

Learning from Women

Although there has been a long history of domestic violence in South Asian communities, only recently have attempts been made to document these issues systematically in these communities in the United States. Our experience is that focus group discussions are extremely effective in exploring a variety of issues regarding domestic violence in these communities. Our work with South Asian women revealed that violence experienced by South Asian women was defined by a variety of unique cultural, familial, and community factors and norms. Socioeconomic factors, immigration status, and a host of perceived barriers, including linguistic ones, further defined their experiences. Our focus group discussions revealed a complex picture of domestic violence among the participating South Asian women. Issues of patriarchy, gender roles and expectations, constricting family and community norms, attitudes and traditions about spousal violence, lack of decision-making power, and economic independence are still important in South Asian communities and have aggravated the problem domestic violence further. Despite this bleak picture, the South Asian women who participated in our groups exhibited enviable resiliency and coping abilities. Their hopes for a peaceful and violence-free life for themselves and their children spoke volumes about their courage. With the help of South Asian women's organizations and other community-based organizations, and through their own willingness to speak out, South Asian women have begun to challenge their communities to confront domestic violence with sensitivity and urgency. Although the process has been initiated, there is much work to be done. Part of the task is to document the nature and incidence of this atrocity systematically and implement culturally sensitive, as well as effective, interventions that address issues in South Asian contexts.

Notes

1. K. A. Huisman, "Wife Battering in Asian American Communities," *Violence against Women* 2 (1996): 260–83.
2. M. P. Koss, L. A. Goodman, A. Browne, L. F. Fitzgerald, G. P. Keita, and N. F. Russo, *No Safe Haven: Male Violence against Women at Home, at Work, and in the Community* (Washington, D.C.: American Psychological Association, 1994).
3. J. Abbott, J. McLain-Koziol, and S. Lowenstein, "Domestic Violence against Women: Incidence and Prevalence in an Emergency Department Population," *JAMA: Journal of the American Medical Association* 273 (1995): 1763–77.
4. D. Berrios and D. Grady, "Domestic Violence. Risk Factors and Outcomes," *Western Journal of Medicine* 155, no. 2 (1991): 133–35.
5. V. F. Parker, "Battered," *RN (TWP)* 58, no. 1 (1995): 26–29.
6. A. L. Kornblit, "Domestic Violence: An Emerging Health Issue," *Social Science and Medicine* 39 (1994): 1181–88.
7. S. D. Dasgupta and S. Warrier, "In the Footsteps of 'Arundhati': Asian Indian Women's Experience of Domestic Violence in the United States," *Violence against Women* 2, no. 3 (1996): 238–59.
8. M. Abraham, "Addressing the Problem of Marital Violence among South Asians in the United States: A Sociological Study of the Role of Organizations," paper presented at the meetings of the International Sociological Association (1994), and "Transforming Marital Violence from a 'Private Problem' to a 'Public Issue': South Asian Women's Organizations and Community Empowerment," paper presented at the meetings of the American Sociological Association (1995). These papers have since been published as: "Ethnicity, Gender, and Marital Violence: South Asian Women's Organizations in the United States," *Gender and Society,* 9 (1995): 450–468; and "Speaking the Unspeakable: Marital Violence against South Asian Immigrant Women in the United States," *Indian Journal of Gender Studies,* 5, 2 (June-December 1998).

9. U.S. Bureau of the Census, *1990 Census of the Population: Social and Economic Characteristics, United States* (Washington, D.C.: Government Printing Office, 1993).

10. Koss et al., *No Safe Haven.*

11. C. K. Ho, "An Analysis of Domestic Violence in Asian American Communities: A Multicultural Approach to Counseling," *Women and Therapy* 9 (1990): 129–50.

12. Abraham, "Addressing the Problem" and "Transforming Marital Violence."

13. T. L. Greenbaum, *The Practical Handbook and Guide to Focus Groups Research* (Lexington, Mass.: Lexington, 1988).

14. Names of all participants have been changed to protect their identity.

Nation and Immigration

RETHINKING THE "MODEL MINORITY"

The Habit of Ex-Nomination

NATION, WOMAN, AND THE
INDIAN IMMIGRANT BOURGEOISIE

—

ANANNYA BHATTACHARJEE

Confronting accusations of having be-
trayed one's national cultural heritage is not an uncommon experience for
members of Sakhi, a women's organization which deals with domestic violence in South Asian communities in New York City.[1] Such accusations, which
have their source in the kind of identities immigrant communities assume,
have inspired me to examine the problematic ways in which an immigrant
community creates its own world in a country where it sees itself as different. As a cofounder of Sakhi, my encounters with South Asian immigrant
worlds have enlarged my knowledge of violence against women, particularly
in the lives of Indians, Bangladeshis, Pakistanis, and Sri Lankans.

Central to the creation of immigrant worlds is the idea of the nation—
not the nation as a bounded geographical unit but the nation as an ideological force. In working with domestic violence, I have come to appreciate how
the question of women is inextricably linked to nation-ness. Here I take a
close look at this link in the context of the "Indian community" in the United
States.[2] Although I came to this discussion through my position with Sakhi,
my primary focus will be the construction of a "national" culture in the Indian

community rather than domestic violence in the lives of Indian immigrant women. It is in the context of such constructions of identity that the pressing issue of domestic violence must be situated.

That there is a connection between domestic violence, women, and nationality occurred to me at a celebration of a popular annual Hindu festival called Divali in New York City in the South Street Seaport. Divali is a festival of lights which celebrates the return of the epic figure of Rama to Ayodhya (in North India) after fourteen years of exile in the forest. At the New York celebration, displays of handicrafts, dance, and food from different states of India were some of the many modes by which the diversity of India was exhibited. Amidst this assortment of booths there was also another style of display—one, for example, periodically demonstrated a mock Hindu wedding—that may be referred to as the "public" displays. In this same vein but by contrast, there was another, more "private," scene.[3] Not only was this other scene never meant to happen at this cultural extravaganza, but its participants were specifically excluded from these festivities by the organizers. It is this latter event in the context of bourgeois Indian immigrant identity that I will explore. Before I turn to this private scene, it will be useful to establish a context for this discussion by looking at some important aspects of the world of the Indian community.[4]

The Habit of Ex-Nomination

In *Mythologies*, which is "an ideological critique bearing on the language of so-called mass culture" in bourgeois French society, Roland Barthes explains his motivation for writing (1988: 9): "I resented seeing Nature and History confused at every turn, and I wanted to track down, in the decorative display of *what-goes-without-saying*, the ideological abuse which, in my view, is hidden there" (11). Bourgeois society, as the privileged regime in which History is transformed into Nature, is his object of study (137). He defines the bourgeoisie as the class which does not want to be named, indeed needs no name, as it postulates itself as the universal. It needs no name because it names everything, or, as Barthes puts it, it is at "the locus of an unceasing haemorrhage: meaning flows out of [it] until [its] very name becomes unnecessary" (138). The power of bourgeois ideology, which spreads over everything, lies precisely in the bourgeoisie's ability to name but itself remain unnamed. Barthes calls this characteristic of the bourgeoisie's power to remain ideologically unnamed, "ex-nomination" (138).

Ex-nomination, which Barthes demonstrates in the case of the French bourgeoisie, is a useful idea for examining the life worlds of the immigrant Indian community in the United States. The persistence of this habit of ex-nomination in the bourgeoisie of this community, which is made up of immigrants/expatriates, is the focus here. But first, what/who is an immigrant/expatriate? The two terms "immigrant" and "expatriate" are not unambiguously synonymous. Unlike the term "immigrant," which has come to mean "one who migrates into a country as a settler," the term "expatriate" in modern usage suggests "a person who lives in a foreign country." Expatriate, then, appears to be a stage prior to the more permanent one that is designated by immigrant. However, the difference between the two is not simply a difference in linear temporal progression, where one begins as an expatriate to later become an immigrant. The expatriate always already carries the seeds of an immigrant in his/her deferred, but nevertheless prospective, immigrant's state; and the immigrant carries the seeds of an expatriate, as the return to one's native place always remains a distant possibility. The difference between the two can also be seen as a deferring of commitment, an anguish over allegiances. To choose one of the words over the other is to dismiss this difference, which is central to the immigrant's experience. When I use the words "immigrant community," I do not want to be understood as privileging the word "immigrant" over "expatriate." It is difficult to unambiguously describe a collective condition as either immigrant or expatriate, and I would like to retain in my use of the word "immigrant" the shifting grounds produced by the tension between the two terms. This tension also captures well one dimension of that crisis of identity that such a community faces.

The bourgeoisie, then, upon displacement from the nation of its origin, finds itself contained in the form of an immigrant community in a foreign country. In particular, the Third World bourgeoisie, as an immigrant group in the First World, finds itself in a position of subordination to the native bourgeoisie: a position defined partly by the experiences of Western colonialism and imperialism.[5] For the Indian immigrant community, which is considered to be predominantly highly educated and relatively wealthy, this subordination is defined more through race/nationality than through class.

As a minority community in a foreign nation, the Indian immigrant bourgeoisie experiences the loss of its power of ex-nomination. Where once it had stood for the no-name universal in the nation of its origin, it now perceives itself (and is perceived) to be in a position defined by difference. It now risks being named. The immigrant bourgeoisie's desire to overcome this condition manifests itself through its grasping for familiar essentials in whose shadows it can regain the power to remain unnamed. This essay explores this desire to remain anonymous; its relation to the nation and to the past; and woman as one of the central elements in forging this relation. Even though I shall discuss woman as an element in the bourgeoisie's negotiation of its own position, I would like to emphasize that such negotiations are, as Lata Mani has pointed out, "in some sense *not primarily* about women but about what constitutes authentic cultural tradition" (1989:90; emphasis mine).

Nation and Ex-Nomination

The landscape of the Indian immigrant bourgeois community reveals a proliferation of organizations reflecting the geographical and linguistic boundaries of India.[6] Linguistic/state/religion-identified organizations such as those of Gujaratis, Tamils, Bengalis, Muslims, and Sikhs are one kind of formation. Another kind of grouping, motivated by a desire to create a unified Indian community across the United States, is exemplified by the National Federation of Indian American Associations (NFIAA) and the Association of Asian Indians in America (AAIA).[7] These two kinds of organizations exhibit a tension where the latter attempts to create an "all-India" community and the former attempts to express their specific unities through their state/linguistic/religious heritages.

The organizations profiled as "all-India," which have large memberships and financial resources, are in a position to become the vehicles through which an Indian identity is articulated in the United States. A discussion of the construction of such an identity is essential, especially in light of the fact that the Indian community is among the fastest-growing Asian groups in the United States.[8]

What is the vision of these all-India organizations? The president of the NFIAA articulated the following vision for the Federation of Indian Associations (FIA) at the time of his presidency of that organization:[9] "If the Federation can justify its existence by providing a *united front of Indians* in the New York region, the next step would be to activate or form such independent Federations in other metropolitan areas so that the National Federation of Indian Associations could finally be formed to *represent the Indian community all over the United States*. We should look forward to the time when we can have . . . convention[s] under the auspices of the national body" (emphasis mine).[10]

The phrase "united front of Indians," in the above passage, seemingly needed little elucidation for the president, as he does not give any: it is supposedly that natural spirit of unity fundamental to Indians awaiting realization in and through an organizational body. This well of natural unity among Indians that the president invokes has historical parallels in the Indian independence movement. Post-1920 Indian nationalists constructed historical narratives that assumed "the almost *automatic* commitment of India's inhabitants . . . to the Indian 'nation' in the centuries past" (Pandey 1990: 247; emphasis mine).[11] Since the 1920s, Pandey notes, "Indian nationalism as we know it . . . [has taken] as its unit the individual citizen, a 'pure' nationalism unsullied " (235).[12]

This comparison of an organization like the FIA with Indian nationalists who have dominated twentieth-century Indian history, first in the freedom struggle against the British and then as the leaders of independent India, is not fortuitous. The FIA president later became the president of the NFIAA, whose description conveys the sense of being a body distanced from and above the vagaries of the community, rather like a nationalist state as it watches over its citizens. The NFIAA, we are told, "*represents and advances* the interests of Indians in the U.S. . . . *disseminates* information on the political, economic and developmental affairs of India . . . *monitors and reports* on social and cultural status of Indians in the U.S. and India . . . *observes and comments* on legislative activities" (emphasis mine).[13]

Indeed, at one point the NFIAA could be confused with a ministry of cultural affairs, as it "seeks to promote and preserve Indian culture and heritage and foster friendship and understanding between Indians and the people of North America." The foresightedness of great leaders, who guard and propagate the essence of India, shines through in the passage. The passage's evocation of "Indian culture and heritage," like that of the "united front of Indians," seems to require no elaboration. In this, the words echo Pandey's characterization of "the Spirit of India, the Essence, an already existing Oneness" as invoked by the nationalist movement, particularly since the 1920s (1990: 252). This Essence lay in "the ideal of Indian unity," resurrected by these nationalists, who attributed such a unity to "the Spirit of India" from time immemorial and to "the great rulers of the state" in the years before the arrival of the British (250).

I point to the absence in the above passages of analysis of concepts such as the "united front of Indians" or "Indian culture and heritage," not in order to expose a negligence, but to demonstrate the opposite: that there is no negligence here. The absence speaks volumes. This absence can be seen as a demonstration of Barthes's "ex-nominating operation": Indian culture and the unity of India are for all Indians to possess by the sheer magic of their being Indians; it permeates their essence. Thus, it is in the shadow of this national cultural essence, this Oneness, defined by it for its own purposes, that the Indian immigrant bourgeoisie takes refuge, under the threat of losing its power to stay unnamed, in its form of an immigrant community. It is this essence, expressed here in "the ideal of Indian unity," that Barthes described in another context as "the haemorrhage of the name 'bourgeois' . . . effected through the idea of nation" (138).[14]

While certain analogies between the nationalist spirit in India (prevalent since the 1920s) and that of the Indian immigrant bourgeoisie in the United States are worth noting, they are not meant to suggest that there is a complete synonymity between nationalists in India and a leader in a bourgeois immigrant community in the United States. The analogy is limited to the nationalist consciousness pervasive in both rather than the actualities of the Indian nation-state apparatus to which a nationalist leader in India would be connected. This nationalist consciousness seems much like a "blueprint" of nationhood, that is to say, its elements have ossified to form a model for nationalist consciousness (cf. Anderson 1991:80). This model, then, becomes available for use as easily by the bourgeois immigrant as by the nationalist leader in India.

Certain elements of Indian nationalist thought help to clarify the nature of this model. It is possible to identify a dominant nationalist spirit in India which has been one of learning Western technology and economics while protecting the culture and spiritual essence of India (which exemplifies the East). Partha Chatterjee describes this nationalist project as one which "cultivate[d] the material techniques of modern civilization while retaining and strengthening the distinctive spiritual essence of the national culture" (1989a:623). Such an essentialization of the West and the East continues to be evident among the Indian immigrant bourgeoisie in the United States.

Of course, Indian nationalist thought is not a monolithic construction. Gandhi, for example, differed from the dominant nationalist thought. He believed that "as long as Indians continue[d] to harbour illusions about the 'progressive' qualities of modern civilization, they would remain a subject nation" (Chatterjee 1989b:157). He was passionately opposed to heavy industrialization and called for a politics that would be "directly subordinated to a communal morality" (164). His success in uniting the peasantry during the Indian independence movement was unprecedented. He was committed to localized, village democracies. However, he too, like most nationalists, invoked the idea of an Ancient India, a changeless and timeless India. His critique of modern civilization was based on the original principles of this ancient India, which he took to be the repository of civilizational values and a guide to a new future. In the final analysis, Gandhi compromised on questions of the organization and construction of modern India with the dominant nationalist classes (192).

By contrast, leaders like Jawaharlal Nehru were exemplary of what has come to be seen as the dominant nationalist thought. Nehru stood squarely behind modern industry and a centralized Indian state supported by a mass electoral apparatus at the same time that he idealized a society that was Indian in sentiment. Nehru understood Gandhi's appeal for mass mobilization and successfully aligned himself with Gandhian principles at the same time that he continued to foster the construction of modern India.

For a diasporic organization like the NFIAA, the nationalist spirit translates into "advanc[ing] the interests of Indians" and "preserv[ing] Indian culture and heritage" (Burek 1992:1861). The interests of Indians in the United States, in the words of the FIA and later NFIAA president, lie in acquiring "political clout commensurate with [their] potential economic strength" (Guthikonda et al. 1979:1). The tension between the terms "advance" and "preserve" reveals a significant opposition between political/economic interests and cultural heritage. "Indian immigrants to America" are exhorted to "preserv[e] their cultural individuality while joining the mainstream of American life" (1). The bourgeois immigrants' role is then to learn to participate successfully in the U.S. economy, and to protect their "cultural individuality." Their success can erase their personal identification with memories of an economically struggling India, and can demonstrate that economically Indians are not "essentially backward." What emerges in the president's comments is a satisfying resolution for the bourgeois Indian immigrant: economic advancement through the model of the envied West and cultural preservation of the Indian Essence. In the emerging binary India signifies nation, culture, tradition, God; and the United States signifies material prosperity, participation in legislative politics, economic advancement, and industrial and technological development. In this, immigrant Indian constructions of national identity are revealed to be predictably similar to dominant nationalist thought in India.

Figure of the Woman

In pursuit of the goal to "preserve Indian culture and heritage," Indian immigrant organizations like the NFIAA and the AAIA organize celebrations of predominantly Hindu religious festivals, such as the Divali celebration that I attended. A Bharatanatyam dance performance, handicrafts from Gujarat, and a food stall from Punjab were some of the featured items which served as a museum for the older generation to affirm its heritage and for the younger generation to realize its.[15] Each such display appeared to function as an emblem for a particular state in India. The assortment was meant to represent the unity of India magically produced out of its diversities. The absence of any historical context helped to create a sense of this timeless essence of Indian unity in diversity: Punjab became a symbol for delicious food; Gujarat, for excellent mirror work.[16] The larger project of the festival sought to construct the "India of our dreams."[17] I do not want to discount the importance of remembering one's cultural heritage, especially for immigrants. I do want to point out the ahistorical ways in which this is often carried out.

It helps at this point to reflect on one of Frantz Fanon's definitions of culture. Fanon warns of the dangers of a thoughtless appropriation of customs, divorced from their historical contexts, as that can lead only to an objectification that is ultimately against a positive transformation of history: "Culture has never the translucidity of custom; it abhors all simplification. In its essence it is opposed to custom, for custom is always the deterioration of culture. The desire to attach oneself to tradition or bring abandoned traditions to life again does not only mean going against the current of history but also opposing one's own people" (1968:224). Fanon rejects those customs which arise out of objectification and which finally oppose "one's own people." The immigrant bourgeoisie's efforts to create the "India of [its] dreams" removed from "the current of history," results in a cannibalization of a mummified heritage. In taking culture to be an assortment of fragmentary customs, as it did in the Divali festival, it succeeds only in the construction of a reified "India-ness."

Now I want to return to the booth demonstrating a mock Hindu wedding. The actors were a smiling bride and groom dressed in traditional Punjabi wedding clothes, who were led by an understanding-looking and ever-smiling priest. This symbolic enactment of the Hindu ritual of marriage carried no trace of its concrete aspects such as the relations between the people concerned and their histories. This display of the wedding ritual is reminiscent of Georg Lukács's description of the phenomenon of reification as one in which "a relation between people takes on the character of a thing."[18]

Such a reified display is what leaves the audience with a ritual insulated from those questions which would place it in a historical context, subject to change, protest, or overthrow; questions such as: Who is the priest? From where does his divine authority come? Who is paying him? Whom does he represent? Who is the groom? Why is he marrying the bride? To have someone to cook and clean for him? To get a servant he does not have to pay for? To maintain his respectable image in the community, while he continues the affair with his American girlfriend? To indulge his own sexual fantasies which he is not able to do otherwise? Who is the woman? Did she marry of her free will? What might become of her? Will her husband rape her, claiming consummation to be his birthright? Will he use his power over her immigration status to extract her obedience? Will she be condemned to smile like the bride in the mock wedding, even as she conceals the bruises beneath her clothes? Will he succeed in ultimately destroying her sense of self?

Admittedly, there are numerous possible interpretations of this mock wedding, some of which may be happier than mine. My choice of questions is motivated by another scene that took place at the festival. Sakhi, the South Asian women's organization that focuses on domestic violence, had requested permission to participate in the cultural events of the festival. Sakhi wanted to stage a play that would highlight select aspects of the family and women's roles in Indian society. Its request was denied by the organizers of the event on the grounds that the topics were too political and had no place in this exclusively cultural celebration.[19] We, in Sakhi, decided to attend the event anyway, to distribute fliers protesting a decision that we took to be arbitrary. We distributed information about domestic violence and about Sakhi's services for battered women. However we had to restrict our activities to an area outside the grounds of the main event. This marginal location mirrored the marginal attention given to abuse against women in the Indian community. A few days later, a woman secretly called Sakhi: she had picked up one of our fliers but had shied away from talking to us at the festival. She had been afraid that her husband would beat her if he found Sakhi's literature in her possession or if he saw her making contact with us. She reported that she had been severely abused by her husband and wanted to know what her options were.

The woman—a wife, like the prospective bride in the mock wedding—fearfully hiding the domestic violence flier at the festival, even as she craved to read and use it, became a potential subversive at the mock wedding which drained her of her story at the same time that it used her figure to create the myth of Indian womanness as a signifier for the Spirit of India from time immemorial. Her story, as well as organizations like Sakhi which affirm her story, became a potential threat to the preservation of the India which her womanhood signified.[20] The Indian woman is allowed no history of her own by those who adopt the spirit of Indian nationalism in a problematic way; she is allowed no content of her own. In protecting all that is meaningful, she must sacrifice her own life. There is usually a woman who pays a price for the preservation of the essential (nationalist) spirit; always a woman who must keep smiling and hide her pain so as not to betray the fragility of this spiritual heritage, the high cost of its maintenance, and the euphoric security of its myth. As Lata Mani has noted for another historical context, "Women become emblematic of tradition, and the reworking of tradition is largely conducted through debating the rights and status of women in society" (1989:90).

A persistent theme of Indian nationalism has been the re-processing of the image of the Indian woman and her role in the family based on models of Indian womanhood from the distant glorious past. The woman becomes a metaphor for the purity, the chastity, and the sanctity of the Ancient Spirit that is India. As Chatterjee puts it, the national construct of the Indian woman attributes "the spiritual qualities of self-sacrifice, benevolence, devotion, religiosity, and so on" to femininity, which then stands "as a sign for 'nation'" (1989a:630). Consequently, anything that threatens to dilute this model of Indian womanhood constitutes a betrayal of all that it stands for: nation, religion, God, the Spirit of India, culture, tradition, family. Thus, Sakhi is seen as a betrayal of India's heritage and as contaminated with Western values when it challenges this model of the Indian woman. Sakhi becomes a home breaker when it exposes abuse against women and questions the patriarchal family even though Sakhi explicitly does not advocate that any woman leave her abuser unless that is what she wants to do. Sakhi provides women information about their alternatives so that they can make an informed decision about themselves—alternatives which may vary from how she can best protect herself if she wishes to stay in her current situation to what her options are if she does choose to leave. In providing information to an Indian woman which could make it possible for her to end an abusive situation and reject a role which she is told she was to fulfill, Sakhi's presence poses a threat to the Indian community's construction of its Indian-ness.

Sakhi's presence is a continual reminder of the presence of the historical self behind the mythical Indian woman. This historical self is the other-woman who is never meant to be present, just as the other-scene was never meant to happen. To follow this train of thought to its logical conclusion, any organization that recognizes the other-woman and challenges her displacement also becomes the Other: the Other as a repository of that which threatens to crumble the imaginary world of bourgeois solidarity, and to expose the artificiality of the bourgeois landscape. Ostracization of Sakhi serves as a warning to the other-woman of her fate if she tries to tell her story. It appears therefore that from the perspective of the Indian immigrant organizations, Sakhi is neither too political nor is it too social. In fact, it is whatever the Indian bourgeoisie is not, at any moment. It is simply the Other.

These comments on the Divali festival confirm my insight gained from feminist thought that the site for preservation of India, its culture, and its tradition is the family—the domestic space in which the figure of the woman stands. On the other hand, the site for economic/political advancement in the United States is the workplace, the legislature—the public space in which the figure of the man stands. This binary continues to work even for women who work outside the home, as the home still remains a place to affirm one's Indian-ness and the Indian woman is expected to be responsible for maintaining this Indian home in diaspora by remaining true to her Indian womanhood.

Construction of a Model-ness

The bourgeois immigrant, like the bourgeois nationalist, sees the preservation of the nation's cultural essence as a domain that can be defended against outside intervention: this is the area where the colonial power's interference was most abhorrent; this is also the area where one must stay ever vigilant against contamination by Western values as an immigrant. Through the changeless and timeless Spirit of India the Indian bourgeoisie, whether immigrant or still in India, seeks to anonymously eternalize its own existence. What is ironical is that the terms of cultural preservation and negotiation are, in fact, set by the dominant power: the desire for an untouched, ancient Indian heritage can be seen to be partly a reaction to the continual threat of the universalizing nature of Western, and particularly white American, culture. Another phenomenon is also illustrative of this. In the United States, Indians, along with other Asian, communities, are regarded as a model minority, exemplifying high educational status and strong financial success. The compelling and approving image of model minority can be an inducement for building an image of a model India that is commensurate with this minority standing. The timeless essence of India, derived from its distant past and unfettered by the struggles and miseries of the present, fits the model image well. This is the model that must be constructed and reconstructed. At each moment it is eternalized, preserved, and celebrated much like an ancient artifact.

The desire for a model history, also commensurate with this model minority image, may explain the selective amnesia in the Indian immigrant bourgeoisie's memory of the history of the Indian community in the United

States. The beginning of the history of the Indian community is commonly taken to date from the 1950s and 1960s, when Indian immigrants consisted predominantly of educated, urban professionals. In this historical narrative, the arrival of farmers, railroad builders, workers, and political refugees from the Indian subcontinent in the United States prior to World War I goes largely unacknowledged.[21] Sohan Singh Josh describes some of these Indian immigrants in the early twentieth century, when immigration laws fluctuated with the demand and supply for cheap labor. For example, an increased demand for cheap labor to construct railroads near San Francisco around 1910 resulted in a temporary relaxation in immigration laws (1977:60).

Some aspects of this pre-WWI history of Indians in the United States echo a more radical immigrant culture, which was informed by an explicit anti-imperialist politics and an awareness of the international scope of Western (especially British) imperialism at that time. Their immigrant and subaltern history resonates with a consciousness of India's independence struggles, although their nationalism was problematized by an unquestioning acceptance of the Indian nation as the unit of liberation. At the same time, their perspective was diasporic: first, they seemed aware of the worldwide grip of imperialism, and second, they had an appreciation of the dispersed nature of the Indian immigrant communities in Southeast Asia, Canada, Africa, Europe, the Caribbean, and the United States. There are various explanations for their awareness: they were Indian nationalists whose country was at that time colonized; they needed diasporic support not only to facilitate emigration on ships, but also in some cases to form alternative Indian independence movements of their own; and racism in the United States in relation to immigrants was more obvious (if not brutal) then. In any case, the rhetoric and activities of pre-WWI immigrants reveal a consciousness of economic power, racial politics, and imperialism that is more radical than the consciousness that predominates today.[22]

Today the Indian immigrant bourgeoisie remembers the history of the Indian community in the United States largely in terms of its own history since the mid–twentieth century. Its loss of historical memory seriously limits response to other communities who continue to face more virulent forms of racism. And not infrequently intoxicated by its success as a model minority, it fails to perceive racism towards itself. In its eagerness to reach the pinnacle of economic progress symbolized by Western capitalism, the Indian immigrant bourgeoisie disregards an analysis of power and ideology which is crucial to its understanding of its own history.

The category of "model minority," which plays an important role in the

Indian bourgeoisie's construction of an "Indian" community, is double-edged. On the one hand, the term "model" signifies a standard of excellence, set by the dominant power, which is predominantly white and wealthy, and is presumably an invitation to the minority to join the majority once it realizes its model-ness. On the other hand, the term "minority" signifies a relegation to the ranks of the not-majority. This contradiction between invitation and exclusion often escapes the leadership of the Indian bourgeoisie in its eagerness to join the mainstream of American life.

Toward this end, the Indian bourgeoisie, which sees itself as the custodians of the model Indian community in the United States, seems to be drawn to a certain "worldly" discourse of diplomacy, negotiation, and officialdom. This is evident in various activities of Indian associations (cf. Fisher 1980:187–89). Activities and issues of official representation, legislative politics, congressional hearings, and banquets to honor senators on the part of these organizations reveal a desire to participate in the administrative politics of the nation-state. The Indian bourgeoisie assiduously works towards an imaginary ideal of official legislative representation in order to acquire for this model minority the coveted goal of "political clout commensurate with its economic strength." Thus, the politics of minority status and representation within the U.S. government become an important focus for legislative activity.

The concerns of such politics focus on a confusing array of racial categorizations based on biological and cultural essentialisms. Such racial categories are constructed, bolstered, and sustained by such devices as the census, which Benedict Anderson describes as fictional: "the fiction of the census is that everyone is in it, and that everyone has one—and only one—extremely clear place. No fractions" (1991:166). Census categories (in relying on counting) profess but fail to capture the complex relationships between place of birth, ancestral origin, language, physical characteristics, and cultural affiliations. The inadequacy of such categories, however, does not seem to deter the leaders of Indian bourgeois organizations from participating in the official thrust towards an exhaustive racial categorization. This effort at categorization, divorced from history and politics, can only make race into a number game and a policy issue rather than an area of radical social change and action. It is further evidence of the limitations of the Indian bourgeois organizations' understanding of racial politics in the United States.

I do not mean to devalue the importance of a minority group's efforts to create a voice for itself. However, the focus on legislative politics by the bourgeois leadership of the Indian community is indicative of how its awareness of racial politics is dominated by the official discourse on race. This community's relationship with other communities, especially those of color, is dictated by competition over limited resources reserved for people of color as well as by rivalry over an imaginary standard of acceptance by the majority. Race as a problematic, with its complex manifestations in our daily lives, goes unacknowledged, let alone articulated. The result is a blind, often intense racism towards other communities, especially towards people of color.

The urge of the Indian bourgeoisie in the United States to engage in activities that have a nation-state-like character is also evident in their organization of annual celebrations of Indian national holidays such as Independence Day, which hold a sacrosanct place in official Indian discourse on the subcontinent. Independence Day is seen as the day when the timeless legacy of the nation of India is foregrounded and as the day to remember the liberation of India from a period of oppressive colonial rule to freely reign over itself again in all its glory. Triumphant images of Indian nationalist leaders liberating the *mother*land from British rule often crowd out questions regarding the origin(s) of this nation-state that was liberated, questions of the identity and the methods used by the liberators to gain India's "freedom." Liberating a colonized country from a racist and otherwise oppressive British regime was (and is) important, as is the acknowledgment that such a struggle for independence was laudable. However, it is necessary to point out that these historic events in a nation's biography become emblems of nationhood, alongside the flag or the national anthem. They are imbued by the nation's official discourse with an unquestioning and undiluted euphoria which places any historical accountability in suspension.

The Not-Model Community

The changing composition of the Indian immigrant community is radically altering the contours of a community that was until recently predominantly bourgeois. The bourgeoisie sees the illegal (Indian) immigrant, the unpaid (Indian) worker and the ill-paid (Indian) laborer in the United States as mere aberrations from its coveted place as a model minority. It denies the existence of gays, lesbians, and battered women as inconsistent with that Indian heritage under which it has taken refuge: for the bourgeoisie to acknowledge their existence would be an act of self-destruction.

In Sakhi, our work directly involves women in these marginalized categories, especially those of unpaid workers, battered women, and illegal immigrants. Women in abusive situations who call Sakhi come from all classes, educational backgrounds, and socioeconomic positions, much as the bourgeoisie would like to relegate them to the working class. By insisting that only cabdrivers or factory workers abuse the women in their lives, the bourgeoisie intends to develop its own image as the model minority in opposition to those it considers aberrant.

In this context, Indian owners of such commercial enterprises as magazine stalls, restaurants, or shops often have their wives work for them. Usually, the owner does not pay his wife for her work. Many times, her working conditions can be worse than those of paid workers in terms of hours and health conditions. Her unpaid labor is rationalized on the grounds that she is her husband's helpmate; indeed, her labor becomes an extension of her household duties. This situation has a historical parallel when the Indian nationalist leaders constructed Indian womanhood as having emerged out of a golden age of the Aryans. Early nationalist historians explain that just as women in ancient India were helpmates in the Vedic sacrifice, so also women in the nationalist cause were to play helpmates' roles (Chakravarti 1989:51). This translated into "energizing the husband for the goal of regenerating the motherland" (53). In the example of the diasporic woman, her unpaid labor is now glorified and romanticized to generate the wealth of her immigrant husband.

By our estimations at Sakhi, women form a large portion of the precariously placed/illegal immigrant population in the Indian community. An Indian woman's immigration status is often contingent on her husband's sponsorship because she usually enters the United States as his wife. Her dependence on him for legal status adds to her vulnerability, and is a threat that her husband often does not hesitate to use to his advantage.

The position of these women reveals the poverty of terms such as "expatriate" and "immigrant" which the U.S. Immigration Service officially uses to categorize them. Both terms usually convey a sense of agency or voluntary will on the part of the expatriate or immigrant, and assume that the presence of the "resident" alien in the United States was (and is) a freely chosen status. For an Indian woman, who is often forced implicitly or explicitly to marry through a process over which she has little control, the question of free will may be a matter of life or death. If she arrives in the United States through a decision that she did not participate in or agree to, then her classification as an immigrant which implies agency and free will is at best inadequate. When a woman abandons her abusive spouse in order to save her life, she may be out on the streets overnight with no legal status, no home, no money, and, more often than not, no community. She is now the other-woman whose presence is inconsistent with the image of the Indian community that the immigrant bourgeoisie constructs.

Naming a Space

My attempt to expose the space that the other-woman occupies leads me to an area which is fraught with ambiguities and contradictions: the discourse of the private. Antonio Gramsci, in this context, identifies two major superstructural levels in society: "the one that can be called 'civil society,' that is the *ensemble of organisms commonly called "private*,*"* and that of 'political society' or the 'State.' These two levels correspond on the one hand to the function of 'hegemony' which the dominant group exercises throughout society and on the other hand to that of 'direct domination' or command exercised through the state and 'juridical' government" (1971:12; emphasis mine). Although Gramsci's superstructural levels need to be complicated, his use of the phrase "commonly called 'private'" suggests that private is a deliberate discursive construction. In common usage, the concept "private" that Gramsci points to carries a sense of seclusion, isolation, and freedom from intervention and state control. Three common usages of this concept are the private world of the individual, the private world of home/family, and the private sector of the capitalist economy. All three spaces share a sacred sense of isolation in bourgeois society, especially with respect to state intervention and the public gaze.

Yet it is the bourgeoisie, by its historical creation of a regulated society, that has homogenized these three entities and imbued them with authority. Thus, the historical agency of the bourgeoisie in formalizing these entities contradicts its declarations regarding their private nature. In its assertions of the sanctity of the private spaces, the bourgeoisie succeeds in obliterating traces of its own agency. In doing so, it roots these entities—these spaces—in eternity. In fact, the production and regulation of each of these private life worlds is crucial to the construction of the nation-state, the emblem of bourgeois society.

In order to determine the space of the woman described above, we need to examine the private spaces constructed by the Indian immigrant community.[23] It is in this space that the immigrant bourgeoisie guards what it perceives to be the nation's cultural essence against contamination by dominant Western values. It is here that the immigrant bourgeoisie steadies itself in the face of changes in a foreign country. This private space appears to be defined at two different levels: the domestic sphere of the family, and the extended "family of Indians" which is separate and distinct from other communities. It is in these spaces that the immigrant bourgeoisie recognizes the woman; in the private individual and the private sector it recognizes the man. Thus, we may note the different deployment of the idea of the private by the bourgeoisie in various contexts.

Community events, such as festivals, play an important role, as these events become the space in which the bourgeois immigrant controls the fate of national culture in the "family of Indian immigrants." A restriction on the kinds of organizations which can participate (such as feminist or gay/lesbian or working class), a careful selection of the kinds of activities that are permitted and invited, and the persistent visibility of women in certain kinds of culturally appropriate roles (such as in a stall for applying *mehendi* [henna], for teaching *bhangra* [dance], for displaying wedding ceremonies [usually Hindu], or coordinating food-related activities) characterize the mood and organization of celebrations of national culture.

The pure, unsullied, and heterosexual family is another space that the bourgeoisie in its construction of national identities seeks to preserve. The responsibility for the preservation of this unsullied space lies with the woman, and the honor of an Indian woman is contingent upon her ability to suffer in silence and maintain this space. Her role assumes an unrivaled sanctity even as her life requires the utmost control. As Kumkum Sangari and Sudesh Vaid say, "Womanhood is often part of an asserted or desired, not an actual cultural continuity" (1989:17).

The private space of the family is, as I said above, fundamental to national constructs. Anderson points out how both family and nation denote eternal and sacred ties whose origins disappear into the mythical and distant past: "Both idioms [family and nation] denote something to which one is naturally tied . . . all those things one cannot help. . . . Precisely because such ties are not chosen, they have about them a halo of disinterestedness. . . . For most ordinary people of whatever class the whole point of the nation is that it is interestless. Just for that reason, it can ask for sacrifices" (1991:143–44).

Thus, any challenge to the family or the Indian community translates for the national bourgeoisie into a betrayal of national cultural values. For a woman (who is mother, wife, bride, daughter-in-law, or daughter-to-be-married) to disown her role(s) is to betray not just the family, but also the nation. It has been suggested that "nation-ness is the most universally legitimate value in the political life of our time" (Anderson 1991:3). In this respect, the woman who occupies the space outside the heterosexual, patriarchal family is in a space unrecognized by the nation, currently a highly valued construct. The displacement of her history is crucial for the construction of the nation; in reclaiming her voice, her story, she risks displacing the nation.

A Twice-Imagined Nation

Anderson suggests that there are three paradoxes of nationalism: "(1) The objective modernity of nations to the historian's eye vs. their subjective antiquity in the eyes of nationalists; (2) the formal universality of nationality as a socio-cultural concept—in the modern world everyone can, should, will 'have' a nationality, as he or she 'has' a gender; (3) the "political" power of nationalisms vs. their philosophical poverty and even incoherence" (1991:5). Anderson captures the way in which national constructions, despite their relative newness, have assumed self-evidential proportions and have lost their historicity. National identity, national allegiance, and nation all appear as an essential and eternal part of ourselves regardless of where we reside.

In the twentieth century, a time when the myth of the nation has played a major and sometimes positive role in liberation struggles in the Third World, the importance of a collective identity, especially for oppressed (or colonized) peoples, cannot be overstated. Independence movements, however, are often dominated by the nationalist bourgeoisie, which unquestioningly imagines the nation to be the unit of liberation. Assertions of other loyalties have often been considered disruptive and disloyal to the cause of liberation and unity. Today, liberation struggles are frequently defined in terms of the nation: struggles which threaten national constructions are seen as random (contrary to the systematized nation), biased (not involving national loyalty), disruptive (addressing a construct other than the nation), subversive (threatening the essential national spirit), regional (not nationwide), and narrow-minded (not including the nation). Women's organizations, for example, are often called "disruptive" in raising questions about gender, a construct other than the nation; communal loyalties are seen as "subversive" when they challenge the idea of an essential national unity and assert regional or religious loyalties.

Through this myth of the nation, the Indian bourgeoisie in the United States establishes once again its universality and eternalizes its own existence in the soil of the community. Cloaked in nationalist consciousness by the habit of ex-nomination, it sets about recreating a community in its own image. Thus cloaked, it succeeds in eliminating any record of its agency in the making of the community—whose creation can then be attributed to the divine agency of the ancient Indian spirit.

The trope of the nation as members of the Indian community draw on it here can be seen as a strategy that they follow as they construct themselves *politically* not as a nation but as a model minority. This community finds itself caught up in the American national project as an exceptionally civil minority which, unlike its counterpart in India, does not occupy the central ground of either the nation or the state. The idea of the nation in the discourse of the Indian bourgeoisie here subserves the project of being a model minority in a culturally plural nation-state. The Indian community is thus under special pressure to present an image of homogeneity and internal discipline, which are crucial components of the twice-imagined nation.

The "figure of the woman" describes one of the foundational elements contributing to the construction of this twice-imagined nation, through which the immigrant bourgeoisie gives itself an identity. The "figure" is the woman reified: it is a "thing," a signifier to help unify the incoherent, impoverished world of the bourgeoisie, a receptacle to be filled, by the bourgeoisie, with any static ahistorical meaning, at any given moment. In the shifting grounds of an immigrant community, the bourgeoisie uses this figure of the woman to steady itself. Sakhi, in exposing the violence behind the figure of the woman, through its concerns with the marginalized, the dispossessed, and the abused, then becomes a betrayal to the twice-imagined nation.

Resisting a Habit

The importance of filling the void created by uncertain identities and changing geography, in the context of peoples of migratory movement, should not be underestimated. That Indian-ness describes a certain historical connection to a geographical area now called India, and provides a means of cohesion, also cannot be denied. However, it is only through an understanding of one's historical conditions that an immigrant can resist the appropriation of this void by ahistorical essentialisms, such as the assumption of a mythical "Indian" identity created in antiquity and existing from time immemorial. Such essentialisms can only be a denial of history.[24]

That which the Indian bourgeoisie calls "betrayal" on the part of Sakhi is what I call a questioning of the appropriation of the Indian immigrant identity by the Indian immigrant bourgeoisie in the name of "national" culture that it constructs for its own purposes. Indian-ness is not a natural excretion of a genealogical tree, but a continual struggle along multiple modes through a negotiation of the inescapable tension between secure definitions and a consciousness of the oppressions that such definitions rest upon. The struggle

in the shifting grounds of immigrant experience holds numerous possibilities for liberation and for the invention of new social arrangements.

The immigrant Indian bourgeoisie, through its habit of ex-nomination,
intends to render historical analysis unnecessary by creating a seamless unity
called "nation." This seamless unity renders invisible the many violences which
lie behind the figure of the woman. The invisible violence which lies hidden
by the reified figure of the woman is a seam in this seamless unity. The
woman who survived domestic abuse, and who decided to call Sakhi to tell
her story after the Divali celebration, makes this violence visible. By reclaiming her voice and asserting her historical self, she created an opening for an
intervention into the imaginary unity of the immigrant bourgeoisie's nation.

Notes

1. The organization Sakhi for South Asian Women was founded in 1989 by women
   of South Asian origin in New York City. It provides such services as crisis intervention, legal advocacy, and referrals to shelters and counselors. Sakhi is committed to the view that only through empowerment can women ultimately resist
   violence in their lives. Sakhi also actively engages in community education because it believes that the community must take responsibility for violence against
   women and that it is through the raising of awareness that fundamental change
   can occur. I am writing this paper from a personal perspective and not on behalf
   of Sakhi. I am indebted to S. Shankar for his valuable suggestions. And I thank
   Purnima Bose, Supriya Nair, Jael Silliman, and Ann Cvetkovich for their thought-
   ful comments.
2. This link may not be unique to the Indian community in the United States, but I
   will restrict my discussion mainly to this community.
3. My discussion of the festival below may seem to contradict my use of the word
   "public" here. However, this contradiction is only apparent, and I have decided
   to let it remain, as it is to help show that words like "public" and "private" carry
   multiple meanings. A festival defined as public in certain contexts can also be
   defined in very different ways in other contexts, as will become clear.
4. Some general studies of Indian immigrant life in the United States include: A.
   W. Helweg and U. M. Helweg, *An Immigrant Success Story: East Indians in
   America* (Philadelphia: University of Pennsylvania Press, 1990); P. Saran, *The
   Asian Indian Experience in the United States* (New Delhi: Vikas, 1985); R.
   Daniels, *History of Indian Immigration to the United States* (New York: Asia Society, 1989).
5. A detailed discussion of the contradictions and paradoxes of the relationship between a recently immigrant Third World bourgeoisie in the First World and First
   World bourgeoisie is beyond the scope of this paper, but the topic would be appropriate for exploration.
6. The term "bourgeois" is a complex one signifying a historical class as well as a
   particular culture and ideology. Thus a person can belong to the class based on

his/her material conditions, but may consciously attempt to dissociate him/her-self from its culture and ideology. In my use of term, I refer to that portion of the bourgeoisie which uncritically satisfies both material and cultural and ideo-logical conditions of the class: it is to this group that ex-nomination is attrib-uted.

7. NFIAA is popularly known as NFIA; AAIA is popularly known as AIA.

8. U. Segal, in "Cultural Variables in Asian Indian Families," says that the Indian community in the United States, whose current size is bout 750,000, is estimated to grow to one million out of a total Asian population of eight million by the year 2000, and to two million by 2050 (1991, 233).

9. I have not found documentation stating that the FIA was the precursor to the NFIAA. However, the FIA president became the NFIAA president, which sug-gests the possibility. It is important to point this out because I will be discussing later how the NFIAA is described in the *Encyclopedia of Associations in the United States* (Burek 1992).

10. *Indian Community Reference Guide* (Guthikonda et al. 1979).

11. In his book *The Construction of Communalism in Colonial North India*, Pandey's discussion of communalism and nationalism in India spans the nineteenth and earlier part of the twentieth century. Even though his comments refer to an ear-lier historical period, I find them to be relevant today in the context of the In-dian community in India as well as the United States because this historical period in India is the one during which the discursive mechanisms used by Indian na-tionalists today evolved.

12. According to him, "Before [the 1920s and 1930s] the nation of Indians was vi-sualized as a composite body, consisting of several communities, each with its own history and culture and its own special contribution to make to the com-mon nationality. . . . Sometime around the 1920s . . . India came to be seen very much more as a collection of individuals, of Indian 'citizens'" (210).

13. Burek (1992, 1861).

14. Though I focus only on the idea of the nation, it is not the only essentialist cat-egory available for the purpose of ex-nomination.

15. Bharatanatyam refers to what is now understood to be the classical dance of South India, and is closely identified with Tamil culture. In the twentieth century, this dance genre was standardized and is now associated with the nation as a national dance form.

16. "Unity in diversity" is a popular phrase in Indian nationalist discourse, especially today, in the midst of communal struggles that occupy center stage in challeng-ing the very survival of both the state and the nation in India. According to G. Pandey, the use of this phrase has waned somewhat with the rise of a "'main-stream' (Brahmanical Hindu, consumerist) culture" which flaunts itself as *the* national culture, expecting all other "minority" cultures to fall in line with it and to which all difference appears threatening and foreign (1992:28). However, given the asynchronicity of social processes, we continue to see evidence of the con-cept of "unity in diversity" in the immigrant community.

17. Pandey demonstrates the construction "of a new community—the 'India of our dreams'"—in the 1920s, by Indian nationalists. One of the changes, he notes, is

the use of terms such as "purely national," raising the nation to a transcendent level (1990:239).

18. This discussion is contained in G. Lukács, "Reification and Consciousness of the Proletariat," where he examines the structure of the commodity (1971:83).

19. We did not complete the script for the play, but its preliminary sketches consisted of a domestic scene juxtaposing the living room with the kitchen. A gathering of friends and family was to take place in the living room while food preparations were to continue in the kitchen. We were attempting to bring out the differences in interactions between the man (husband) and the woman (wife) in these two areas, in order to demonstrate the different faces of abuse and the ease with which it remains hidden.

20. T. Sarkar shows, in the context of Bengali nationalists, a "constant preoccupation . . . with the figure of the woman" and with the "conceptualisation of the country itself in her image" through a nationalist "reconstruction of feminine roles and duties" (1987:2011).

21. This was a time before the liberalization of the U.S. immigration laws in the mid-1960s, which abolished discrimination based on place of birth and national origin.

22. J. Jensen describes at length the conditions of these immigrants in *Passage from India: Asian Indian Immigrants in North America* (1988).

23. In my discussion of private spaces as created by the Indian immigrant society, I would like to note a point that D. Chakrabarty makes in the context of colonial India. Even as he traces the origins of the concepts of bourgeois privacy and individuality in India to British rule, he shows how these concepts were not transplanted in an uncomplicated manner into Indian society. He describes the ways in which Indians challenged and modified these ideas through their own cultural operations, and I would like to retain this though in my discussion (1992).

24. In my use of the terms "history" and "historical" I would like to retain D. Chakrabarty's point regarding the subalternity of Third World histories as long as Europe remains the sovereign subject of all histories. He stresses the importance of rethinking "history" on the part of people of Third World origin in ways which "displace a hyperreal Europe from the center" (1992:22).

References

Anderson, B. 1991. *Imagined Communities*. London: Verso.

Barthes, R. 1988. *Mythologies*, trans. A. Lavers. New York: Noonday.

Burek, D. M. (ed.). 1992. "National Federation of Indian American Associations," in *Encyclopedia of Associations in the United States*, 26th ed., pt. 2, sect. 10. Detroit: Gale Research.

Chakrabarty, D. 1992. "Postcoloniality and the Artifice of History: Who Speaks for the 'Indian' Pasts?" *Representations* 37:1–26.

Chakravarti, U. 1989. "Whatever Happened to the Vedic *Dasi*? Orientalism, Nationalism, and a Script for the Past," in *Recasting Women: Essays in Colonial History*, K. Sangari and S. Vaid (eds.). New Delhi: Kali for Women.

Chatterjee, P. 1989a. "Colonialism, Nationalism, and Colonialized Women: The Contest in India," *American Ethnologist* 16 (4): 622–33.

————. 1989b. "Gandhi and the Critique of Civil Society," *Subaltern Studies III*, R. Guha (ed.). Delhi: Oxford University Press.

Fanon, F. 1968. *The Wretched of the Earth*, trans. C. Farrington. New York: Grove/ Black Cat.

Fisher, M. P. 1980. "The Indian Ethnic Identity: The Role of Associations in the New York Indian Population," in *The New Ethnics: Asian Indians in The United States*, P. Saran and E. Eames (eds.). New York: Praeger.

Gramsci, A. 1971. *Selections from the Prison Notebooks*, ed. and trans. Q. Hoare and G. N. Smith. New York: International.

Guthikonda, R., et al. (eds.) 1979. *Indian Community Reference Guide and Directory of Indian Associations in North America*. New York: Federation of Indian Associations.

Jensen, J. M. 1988. *Passage from India: Asian Indian Immigrants in North America*. New Haven: Yale University Press.

Josh, S. S. 1977. *Hindustan Gadar Party: A Short History*. New Delhi: People's Publishing House.

Lukács, G. 1971. "Reification and the Consciousness of the Proletariat," in *History and Class Consciousness*, trans. R. Livingstone. Cambridge, Mass.: MIT Press.

Mani, L. 1989. "Contentious Traditions: The Debate on Sati in Colonial India," in *Recasting Women: Essays In Colonial History*, K. Sangari and S. Vaid (eds.). New Delhi: Kali for Women.

Pandey, G. 1990. *The Construction of Communalism in Colonial North India*. Delhi: Oxford University Press.

————. 1992. "In Defense of the Fragment: Writing about Hindu-Muslim Riots in India Today," *Representations* 37:25–54.

Sangari, K., and S. Vaid. (eds.) 1989. *Recasting Women: Essays in Colonial History*. New Delhi: Kali for Women.

Sarkar, T. 1987. "Nationalist Iconography: Image of Women in 19th-Century Bengali Literature," *Economic and Political Weekly* 22, no. 47:2011–2015.

Segal, U. 1991. "Cultural Variables in Asian Indian Families," *Families in Society: The Journal of Contemporary Human Services* 72, no. 4:233–241.

"Underneath My Blouse Beats My Indian Heart"

SEXUALITY, NATIONALISM, AND INDIAN WOMANHOOD IN THE UNITED STATES

SUNITA SUNDER MUKHI

Indians all over the United States celebrated the 47th anniversary of India's Independence Day—Aug. 15, 1947—with traditional fervor. The events were marked by speeches and nationalist songs. . . . New York's Governor Mario Cuomo issued a proclamation declaring Aug. 15 India Day. The India Day parade in New York City [was] held on Aug. 21.

I was packing my video camera on my way to the Independence Day parade when it struck me that I was going there by myself.[1] I suddenly became frightened and began to sob. I was terrified of being found out by the community that I was not Indian enough: I had short hair, was wearing khaki pants, was born in the Philippines, and I was without a man. I am thirty-five years old, and very single. What kind of Indian woman was I?

The Jewish shopkeeper in Rego Park from whom I bought batteries for my cassette recorder asked me if I was Indian. I said yes tentatively, not wishing to explain that, actually, I was born in the Philippines. He enthusiastically went on to tell me how much he loved to watch the Indian movies of Raj Kapoor and Nargis and began to sing a song from *Shree 420*. I, in good spirits by now, sang along with him—*Ichuk dana, beechuk dana, dane upar dana*. After much giggling, he explained to me why Indian movies were so popular in Israel. "They are so romantic," he proclaimed, "with the songs and dances and no nudity." What's the use of seeing a woman fully naked? There is no mystery left! What's more, the whole family can come and watch these movies. Indian women are more beautiful because they are modest, he assured me.

"To the strains of nationalistic slogans '*Jai Hind, Hindustan Zindabad*' and a popular Hindi film song '*Tu Cheez Badi Hai Mast Mast*,' hundreds of young Indians led by New City Mayor, Rudolph Giuliani, Indian Ambassador Siddhartha Shankar Ray, Miss Universe 1994 Sushmita Sen and film star of yesteryear, Asha Parekh, marched down Madison Avenue in Manhattan to celebrate the 47th anniversary of India's independence here August 21."[2]

The spectacle of the Indian Independence Day celebrations produced by the Federation of Indians in America (FIA) is an exemplar of a vernacular nationalism as expressed by Indians in the diaspora. The parade, which passes through about twenty blocks of midtown Madison Avenue, comprises various marching bands and many floats paid for by merchant associations and commercial establishments, as well as by sociocultural voluntary associations. It culminates in a food fair and cultural program in which local talents and invited celebrities perform their version of "Indian culture."

The FIA is the umbrella organization for ninety-three parochial, merchant, sectarian, and service-oriented voluntary Indian associations in the New York Tristate area. It seeks to "represent a pan-Indian population and image, one rising above the regional and religious boundaries," observes Madhulika Khandelwal in her research on New York immigrants.[3] Besides promoting ethnic solidarity, the FIA seeks to "introduce Americans to India in a convivial setting."[4] Since 1981, the FIA's main activity has been to organize the India Day parade in Manhattan and the cultural program immediately following it, ostensibly to celebrate India's independence from British sovereignty. The events of India Day have become an opportunity for Indians not only to socialize, network, and have fun but also to vent frustrations and express their ambivalence about being Indian in America. Thus, the parade and the celebrations surrounding it become yet another arena wherein various expressions of Indianness are contested and negotiated.

Various Indian merchant associations from the New York Tristate area, restaurants, and retailers of Indian foods and spices march in the India Day parade along with religious organizations such as Asian Indian Ministry, ISKCON, Bochasanyasi Swaminarayan Sanstha, Muslim Federation of America, and Sri Chinmoy Centre. To enliven the parade, there is much dancing, shouting of *Jai Hind* (long live India), and waving of the Indian flags of various sizes. Groups of teenage girls dance with the flags, waving and whirling them to the rhythms of a Hindi film song with a disco beat. They usually appear on stage later, dancing to a folksy film dance. Needless to say, dignitaries like the mayor, or the governor, candidates for political office who need the Indian vote, and members of the Indian consulate march down Madison Avenue and make speeches extolling the Indian community's great importance and contributions to U.S. society. On one summer day in August each year, all Manhattan witnesses Indianness in America.

There is much to tell about the India Day celebration, but I restrict my discussion to two salient themes gleaned from three years of observations and attendance in the parade: 1991, 1992, 1994, especially focusing on the 1994 parade. The first is based on my observation that the performers for the cultural show are mostly young girls. With the preponderance of Hindi film songs and reinterpretations of Hindi film dances at the parade, the question that begs to be asked is, What is the relationship between girl/womanhood, the preponderance of Hindi film songs and dances, and Indian nationalism? The second motif comprises a number of subplots that have a complex relationship with that theme. The first subplot involves the exclusion of the South Asian Lesbian and Gay Association (SALGA) and eventual exclusion of Sakhi for South Asian Women (Sakhi) from the parade.[5] I will contend that this ambivalence on the part of the parade organizers bears upon the definition of the Indian woman and refers to female sexuality in general. The second subplot involves the 1994 float of the Bharatiya Janata Party (BJP), which constructed a Hindu fundamentalist and nationalist "ideal woman" for the immigrant community. Last, the third subplot has a personal focus. In relation to these anecdotes, I try to define my place and involvement as a diasporic woman in the India Day parade.

Dancing to the National(ist) Tune

Manhar Patel, chairman of the cultural program of the 1994 India Day parade, claimed that, despite encouraging the participants to present folk or classical numbers, the more respectable artifacts of Indian culture, most participants had insisted on film dances and were in fact competing to perform two or three currently popular Hindi film songs. He asserted that in response to the call for performances in the India Day variety show, the main source of inspiration generally was Hindi film song-and-dance sequences rather than classical "high" art forms. Out of the nine performances approved in 1994, six were Hindi film song-and-dance reinterpretations, and in 1992, twelve out of sixteen items were. Even when a title indicated that an act was a folk dance, the music or song was taken from regional language films. Furthermore, these song-and-dance interpretations were performed primarily by girls between the ages of twelve and sixteen, fully costumed in folk dresses or classical costumes.

To comprehend this overwhelming influence of Hindi films on immigrant lives, it is important to understand the ubiquity of the industry itself. The Hindi film industry is a big, booming enterprise based in Bombay. On average, at least 500 Hindi films are produced each year, out of which approximately ten become hits.[6] As of 1985, the daily film viewership of Hindi films had reached thirteen million, with an average of 100 million tickets sold every week.[7] The industry is the sixth largest in the world and employs over two million people. Overseas too, these films are viewed by four million expatriate Indians on videocassette.[8] According to Barnouw and Krishnaswamy, to become a hit, a Hindi film calls "for one or two major stars, at least half a dozen songs, and a few dances. . . . The subject matter, with increasing concentration [was] romance."[9]

Within the structure of Hindi films, song-and-dance sequences do have a narrative function. They help in the release of tension, especially sexual tension between the hero and heroine, without portraying actual coitus or related activities. The sequences can be used to arouse pathos or bathos when there is a sad or comic situation. Furthermore, the sequences can move the story from one point in the plot to another. They can cause romance to bloom and strategically distract a villain, as well as change the fate of the characters. A more important function of these sequences is the arousal of *rasa*, sympathetic delight and pleasure evoked in the spectator by the technical and emotive expertise of the performer through theatrical devices such as dance, song, costume, scenery, and poetry. This classical tradition extends into popular performance and takes on a new form (or what elitist critics would describe as corruption) in Hindi film.

My aim in referring to classical art in relation to film song-and-dance sequences is neither to apologize for nor to legitimize the existence of the more popular form. It is to underscore the preponderance of songs and dances in Indian art, in Indian life, if you will. When television became widespread in India in the seventies, the first prime-time, and one of the most popular, shows was the MTV-like "Chitra-Haar" (garland of songs), which depicted song-and-dance segments spliced from various Hindi films. With the greater availability of home video machines in the United States, many people rented Hindi videocassettes consisting of only song-and-dance sequences, expertly put together for the home viewer by Indian merchants.

These song-and-dance sequences on video are one of the first teachers of Indian aesthetics and culture to overseas Indians. The film dances are watched and watched again, imitated and rechoreographed, and subsequently performed at festivals, commemorative occasions, and other community affairs of expatriate Indians. They are a potent marker of Indian ethnicity in the diaspora. Hearing a familiar and well-liked song accompanying the dance movements of a young compatriot is sufficient to create an ersatz experience of community, or to use a Turnerian phrase, "a liminoid experience of 'communitas.'"[10] Kiren Ghei, in her studies of Indian immigrant teenage film-dancers in the Los Angeles area, has remarked on this phenomenon: "Forming one aspect of this rich public life are immigrants' and first generation Indian Americans' interpretations of Indian popular cinema. Film music and dance typically appear in 'cultural programs' which are usually the centerpiece of a larger event celebrating a religious or national holiday celebrated in India (for example, Divali or India Independence Day)."[11] It is through the stylizations of Hindi song-and-dance sequences and their consequent reinterpretations on the North American stage by middle-class Indians that a vernacular nationalism is delineated.

Indian/American? Girl/Woman?

In the 1994 India Day cultural show, one of the marvels was the performance of a young seven-year-old girl, Preeti, who was immediately catapulted to the status of star.[12] Her depiction of the popular and controversial song *"Choli ke peeche kya hai"* (Guess what is underneath my blouse) was a conflation of sexuality, nationalism, rusticity, disguise, and talent.[13] Before I go on to describe Preeti's performance, let me present the background of the song she danced to, which became controversial in India because its sexual innuendoes and explicit earthy dance gestures jarred middle-class sensibilities. In the film, the song appeared when the heroine, a policewoman, tries to lure the villain by playing the role of a prostitute. Thus, we have the respectable, well-bred girl impersonating the woman of ill-repute for the sake of greater good.

"Choli ke peeche" is a parody of prostitution and heterosexual seduction, as the heroine slips in and out of her disguise. She plays at being a prostitute in the line of duty of police work. The heroine boldly puts herself, her womanhood, and her reputation at risk for her profession, her *dharma* (duty). She even becomes heroic in the process, not a passive victim waiting to be saved by a macho hero. In fact, she is the macho hero! Her disguise gives

license for seduction and display. Her duality of lewdness and chastity, badness and goodness, debauchery and heroism, shimmer in her dance.

However, what happens to the dance when a young girl of seven, whose sexuality is still ambiguous or at least unrealized, performs it during Indian Independence Day? Interestingly, much of the sexuality that is implicit in the lyrics and the original dance sequence in the film remains intact in the gyration of Preeti's hips, flirtatious facial expressions, and the sheer control of her body in performance. Her reinterpretation of the dance is not a superficial mimicry of the original. Her mastery of the spirit of the dance can be seen in the choreography, stage presence, and her eye contact with the audience. To accommodate the demands of this particular stage, her immigrant milieu, and middle-class morality, her costume is made more demure. In fact, her modest costume points to the immodesty of showing too much flesh, even in so young a body. Unlike the film's heroine, Preeti's body is fully covered. After all, Preeti is not a movie star, yet! Moreover, the context within which she performs the dance is different from that of the movie. Preeti is still the child of middle-class parents and, therefore, must conform to their restrictive rules.

The song, moved from the narrative context of the film to the diasporic stage, turns into another story. The audience is enchanted by the child mimicking and altering the dance of an adult Indian woman, a superstar playing the role of a policewoman disguised as a prostitute. Overlaid on Preeti's somewhat innocent, and therefore unavailable, body are the not-so-innocent text of the song and the sensual choreography. Integral to these features are the implicit narratives: seduction, disguise, and the child's destiny of "Indianness." As the child moves rhythmically, what shines in this free space of performance is the fact of her being a child now, with the potential of womanhood, of childbearing, in the future. Contained in her tiny dancing body is the "future-past" of Indian culture.[14] The emcee of the show proclaimed in admiration of Preeti's charming performance, "She is only seven now and look how beautiful she already is! What more, when she is seventeen!" The subtext of his declaration seems to be, "Watch out for her, you young Indian studs out there!" The girl-child in this dance is not only a future childbearer, but she is also erotic, a source of delight and pleasure.

As a miniature of Indian culture, Preeti is portable, she can be held and had by the spectating audience in the sheer act of looking. Moreover, the audience can possess with this "optical tactility" the glamour of Madhuri Dixit, the superstar who performed the original dance in the film. For the little girl, the process is similar. Through her mimicry and alteration of the dance, there is a "palpable, sensuous connection between [the] body [Preeti's] and the perceived [Madhuri]."[15] In watching or dancing *"Choli ke peeche,"* the audience and performer both acquire the glamour and talent of the Hindi film and its star, its multilayered narratives, and a vernacular Indianness.

Besides the rechoreographed main part of the dance, Preeti introduced some innovated Bharat Natyam dance steps to fill the gaps left by the absent chorus line, a universal feature of Hindi film dances. This inventiveness would have dismayed Indian classical dance purists. Interestingly, when Preeti was asked who taught her the dance, she proudly claimed that "I did it myself." She watched the videotape of the movie, imitated some of the steps, and innovated others. It is her relationship with the domestic technology of the VCR, her initiative to control the dance's accessibility, and her personal discipline that facilitated her learning of the dance and of Indianness. According to Preeti's mother, Rakhee, the little girl had never taken Bharat Natyam lessons, although this is a typical practice among middle-class immigrant families in the United States. I found in my own research on Indian immigrant children in the San Francisco Bay Area, and corroborated by Ilana Abramovitch's fieldwork on Indian residents of Flushing, Queens, Indian classical dance classes were a respectable way to initiate Indian children into "lessons [of Indian] culture and grace . . . , [a] marking of Indian identity."[16] However, when Preeti chose to use Bharat Natyam steps merely to fill in the gaps of a film dance rather than to dance a full-fledged classical number, she was not only betraying her true affections but also repudiating the official discourse on "respectability." Without having to depend on the precarious sociopolitical structure of the *guru-shishya* (teacher-disciple) tandem, Preeti independently created her own film dance.

It is most convenient that Hindi film videotapes and music audiocassettes saturate the home life of Indians in the United States. Unlike Bharat Natyam and other Indian classical dances, the choreography of the film dance is easy to imitate and does not require years and years of training and large amounts of money for classes. Preeti's teacher is the dancing film actress, who is accessible through video technology, instead of some brahminical master of Indian classical dance. Unlike the arduous rounds of repetitive movement lessons in classical dance, the Indian child, in the comfort and safety of her home, can immediately, with some practice and attention, embody the film dance. Furthermore, by extension, she reproduces the culture by rewinding the video-cassette over and over again while imitating the choreography in a matter of four or five hours. Because of the film dance's accessibility to her and others like her, Preeti can perform almost every other week in a community gathering, wedding reception, or any other such show. Her mother rather unconvincingly lamented that she needed to control Preeti's appearances so that she could concentrate on schoolwork. Performing thus is a cheaper and more democratic way of learning Indian culture. Preeti can perform this artifact of culture at the Independence Day celebration without the burden of classist and classical bias, or without having to wait for a guru to authorize her debut.[17] Preeti becomes the author, as well as the authority of her dance, talent, and expression of Indianness. Furthermore, she celebrates India Day by saluting her own independence and practicing a democratic aesthetic.

This independence and authority bestowed on the performer is supported by Kiren Ghei's research. The following is the summary of an interview she conducted with one of her subjects: "When you have a dance class, there's a planned dance practice, there's a planned time, date, the teacher's there to say this is how you do it, and that how you're going to do it. But here you've got to say, well I'll just do it after I finish my homework or whatever. You sit there and go, I'll do it, turn on the tape and you do it on your own . . . in the class, you sit there and wait for the teacher to tell you, well 'we're going to do this dance this time, and this is how we're going to do it.' . . . There's no one to tell you 'practice your dance'; you've got to do it on your own."[18]

Using Michael Taussig's definition of the mimetic faculty as the "nature that culture uses to create second nature," I can say that the child's self-taught mimicry of the dance naturalizes her talent and her Indianness.[19] Her ability and her talent to copy well, to perform the dance with such confidence and self-sufficiency, persuades us, comforts us, that Indianness is indeed, second nature. As our miniature star sparkles on stage, we are reassured that Indian culture is intact, that it is alive and well in the body of our children and will continue, even on Madison Avenue, New York City, United States of America.

Because Preeti was born in the United States, she appreciates the occasion of Indian Independence in a very different way from how her parents or the show's organizers experience it. Her elders remember the independence struggle, or at least are products of the newly partitioned Indian nation-state. Their lived experience of Indian nationalism can be narrated to her only in the form of stories, if at all. What Preeti knows of India and Indianness includes what she sees on video in her suburban home in New Jersey and what she dances on stage in New York City. The vivid film portrayal of dancing superstars, romance, and sexuality cultivate her allegiance to India, her understanding of what it means to be Indian. She therefore expresses her "infantile citizenship" of India in her reinterpretation of an ahistoric, media-produced and reproduced popular Hindi film dance.[20] To her, the Hindi film song and dance is as nationalistic as the poetry of Nobel Laureate Rabindranath Tagore, the chant of *Vande Mataram* (I worship my motherland), or even singing the national anthem solemnly. It is equivalent to shouting out *Jai Hind! Jai Hind! Jai Hind*! which she in fact does after her dance. The crowd responded likewise with much exuberance, and understanding!

The insistence of the emcee that talent is somehow passed down from mother to child because Preeti's mother also dances may hold some logic. For, indeed, if the mother notices her daughter performing well, she will encourage her by providing her daughter with the tape, VCR, costume, and transportation to and from performance sites, that is, the material requirements for Preeti's dance. After all, her daughter is fulfilling and continuing the genealogical line, a matrilineal one at that, of talent. Her daughter's dancing may even be the vicarious fulfillment of the mother's own personal aspiration to perform, an ambition which may have been curtailed by the obligations of marriage and family life. Indeed, it would be immodest for Rakhee, Preeti's mother, to perform "*Choli ke peeche*" precisely because the erotic explicitness of the dance would glaringly mirror her sexually realized adult body. The thrill of sexual potential is thus made flaccid by its fulfillment.

This decision to separate adult female sexuality from the song "*Choli ke peeche*" is not unique to this particular situation. In a wedding reception I attended recently, I was asked to perform a dance. While I was figuring out which song to dance to, one of my dear woman friends who had come to visit me from Singapore, firmly told me that I was not to dance to "*Choli ke peeche*" under any circumstances. I inquired why, and she said it was not appropriate for a grown woman, who is still looking for a husband, to dance to such a song, especially in front of strangers. It would not look good. People would take me for a "loose woman." Nevertheless, the song was played by the deejay, and my other married friends, my girlfriend, and I all danced to it, enjoying its rhythm and flirtatiousness. My friends formed a circle around me, allowing me to perform the dance for them, veiling me from the malicious and salacious gaze of people who did not know me.

For the mother, it was better that her daughter Preeti, in her innocence, mimic the adult gestures of the dance. Preeti's innocent young body is comparable allegorically to the idea of India being pure, young, and virginal, the newly carved out "infant" nation, untainted by the "lusts" of Westernization, bureaucratic inefficiency, governmental graft and corruption, imbalanced global politics and economics, and communal violence, to name just a few of its postcolonial troubles.[21] Preeti's innocence about the class biases of film dance versus classical and folk dance frees her to innovate, appropriate, and enjoy spontaneously the gamut of ethnochoreographies available to her. She can enjoy dancing per se. A young child dancing a Hindi film song on Independence Day is a tale telling of utopia. And of course, this Indian paradise is not devoid of eroticism.

Dreams Can Come True

The fate of being away from India is underscored by the fact that the movie stars and celebrities feel privileged to make an appearance among expatriate Indians. For example, film actress Meenakshi Sheshadri, who was the grand marshal of the 1993 India Day parade, fulfilled her promise to return in 1994. Meenakshi is not only glamorous, successful, and beautiful, but she also keeps her word. She attempted to share her mystical philosophy of true independence by explaining, "Liberation is not just for a country or a people. True liberation is, even while you are still human, you are liberated from being human." Indeed, as a movie star, she is already much larger than life. By virtue of her profession, economic status, and social position, she can be liberated from the trials and travails of being merely an ordinary human being. The audience present in the United States, in the metropolis par excellence of New York City, experience her three-dimensionality. The celluloid goddess is present, in the flesh, talking about how happy she is to be loved by all.

Indians across socioeconomic classes in New York are more apt to see, take *darshan*, of film superstars, these mythic beings here, than they would in India. Hindi film stars are more likely to give live performances in North America than in India. It is reassuring to the Indians in the diaspora that we are indeed privileged over our siblings who have been left behind. Thus, the phantasm of the movie star bleeds into the reality of the audience. Her live presence somehow cuts Meenakshi down to familial and familiar size. Meenakshi is both giant and life-size. Giant size because she is a screen idol and life-size because she is in our presence, in our life. She is our big sister from Bombay who has come to visit. Audience and star forge a relationship, which in turn promises Indians here that they, too, by virtue of this bond, are extraordinary, liberated from being merely a human trifle. The fantasy of America being the land of opportunity coalesces with the film star come alive in the flesh from our dream world of the Hindi film. It reassures us diasporic

Indians that America is truly a place where our dreams come true, albeit the dream is produced and directed in India. Moreover, we are also reassured that we are not forgotten by these exceptional Indians who come to visit us. The stars in turn are assured a transnational audience, and both star and audience are transformed in their meeting. Ah, only in America!

An even more personal relationship was forged between the 1994 parade's grand marshal, Miss Universe, Sushmita Sen, and the audience. She was not a Hindi film star, though she had expressed ambitions to be one after her reign. However, she shared the same mythic status of the film star, maybe even more, because her fame is international (nay, universal). She inquired at the parade, "Does anyone want to know anything about me?" and promised to answer each personal question asked of her. The fissure between glamour and reality, image and object, was sutured in her intimate proclamation, "I just love all of you!" both in English and in Hindi. Although the proclamations are unrealistic, corny and sentimental, their subtext hints at these celebrities' availability to everybody, class, caste, religion no bar. The result is subjectivity and the result is democracy. With the physical presence of these imports from the motherland, the nostalgia for that imagined place represented by these mythic beings is healed. In these celebrities' presence here, in their evocation of solidarity with the populace, India is here in America.

The narrative of cultural genealogy turned most poignant when the celebrities and the local talent all danced together to another popular Hindi film song. Three young girls, Preeti, Sushmita, and Meenakshi, and two other young girls formed a sorority as they all improvised and interacted with each other, displaying and celebrating the libidinal potential and sensual actuality of their bodies in dance. As the young girls, who are part of our ordinary milieu, danced, touched, and embraced these mythic ideals, mythic idols, we were reminded of, made to believe in, the girl-child's potential to grow up into one of these beautiful embodiments of Indian womanhood. We realize that Indian culture flourishes as the child grows, as the culture becomes her, as she evolves into a Meenakshi or Sushmita. As adult women, these young Indians have the vital capacity to produce more Indians, assuring that the culture will prevail in the bodies of their children regardless of their residence. Needless to say, the lyrics of the song, the hip and pelvic gyrations of the dance, the familiarity and personalism between audience with the performers, reiterate the girl-child's heterosexist fate of marriage and, consequently, a biological family. The production of Indian culture becomes conflated with the reproduction of Indian children. As long as one's heart (that is under her blouse!) beats to the pulse of Hindi film music, Indianness becomes unbound by geographic limits. This new (Indian) patriotism, as described by Arjun Appadurai, is transnational and transported by the very long multiple arms of electronic media, travel, as well as communication.[22] Like Krishna's ubiquity in the *Raslila* (a collective erotic play), India/Indianness appears simultaneously everywhere.

Good Indian/Bad Indian?

Amid the din of the heterosexual fervor manifested in Hindi film songs and dances, yet another sororal performance of a different sort occurred concurrently on a different stage. Hitherto silenced voices proclaimed the underside of the ideal of the heterosexual Indian family. In the 1994 India Day parade, the South Asian Lesbian and Gay Association (SALGA) was not allowed to march because, according to then-FIA President Probir Roy, having such a group in such a parade would have been "out of place." SALGA was considered a misfit, because they placed their gay rights agenda over and above Indian Independence. In the 1994 parade, Roy had requested that SALGA carry posters that saluted India's democracy, which the members apparently refused, arguing that their organization also catered to non-Indian homosexuals of the South Asian subcontinent. In addition, SALGA had not applied to join the parade on time. SALGA's bureaucratic laxity provided a good excuse for Roy and the FIA board's disguised homophobia.[23] To rectify their exclusion, Sakhi, an all-woman advocacy group against domestic violence, invited SALGA to march with them. This act was considered disrespectful and anarchic by the FIA. Roy likened it to bringing along an uninvited guest to a party without informing the host.

To me, Sakhi's inclusion of SALGA expands the concept of the Indian family to include into its fold all other expressions of identity whether mainstream, alternative, populist, or official. To protest the violence of exclusion, SALGA and Sakhi staged a demonstration while the performance on the main stage was going on. Indeed, underneath Sakhi's blouse beats a heart that embraces the recalcitrant, the different, the abused, the out-of-place. In fact, Roy's "party" became even more colorful with the arrival of these bohemian guests.

The exclusion of SALGA by the FIA demonstrates their adherence to what Anannya Bhattacharjee describes as the bourgeoisie's "habit of exnomination."[24] The FIA does not want the Indian community to be marked, named, recognized in the mosaic of the New York multicultural society as different, problematic, or imperfect. Allowing groups like SALGA to march admits to the host country and other minority communities that we are not a "model minority," not free from abuse, racism, disease, and, God forbid, alternative sexualities. In their conservative, bourgeois morality, these ruptures from the norms of the ideal heterosexual family are something to be ashamed of, because they thwart the notion that Indianness necessarily includes the production of Indian children, the reproduction of pure and innocent Indianness, unsullied by reality.

Against the backdrop of this self-proclaimed impeccability, "*Choli ke peeche*" is performed with gusto. But how innocent is the "*Choli ke peeche*" dance, anyway? It definitely is not devoid of sexuality. In fact, a young girl performing it only accentuates her libidinal potential. Nonetheless, this sexuality, though not lauded by official culture, can be tolerated since it is heterosexual. Conversely, by their participation in the India Day celebrations, Sakhi and SALGA affirm an alternative sexuality that some Indians practice and cherish. This assertion destabilizes the belief that there is only one kind of normal sexuality and that being Indian only means reproducing Indian culture through one's legitimate children and biological family. We are forced to recognize that the Indian heart underneath one's blouse can beat to a more complex, nuanced rhythm.

In the 1994 India Day celebration, snubbing the group that announces its alternative sexuality does not invalidate, hide, or extinguish it. SALGA is, in fact, mounted on a valorized stage of controversy with Sakhi as stage manager. Members of the community who watch them parade actually begin to realize that they can be Indian populist and mainstream as well as alternative, homosexual, and unfortunately, a battered woman. FIA's 1994 president, Probir Roy, lamented that the "American" press, the *New York Times* paid much more attention to the exclusion of these groups from the parade than to the fact that the parade included representatives from the varied regional and sectarian Indian communities.[25] Sexual politics make much better copy than racial and religious politics, I guess. However, Roy's point is well taken. It is an achievement well worth noting that in the same parade, in the same "party," in the same "family," Muslims, Christians, and Hindus celebrated their Indianness together. Nonetheless, it is still a sad fact that this famed "Indian tolerance" is intolerant of alternative sexualities!

It is, however, not surprising that Sakhi welcomed SALGA to march with them. As an advocacy group defending the rights of women in the South Asian Community, their activist agenda spills over to all other oppressed and abused groups. Although the FIA considers both groups unacceptable because of their "undisciplined" guerrilla (read, nonbourgeois) tactics, Roy admits that Sakhi does good work for the community in helping battered women.

On the basis of her observations of Sakhi's approaches to the issue of domestic violence, Caitrin Lynch has astutely discussed this ambivalence toward them.[26] She believes Sakhi appears as a threat to the bourgeois community because the activists locate domestic violence in the outdated values of a traditional patriarchal Indian culture. To the Indian in the diaspora, faced with too many changes and dislocations as it is, this is a threat to an Indianness which has been romanticized as perfect and aspects of which give much comfort to the displaced immigrant. Sakhi proposes to bring changes in this culture by modifying the relationships that fortify our home life, which the woman as wife, mother, and child-bearer traditionally runs. The organization criticizes, questions, and exposes the myth of heterosexual marital bliss. In addition, Sakhi's members are perceived as primarily young, unmarried women, which conjures images in the mainstream of these women being unbound to tradition, being homewreckers, man hating, and even lesbian. All in all, being anti-Indian.

Woman: The Tie That Binds

What do the *"Choli ke peeche"* dance, film stars, dancing girls, and the exclusion or inclusion of SALGA and Sakhi have in common? Besides their saturation in two varieties of sexual politics, these two performance events rebuke and refute the official rhetoric of the ideal nationalistic woman. The kind of Indian womanhood that is imported in the persons of Meenakshi and Sushmita, performed in the dances by the young girls, and enacted by the Sakhi women, who defiantly included SALGA in their contingent, is a lively, upbeat, assertive, as well as libidinal one. They seem very unlike the woman redefined in the nationalist project of postindependence India as elaborated by Partha Chatterjee in his analysis of the role of women in the Indian independence movement.[27] He explained that since women are the upholders of all that is spiritual and non-Western, "The home [was] the principal site for expressing the spiritual qualities of the national culture, and women must take responsibility for protecting this quality." The nationalistic Indian woman of postindependence India was further worshiped as goddess or as mother, which "served to erase her sexuality in the world outside the home."

The asexual goddess or mother is reminiscent of the figures of the passive and victimized Sita and the mute and benign "Mother India" represented in one of the largest floats in the parade, belonging to the Overseas Friends of the Bharatiya Janata Party (BJP). There were at least a hundred people in this contingent, a reflection of the unprecedented support this Hindu fundamentalist opposition party enjoys in this country. Their float included a tableau from the Hindu epic *Ramayana*, where Rama, Sita, and Lakshmana, with the help of Hanumana, triumphed over King Ravana of Lanka. Raised on a dais in front of a map of pre-Moghul India was a feminine icon of India, Mother India, implying the similarity of India to Sita, both being saved by Rama from Ravana. Now, of course, the enemy of Hindu India/Mother India/Sita is the Muslims. According to BJP's version of Indian history, which is based on the colonial version, the Indian subcontinent, with its Hindu majority, has repeatedly been subjugated by foreigners, especially Muslims. This version conveniently ignores the Aryan invasion, the invasion of Alexander of Macedonia, and other such forays into the land.

The Hinduism that is propagated by BJP does not take into account varieties of Hindu sects such as Shakti cults (worshipers of Kali), Shaivaites (worshipers of Shiva), and other hybrid forms of Sufi/Bhakti (a combination of Islam and Hindu) denominations which are alive and thriving in India as well as the diaspora. BJP's tableau in the parade was a blatant conflation of a certain form of monotheistic North Indian Hinduism (Rama as the One True God) and nonsecular nationalism. It depicted the triumph of Hindutva (a Hindu state) rather than of India, the triumph of an ahistoric, monocultural political formulation over the reality of a multiethnic, multireligious, intercultural, even syncretic federation. The characters on the float were represented by young adolescents with the most solemn expressions on their faces. They seemed to carry the weight of their fundamentalist and communal mission with a seriousness and stillness unbefitting youth. The spectacle was quite frightening!

In contrast to the BJP Hindutva tableau, the performance of the dancing movie stars, star-struck girls, and activist women of Sakhi expressed dynamic pleasure, talent, initiative, lack of inhibition, beauty, articulateness, success, wealth, confidence, and political assertiveness. Whereas Sita is swallowed up by the earth (after being rejected by her husband, the good God-king Rama), these worldly women are in control of their environment, bodies, and the audience. Furthermore, they announce this message to the public at large. Although these performers appear larger than life (liberated from being merely human, remember!) they are nevertheless very alive in our lives, being in the present and in our presence. It is Sita and her ilk who seem to be quite distant, quite dead in contrast. Dancing to film music which is upbeat, sensual, and on occasion challenging to middle-class sensibilities subverts the official rhetoric as propounded by the narratives of Sita, the artificial and asexual construction of Mother India, and the apathy of the life-denying

spiritual-nationalistic woman. The dancing body performs the earthy pleasures of being in a community, of being Indian. In addition, actively defying
the official edict of the FIA, Sakhi emphasizes a true sororal spirit against
oppression and facilitates SALGA's narrative of homosexuality and homophobia. Here, the Indian woman is active and deliciously loud.

This indeed is a very different kind of nationalism. Through the mimesis and alterity of the popular form of the Hindi film dance display, the
heavy-handed clenched fist of official nationalism is pried open into a wave
of effusive greeting by the movie star and beauty queen, and into the playful
hand gestures of the young girls in their dance. Since the Hindi film and its
systemics as a representative of India travel to other parts of the globe
through the tributaries of electronic media, culture is learned and performed
by Indians in the diaspora. The enthusiastic response to film dance, film stars,
and the consequent recreation and re-creation of community in New York
through Indian Independence Day cultural programs suggest that the relationship between India and Indians in the diaspora "[is not based on] language, religion, politics or economics . . . [but] this relationship is so much
a relationship of the imagination."[28] I would contend that the specialist par
excellence of this Indian imagination is the spectacular and phantasmagoric,
ever-repetitive, and ever-reproducible Hindi film dance, with its accessible
and democratic choreographies, lively and occasional ribald songs, person-
able superstars, and its multiple incarnations in the dancing bodies of Indians large and small.

The resistance to SALGA, Sakhi, and other such groups and the dis-
may over the presentation of film dances rather than the classical or reified
folk dances, spring from the community leaders' earnestness in impressing
the non-Indian community with an identity that is "orientalist."[29] The community leaders want to create Indianness in the image and likeness of how
the West wants to perceive us, have us, and enjoy us. This kind of Indianness
is a reified image of spirituality, exoticism, mysteriousness, and essentially
all that is stereotypically perceived as non-Western. The result of this internalized orientalism is the persistence to keep only the most traditional aspects of Indianness. But who defines what is traditional and also what kinds
of histories, narratives, ideologies sustain the Indian culture? Usually such
decisions are based on the agendas of political parties. Thus, homosexuality,
feminism, and other variations of sexual politics are perceived as Western
interventions, as Western corruptions. They are declared anti-Indian by the
official culture. However, the immobility and sullenness on the faces of the
young adolescents in the BJP float wail of the deadening and reification of

Indian culture. Obviously, there needs to be room cleared for a dynamic, contemporary Indianness. With the insistence of the community on performing the Hindi film dance as an expression of nationalism and including all kinds of Indians, sexual orientations notwithstanding, the celebration of Indian Independence Day dislodges the host country as the reference point from which the leaders base their definition of Indianness.

Indeed, the vernacular, unofficial response to the call for nationalistic allegiance on India Day is to perform what is most pleasurable, what speaks to the needs and values of certain hitherto unheard of or silenced segments of the community. The Hindi film dance subverts the overly refined, sanskritized classical dance, as well as the "authentic" folk dance, by celebrating a heterosexual libido, while Sakhi and SALGA subvert the heterosexist ideology of reproductive sexuality and by challenging the image of unsullied domestic bliss. After all, India could also be a "queer nation" and she could further be Mother India in tricolor drag gyrating his/her hips to a ribald Hindi film song! These subversions proclaim that there are indeed multiple ways of being Indian, and therefore, why not celebrate a multifaceted Indianness free of all oppressive forces from without and within. In Anannya Bhattacharjee's words: "Indianness is not a natural excretion of a genealogical tree, but a continual struggle along multiple modes through a negotiation of the inescapable tension between secure definitions and a consciousness of the oppressions that such definitions rest upon."[30]

My Place in the Sun

Taking my cue from Bhattacharjee, I sought my place in this milieu. Having come with a video camera to the India Day celebration gave me legitimacy as a recorder of culture, a visual historian if you will. I was allowed a place in the front of the stage to document the show. Guided by the stage managers to a position where I could get a relatively good view of the stage, I was able to tape footage of Preeti's dance and look at the celebrities up close. Participants eagerly agreed to have themselves videotaped. Members of the public did not seem to mind my panning the video camera across the audience. Some asked me why I was doing this, not suspiciously, but out of curiosity or to strike up a conversation. I told them I was doing a paper for NYU. They were pleased that I was doing something for "Indian culture" and agreed to pose for me. They played at being movie stars for my camera. They seemed to think I was doing a favor to Indianness. Although subject to negotiations, there is a place for a single Indian woman from the Philippines in the community, after all. Using my intellect, my scholarly enterprise, my voyeuristic video camera, I, too, can actively participate.

Personally, I align myself to the left-of-center groups like Sakhi and SALGA. I have, in fact, acted in an educational video for Sakhi entitled, quite appropriately, "A Life without Fear." I played the role of the Sakhi advocate who persuades a battered woman to seek help. I had my fifteen minutes of fame in front of the video camera and for a good cause, too. In 1995, I acted as moderator of a televised discussion among the groups who were excluded. I am fulfilling my destiny of Indianness—reproducing Indianness in my own ways, I guess. On India Day of 1994, I celebrated the success of my masquerade, my own playing at Indianness, by singing a popular Hindi film ditty along with the crowd:

> *Choli ke peeche kya hai?*
> *Choli me dil hai mera!*
> *Yeh dil mai dungi mere pyar ko! Yaar ko!*
> (Guess) What is underneath my blouse?
> Underneath my blouse is my . . . my . . . heart!
> My heart I give to my love, to my friend.

The FIA, the organizers of the Indian Independence Day parade, deserve accolades for expertly creating a space in New York City where these contested identities can be negotiated and a multifaceted, dynamic Indianness can be played out. Although these were not their original intentions, complex realities have taken charge of their enterprise. It is delightful that in the subversive performances of the Hindi film dance and activist proclamations of leftist groups, all Indians, the marginalized, those who love Hindi films, the activists and the silenced, claim a piece of the territory that has been marked as Indian for a day. Indians become the focus, the referent, replacing the host country. These subversions send the message to community leaders that we practice a true independence in which we free ourselves from being entangled in a sticky web of orientalism and the habit of ex-nomination.

Notes

Earlier versions of this essay were presented at the 1994 South Asian Studies Conference at the University of Wisconsin—Madison and at the 1995 National Conference of Indian-American Identity, sponsored by *Little India* magazine. I am indebted to the valuable discussions I have had with my dear friend Iby de George-Geary and my colleagues Sudipto Chatterjee, Ananya Chatterjea, and Hanna Kim. My thanks to Probir Roy, Manhar Patel, the members of Sakhi for South Asian Women, and the editorial staff of *India Abroad*.

1. Epigraph from *India Abroad*, August 19, 1995, p. 42.
2. *India Abroad*, August 26, 1994, p. 42.
3. M. Khandelwal, "Patterns of Growth and Diversification: Indians in New York City, 1965–1990," Ph.D. diss., Carnegie-Mellon University (1992); and M. P. Fisher, *The Indians of New York City: A Study of Ethnic Identity* (Columbia, Mo.: South Asia, 1980), and "The Indian Ethnic Identity: The Role of Associations in the New York Indian Population," in P. Saran and E. Eames, eds., *The New Ethnics: Asian Indians in the United States* (New York: Praeger, 1980).
4. Khandelwal, "Patterns of Growth."
5. Sakhi for South Asian Women is a New York–based advocacy group for battered women.
6. R. Burra, ed., *Indian Cinema, 1980–1985* (New Delhi: Directorate of Film Festivals, 1985).
7. P. Iyer, *Video Nights in Kathmandu and Other Reports from the Not-So-Far East* (New York: Vintage, 1989).
8. V. Mishra, "Towards a Theoretical Critique of Bombay Cinema," *Screen* 26 (1985): 133–46.
9. E. Barnouw and S. Krishnaswamy, *Indian Film* (New York: Oxford University Press, 1980), 155.
10. V. Turner, *Anthropology of Performance* (New York: *Performing Arts Journal*, 1986).
11. K. Ghei, "Accessible Choreographies: Hindi Cinema on Videotape in Los Angeles," *UCLA Journal of Dance Ethnology* 12 (1988): 36 .
12. I have used pseudonyms to protect the privacy of individuals. However, community leaders and professionals in the entertainment industry have been named.
13. "*Choli ke peeche kya hai*" from the film *Khalnayak* (1993), music by L. Pyarelel and lyrics by A. Bakshi.
14. S. Stewart, *On Longing: Narratives of the Miniature, the Gigantic, the Souvenir and the Collection* (Baltimore: John Hopkins University Press, 1993).
15. M. Taussig, *Mimesis and Alterity: A Particular History of the Senses* (New York: Routledge, 1993).
16. S. S. Mukhi, "The Imagined Audience," MA thesis, San Francisco State University (1989); I. Abramovitch, "Flushing Bharat Natyam: Indian Dancers in Queens," unpublished ms. (1987)
17. For a discussion of the upper-class bias of Indian classical dance, see A. Meduri, "Bharat Natyam: What Are You?" *Asian Theatre Journal* 5, no. 1 (1988): 1–22.
18. Ghei, "Accessible Choreographies."
19. Taussig, *Mimesis and Alterity*, 233.
20. L. Berlant, "The Theory of Infantile Citizenship," *Public Culture* 5 (Spring 1993): 3.
21. Ibid.
22. A. Appadurai, "Patriotism and Its Futures," *Public Culture* 5 (1993): 411–29.
23. In 1995, SALGA as well as Sakhi, together with the South Asian AIDS Action, Lease Driver's Coalition, and Committee against Anti-Asian Violence were banned from joining the India Day parade. The official reason given for this exclusion was that these organizations catered to a general South Asian population and that the parade was meant only for Indian organizations. The boards of

Sakhi and SALGA responded that this was FIA's strategy to exclude SALGA without appearing homophobic. These excluded organizations staged a protest during the parade.

24. A. Bhattacharjee, "The Habit of Ex-Nomination: Nation, Woman, and the Indian Immigrant Bourgeoisie," *Public Culture* 5 (1992); reprinted in this book.

25. "South Asian Gay and Lesbian Group Marches for India," *New York Times*, August 22, 1994, B2.

26. C. Lynch, "Nation, Woman, and the Immigrant Bourgeoisie: An Alternative Formulation," *Public Culture* 6 (1994): 425–37.

27. P. Chatterjee, *The Nation and Its Fragments: Colonial and Post-Colonial Histories* (Princeton, N.J.: Princeton University Press, 1989), 126, 129–31.

28. A. Ghosh, "Diapora in Indian Culture," *Public Culture* (Spring 1990).

29. E. Said, *Orientalism* (New York: Vintage, 1979).

30. Bhattacharjee, "The Habit of Ex-Nomination," 41.

Three Hot Meals and a Full Day at Work

South Asian Women's Labor in the United States

Sonia Shah

*"Well, those ladies on the lines, they have it pretty easy," Mr.
Singh replied when I asked Mrs. Singh about her job as a
cannery worker. Mrs. Singh's husband continued to answer for
her: "And now that she has seniority, you know, she can sit
around and drink tea or something like that." While I tried to talk
to Mrs. Singh about her life and work at a nearby food-
processing plant, she moved industriously around the kitchen,
preparing snacks for her two little granddaughters and
me. . . . Although the entire family was very gracious and
hospitable, whenever I asked Mrs. Singh questions about herself,
the other members present frequently answered instead.
"My work is sort of my family, you know, with all my relatives
and friends there; and, of course, my family is my work."
[Mrs. Singh]* [1]

There's a story my mother tells about
when I was around five years old or so and playing "doctor" with the little
boy next door. My mother immigrated to the United States from Coimbatore,
India, in 1968, having recently married my father, who hailed from Bombay.
"I have to be the nurse," I apparently declared, "and you have to be the doctor." My mother likes to tell this story because she is, and was, as I was supposedly aware at the time, a practicing physician. Yet, even given this real-life
example of a woman doctor, my own mother, I was convinced that women
were meant to be nurses, while men were supposed to be doctors.

My earliest memory of a career ambition was to be a baby-sitter. I also remember wanting to be a secretary, as I liked to fill out the blanks on the medical forms my parents used to bring home. My father is also a physician. When I was around eleven years old or so, he used to bring me to his office in the summers, where I would "work" with the women in the secretarial office. They gave me the oversize, heavily bound appointment book, which I would date years into the future. I remember enjoying this work, and feeling it was useful to the secretaries.

At home, I did very little work, as I recall. My mother seemed to do most of the housework, including buying groceries, cooking at least three hot dishes for dinner each night, cleaning the kitchen, vacuuming, sweeping, and doing the laundry. At the time, she was working part-time as a physician while my father was working full-time. My father would often put me and my sister to bed or give us baths. I liked to draw and to write stories, and my parents encouraged me to channel those proclivities into applied crafts, such as architecture and journalism.

When I was about fifteen, I went to India to visit my extended family there. One stop on my trip was Tirupur, a small town where my aunt and cousins lived. I hated visiting Tirupur, as I found it a stultifying town. There were no restaurants or theaters in Tirupur and no running water or electricity. But it wasn't a poor town; there were several successful factories located there. My cousin's factory, for example, produced cotton clothing for export on contract. He brought me to see the factory one day.

I was surprised to find that he employed dozens of young girls, even younger than I was at the time. The vision of these disheveled little girls clambering over the mounds of bright white cotton is still vivid to me. They crawled over the cotton like mice, twisting and cutting and sewing it. Their brownish rags contrasted with the brightly colored and starched oversize cotton T-shirts that they were making to be sold to little girls in France. My cousin told me proudly that he preferred hiring the little girls, as he could pay them significantly less than the little boys.

It was disturbing to me that my cousin didn't feel it was wrong to exploit children. And the obvious misuse of their and his labor struck me. Because the little girls would work for so little money, my cousin could offer competitive contracts to foreign buyers, who could then make a healthy profit by selling the cheaply bought products abroad. It seemed so clear that the girls, my cousin, and the town could all benefit themselves much more if they were to direct their energy and labors toward meeting their own material and social needs; if the girls went to school to develop their skills while my cousin used his resources to help build the town, which the girls would one day inherit. Instead, the men exploited the girls and all worked too hard, just to make a throwaway item for some kid—a rich one, relative to the workers—across an ocean.

What were the forces that resulted in such a wasteful and unjust situation? I wondered. And how would these forces affect my own place in society? Until then, my main goal was to find work that was interesting and meaningful to me. I started asking myself a different question: Who and what do I want to work for?

U.S. feminists have long fought for expanded employment opportunities for women, for more and better jobs for women. They have been concerned with the *quality* of women's work. In terms of quality, Indian women in the United States—myself and my mother included—have been relatively successful. By and large, we are better employed than our white counterparts, as are the men in our community (see figure 1). If quality of work were the sole criterion on which to judge our labor, then Indian women would have much to celebrate.

And so we should. But we must also look at our labor in terms of the greater historical and economic forces that dictate its role in society. For, while it is true that Indian women have predominantly better jobs than their white counterparts, as do Indian men, it is also true that our labor has contributed to the underdevelopment of India, and to racial antagonism and exploitative capitalism in the United States. And, our resources—our education, our paid and unpaid labor, and our social relationships—have been devalued and used for others' gain.

South Asian Labor under Imperialism

My mother was the first physician and the first to immigrate to the United States in her family of six children. Her father worked hard all his life in a family-owned warehousing business, his long hours of paid work made possible by his wife, my grandmother, and some poorly paid servant women, who performed the unpaid labor of child rearing and housekeeping. Since my mother was the only child to pursue an advance degree, one can assume it was at the cost of the other children's not being able to do so.

But why did she, and my father, want to leave India? Then, as now, emigrating to the United States was considered a path to certain upward mobility. It was and is possible for elites to accumulate much wealth in India. But Indian immigrants to the United States consistently cite economic-related reasons for leaving: corruption, poverty, lack of opportunity. For example,

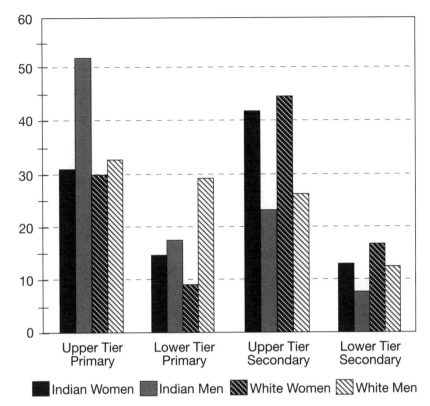

FIGURE 1. Percentage in U.S. Labor Sectors Indians and Whites by Gender. *Source: U.S. Census Bureau, 1990.*

when my mother graduated from medical school in the late 1960s, the postcolonial Indian economy suffered a surplus of educated labor. India's educated unemployed numbered 1.53 million in 1969, and 3.3 million in 1972.[2]

The postcolonial Indian economy was and continues to be weak and unstable, not least because of the legacy of British imperialism. As Edna Bonacich and Lucie Cheng write:

> Imperialism distorts the development of societies that are subjected to it. Imperialism has often led, especially in the early phases of contact, to the extraction of tribute of simple stripping of some of the wealth of the invaded area. This can take the form of looting, payment of war indemnities, or taxation. Whatever the form, the effect is an initial transfer of some wealth from the colonized people to the colonial power. A second effect is unequal exchange. . . . Even

if no special barriers to free trade (such as protective tariffs) are set up, exchange between more and less advanced economies will redound to the benefit of the former. As a result, indigenous craftsmen and incipient entrepreneurs are undermined. . . . Even the establishment of unequal treaties, such as the forced opening of a port for free trade, can be devastating to local industry. Furthermore, imperialist powers can use their political advantage to subvert industrial development in the colonized societies. They can, through selected tariffs and other policies, force dominated countries to concentrate in raw material production and prevent them from producing manufactures that could compete with the advanced capitalist country.[3]

At the same time that more and more Indians pursued higher degrees in a postcolonial economy that could not absorb them, the United States experienced a shortage of skilled professional workers, physicians in particular. The expansion of hospital-based medical care, and the institution of broad social programs, such as Medicare and Medicaid in 1965, resulted in the need for thousands of skilled professionals. The 1965 Immigration Act, which abolished national quotas in favor of those based on professional status, aimed to encourage the immigration of such professionals.[4] Thousands of unemployed professionals from India and Pakistan flocked to the United States, my parents among them. Medical graduates especially were encouraged, with offers of free apartments and secure jobs at hospitals.[5]

While the U.S. economy may have benefited, it was the Indian economy that bore the cost of the investment in these professionals. If one considers the colonial practice of siphoning resources from the colonized nation to be one reason for India's poverty relative to the West, the 1960s' flow of educated emigrants from India to the United States deepened the inequity. If the per-capita average education cost for these emigrants is estimated at $20,000, then skilled emigration to the United States between 1962 and 1967 represented a loss of $61,240,000 for India.[6] While, according to some commentators, a lesser-developed country such as India does not need highly skilled workers as much as it needs semiskilled workers, the loss of highly skilled workers still means a loss of intellectual leadership, and thus "widens the technological gap" between less-developed and more- developed countries.[7] Ironically, while Western intervention in India led to underdevelopment in the first place, postcolonial emigration to the West further deepened India's relative poverty.

Indian immigration to the United States is thus most accurately characterized as a transfer of wealth from an underdeveloped country to a developed country. The fact that Indian immigrants' relative economic success in the United States is due to the resources they brought with them from India—their work skills and educations—is in direct contradiction to the second of two assumptions of the "model minority" myth. The model minority myth holds that Asian Americans have been more successful in the United States than native ethnic groups and that they have been more successful because of their cultural heritage, not the material resources they brought with them. Of "uptown" Chinese immigrants to the United States, who are as well educated as many of the 1960s Indian immigrants, Teresa Amott and Julie Matthaei write:

> Uptown Chinese, many of them women, come to the United States
> with excellent English, top-level educations, and often with consid-
> erable financial resources. Since these credentials allow them to find
> lucrative professional jobs, their presence raises the average income
> statistics for Chinese Americans and gives the false impression that
> Chinese are easily upwardly mobile in the United States. In reality,
> uptown Chinese were already educationally and socially advantaged
> in Taiwan and China, and simply transferred these achievements and
> status to the United States. Indeed, their experience in the United
> States is one of *downward* mobility. Discrimination exists even
> against such "model" immigrants, who earn less than whites with
> equal educations and have less access to managerial promotions than
> equally qualified whites.[8]

Indian government and industry encourage their emigrants to the West to invest in India. Possibly such investment could help balance the loss of these productive workers. At least in one case, however, such balancing was not so simple. According to Roger Ballard's study of peasant emigration from Pakistan to Britain and the Middle East, workers' remittances sent back to Pakistan, while totaling over half of Pakistan's foreign exchange inflow, for various cultural and political reasons were not invested in the productive base of the country. At the same time, this inflow of remittances allowed Pakistan's rich elite to export a large part of their own capital. "So should the current edifice collapse," Ballard writes, "those who have been running it for the last few years will only need to find their way to the nearest Jumbo Jet to begin a prosperous life elsewhere. The fruits of the labours of millions of Pakistanis overseas will largely have been transferred into other, more prosperous hands."[9]

South Asian Labor under Capitalism

According to the 1990 U.S. Census, 58 percent of all Indian women in the United States are employed outside the home, 45 percent of whom work in high-paying, upwardly mobile fields, as opposed to 39 percent of white women (see figure 2). Over 80 percent of Indian men in the United States are employed outside the home, and over half of them, compared with a third of white men, hold high-salary, upwardly mobile, secure jobs.[10] But these professionals have not necessarily enjoyed the full benefits of their skills and education. Once in the United States, many of them encountered a number of obstacles that prevented them from reaching the most lucrative private-sector jobs, steering them into the government-run jobs in the inner-city and rural areas where native professionals were unwilling to go. According to the U.S. Commission on Civil Rights, Asian immigrants encountered a glass ceiling that prevented them from moving up the ladder as fast as their white counterparts. They encountered racist attitudes, difficulties in networking with other professionals, a lack of mentors, and a corporate culture hostile to outsiders. Their accents were the basis for exclusion and harassment on the job. And their foreign educations have been devalued and held to higher-than-usual standards than those for U.S.-educated professionals.[11] Some of them ended up not working in the fields for which they had trained: "College-educated, they can be found operating travel agencies, sari shops, and luncheonettes featuring pizza, souvlakia, and Indian 'fast food.' They are also news-stand operators in the subways of Manhattan. . . . Asian Indians have also found a niche in the motel business: they own fifteen thousand motels, or 28 percent of the nation's 53,629 hotels and motels."[12]

Immigrant medical graduates "serve in disproportionate numbers in rural areas, often in solo and partnership practices, in public hospitals, in smaller not-for-profit hospitals, and in regions of the country that have experienced emigration of population because of declining industry and high unemployment. Poor populations and Medicaid recipients also are often reliant on FMGs [foreign medical graduates]."[13] According to sociologist Paul Starr, immigrant physicians from India, Korea, and the Philippines "often took jobs that Americans did not want (for example, in state mental institutions). In effect, the peculiar slant of American health policy (expanding hospitals, but keeping down medical enrollments) was producing a new lower tier in the medical profession drawn from the Third World."[14]

According to Cheng and Bonacich, such discriminatory treatment renders immigrant workers especially exploitable by employers, and thus well serves the needs of the capitalist economy: "Employers want to keep them

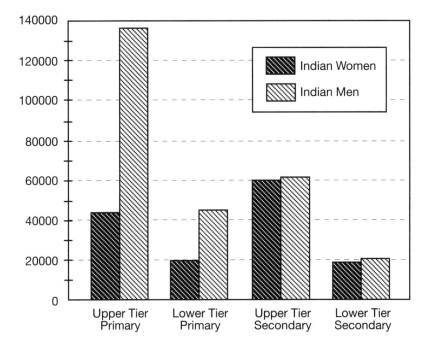

Upper Tier Primary: High Salary Stable, Upwardly Mobile, Requires Elite Training
Lower Tier Primary: High Earnings, Stable, Does Not Require Training
Upper Tier Secondary: Low Wages, Few Benefits, Unstable, Little Mobility
Lower Tier Secondary: Low Wages, few Benefits, Unstable, Poor Working Conditions

FIGURE 2. Indian Men and Indian Women in the U.S. Labor Market. *Source: U.S. Census Bureau, 1990.*

as an especially exploitable sector of the working class, a position rationalized by such ideological concomitants of imperialism as racism. Local workers, however, are fearful of being undercut by the presence of an especially exploitable group of workers. These competing interests give rise to anti-immigrant movements. . . . Thus, the treatment of immigrant workers, including the prejudice and discrimination they face, must also be seen as part of the world capitalist system."[15]

South Asian Women's Work under Patriarchy

While imperialism and capitalism have shaped South Asians' work experiences in the United States, the specific work experiences of women have also been shaped by their gender. Women bear much of the direct loss of the transfer of resources from poor nation to rich nation. Such was the case with the first immigrants from South Asia, the 6,400 young Indian men who came to the United States between 1900 and 1920, the majority of whom were Sikh. U.S. industrialists were eager for the opportunity to employ workers whom the 1908 *Overland Monthly* deemed "willing to work for 'cheap' wages and able to 'subsist on incomes that would be prohibitive to the white man.'" Many came from a farming background but were mostly employed as railroad workers in the United States, and as replacements for striking workers.

Although between one-third and one-half of these immigrants were married, of the five thousand Indians in California in 1914, only twelve were women. In the beginning, the men hoped either to return to India with newfound riches or to send for their wives and children. By and large, having mortgaged their farms in India to work for low wages in a discriminatory U.S. environment, they did not make enough money to do either. By 1917, anti-Indian sentiment—sometimes violent—among the white workers who considered them competitors resulted in an immigration restriction law that barred Indians from immigrating to the United States.[16]

Ronald Takaki recounts the story of a married Indian worker who tried to bring his wife to the United States to join him:

> Moola Singh had left his wife in the Punjab in 1911 and had saved enough money to pay for her passage to America. But by the time he had sent the money to her, the law had already been enacted. "She worry," Singh told an interviewer many years later. "She good, nice looking, healthy, but she love. You know love, person no eat, worry, then maybe die. Mother wrote one time letter, 'she sick, you gotta come home.' Then I write her letter from Arizona, to her I say, 'I'm coming, don't worry, I be there. . . .'" But she passed away in 1921 before Singh could return. "If we had our women here," said a fellow countryman, "our whole life would be different."[17]

These workers could work for low wages in large part because their female relatives bore the cost of caring for their families in India and ensuring their long-term social security at home. These were costs that U.S. employers did not have to bear, as they did for local white workers.[18] This is not to imply that those women who provided this unpaid labor were somehow at fault for following the cultural dictates of the sexual division of paid and unpaid labor. It does show, however, how capitalist economies were able to exploit such a gendered division of labor to their advantage in ways that these workers and families were not able to interrupt. Finally, between 1920 and 1940, half of the Indian population left the United States. Their cheap labor no longer needed in the United States, the men returned to India no richer, and those who stayed started families with Mexican and other non-Indian women.[19]

Among the 1960s-era educated Indian immigrants, there is evidence that the relative success of some of the women has been because they have worked longer and harder than their white counterparts. Asian-American women were found to work more hours per year and more consistently through their life cycle, regardless of family circumstances, than white women. They were also found to receive lower economic returns than white women with comparable educational backgrounds.[20] Finally, according to studies from around the world, women's income is more likely to be invested back into the household than men's.[21] Thus, women are less likely personally to enjoy the benefits that accrue to them from their employment. The many Indian motel-owning families are an example of this. According to Suvarna Thaker's study of Indian motel-owning wives in Los Angeles:

> Women do most of the work involved in running motels. . . . Though she does hard work in the motel, she has no help in the kitchen or [with] other household work which is traditionally considered "women's tasks." When asked if her husband ever helps her with the dishes, etc., Mrs. C's quick reply is "No, never, I cannot think of him doing that!" For many, what they do in the motels is in a way an extension of their household work. The type of work involved in running a motel does not require any special skill. It is like an extension of domestic work so some women do not get the feeling that what they do is really one kind of employment, and they derive little job satisfaction from it."[22]

In addition to their paid work, South Asian women in the United States, like women everywhere, perform the lion's share, if not all, of the labor in the home.[23] According to the United Nations, women perform almost two-thirds of the world's labor, but receive only one-tenth of the world's income and own less than one-hundredth of the world's property.[24] Also according to the United Nations, $16 trillion worth of women's work in the home, family businesses, and in child care is unpaid and undervalued in economic statistics.[25]

"Most women have to work . . . a 'double day': they work for wages in the labor market and work without pay in the home."[26] This is true for women everywhere. In addition, South Asian women in the United States are less likely than other similarly well-employed women to rely on restaurants, laundries, hired help, paid child care, fast foods, and other bought conveniences that cut down on home labor. Further, the cheap household help and the help of extended family members that were available in South Asia are by and large not available in the United States. Yet given all these differences between the South Asian and U.S. environments, South Asians in the United States have not significantly altered their standards of cleanliness, cooking, and child rearing. Evidence shows that South Asian communities in the United States have "retained their taste for traditional food, along with their values concerning home, family, children, religion, and marriage," and have "transplanted old-world gender ideologies and clearly dichotomized sex roles in their adopted country of residence."[27] Religious, cultural, and linguistic traditions thus prevent such South Asian families in the United States from using McDonald's, European nannies, or microwave ovens as comfortably or as easily as a white family, even if they can afford to.

Why do women perform so much unpaid work? According to Teresa Amott,

> Historically, men have been able to command women's unpaid labor through direct intimidation (domestic violence), by excluding women from the paid workforce, by controlling the politics and technology of biological reproduction so that it has been difficult for women to plan childbearing, and by dominating the government so that laws and policies are passed that maintain men's control over women's lives. These efforts not only contributed *directly* to male dominance in the household, but did so indirectly as well, by ensuring that women earned less than men and making them dependent on men for support.[28]

Among South Asian women in the United States, the men are more and better employed outside the home than the women. Over 80 percent of Indian men in the United States are employed outside the home, and over half of them, compared with a third of white men, hold high-salary, upwardly mobile, secure jobs. While it is true that South Asian women are better employed than white women, it is also true that, like all women, they are employed in worse jobs than men. According to the 1990 U.S. Census, over half of working Indian women work in low-wage, low-mobility, unstable positions such as clerical, service, and certain low-ranking sales fields. This discrepancy between Indian men and Indian women, in fact, is even larger than that between white men and white women.[29]

About 55 percent of working Indian women work in the secondary labor market; 42 percent in the "upper tier" and 13 percent in the "lower tier." While both tiers of the secondary labor market comprise low-paying, unstable positions with little or no possibility of upward mobility, jobs in the lower tier also entail poor working conditions. These positions include private household occupations, some service occupations, farming, forestry and fishing, and handlers, equipment cleaners, helpers, and laborers. In contrast, just over 30 percent of Indian men are in the secondary labor market; of these, the majority are in jobs with the better working conditions of the upper tier secondary market.[30]

These census statistics probably do not reveal the whole picture either. South Asian women who make *chapatis* and *samosas* for South Asian grocery stores and cater South Asian food may not be considered "working" by the census. As well, the many women, including motel owners' wives, who work for free in their family's convenience stores and newspaper stands may not be counted.

Growing South Asian Class Disparity

Since 1976, Indian immigrant professionals have been sponsoring their less-educated relatives for immigration to the United States. Between 1980 and 1990, the Indian population in the United States more than doubled, growing from 247,801 to 786,694. While the 1960s immigrants were primarily professionals ready to be incorporated into the middle- and upper-middle classes, the 1980s and 1990s immigrants are more likely to be semiskilled and working class.[31]

Given capitalism's tendency to use race and gender differences among paid and unpaid workers to exploit labor and maximize profits, it seems likely that the growing class disparity in the South Asian community may well be fodder for such manipulation as well. Racial differences among native and immigrant workers have ended up weakening worker solidarity against employers. The sexist division of labor between men and women in immigrant communities has been instrumental to keeping immigrant labor cheap and expendable for employers.

For South Asians and other Asians in the United States, the myth of the "model minority" is key to providing the rationale for racial and class divisions—and for their manipulation—between South Asian and other communities. By promoting this myth, mass media outlets serve the interests of capitalist employers and the government and other elites that support them. For example, the model minority myth obscures the role of South Asian investment in its emigrants and in their subsequent relative success as immi-grants and, with it, the continued transfer of wealth from poor Third World countries to the West. It deceptively offers as evidence that culture rather than resources creates economic success, thus strengthening arguments against material benefits for poor workers and communities. It creates the false impression that South Asian communities are monolithically successful, ob-scuring the class and gender divisions within the community. Obscuring those divisions makes cross-cultural women's and workers' solidarity less likely, and the divisions themselves, with the competing interests they create, frag-ment South Asian community organizing.

Many members of the South Asian immigrant professional community are employers themselves. They, along with other employers and capitalist elites, will also have an interest in protecting the model minority myth of a culturally superior, monolithically successful, non-gender-stratified commu-nity. A recent and obvious attempt to nurture the model minority myth, by not admitting contradictions to it, was the 1995 India Day parade in New York City, in which parade organizers excluded South Asian feminist, gay and lesbian, and working-class groups from participating.[32]

Strategies for Change

Any strategy for securing more just work conditions, opportunities, and compensation for South Asian women needs to take into account the various divisions in the South Asian community and how they are manipulated by capitalist elites. As Evelyn Nakano Glenn explains, the white women in the early feminist movement who claimed to represent the best interests of all women in fact worsened conditions for women of color. Their demand for a less-burdensome labor load was much more easily met by pushing more la-bor onto women of color than by getting men to do their share:

> Most middle-class women did not challenge the gender-based divi-sion of labor or the enlargement of their responsibilities in the do-mestic sphere. . . . Nineteenth century middle-class White women helped to elaborate and refine, rather than overthrow, the domestic "code." Instead of questioning the inequitable gender division of la-bor, White middle-class women delegated the more onerous house-hold tasks onto women of color. . . . [Thus] White middle-class women benefited from the exploitation of women of color. The la-bor of Black, Hispanic, and Asian-American women raised White women's standard of living.[33]

If upper-sector South Asian women similarly agitate for opportunities equal to South Asian men without considering the ramifications of such a demand on poorer women, a similar rift is likely to appear. That is, if upper-class South Asian women stop making fresh *roti* without protecting the interests of poor South Asian women who will not be able to do the same, poor South Asian immigrant women will start making them before men do. Any strategy to secure a more equitable labor load for South Asian women must therefore protect the interests of both rich and poor South Asian women.

To organize for better labor conditions, opportunities, and compensation, South Asian women have an interest in breaking the elite-manufactured image of the model minority and organizing workers across race, class, and gender. In Los Angeles, for example, organizers were able to subvert racial polarization based on the model minority myth and secure just compensation for poor immigrant workers. In south Los Angeles, the model minority myth obscured the role of cheap Korean immigrant labor in nurturing the relative success of the local Korean business community, thus inflaming relations between the local, poorer African-American community and the Korean community in an area devastated by white flight and underdevelopment. Organizers from Korean Immigrant Worker Advocates (KIWA) blew apart the myth of a monolithically successful Korean community by organizing immigrant Korean workers to demand reparations due them from Korean business owners. At the same time, KIWA organizers worked to support African-American and Latino workers and to build alliances between them and Korean immigrant workers.[34] Organizers from the Committee against Anti-Asian Violence (CAAAV) are similarly working to organize working-class South Asian taxi drivers in New York City.[35]

Conditions for these and other campaigns in the South Asian women's community will vary according to industry and locale. Regardless, their success will depend on their ability to transcend class, race, and gender divisions that keep South Asian women's labor—and most everyone else's labor—supporting unjust imperialistic and capitalist relations.

Notes

1. Epigraph is from M. Williams, "Ladies on the Line: Punjabi Cannery Workers in Central California," in *Making Waves: An Anthology of Writings by and about Asian American Women*, Asian Women of California, eds. (Boston: Beacon, 1989), 148–49.
2. B. N. Ghosh, "Some Economic Aspects of India's Brain Drain into the U.S.A." *International Migration* 17 (1979): 281.

3. L. Cheng and E. Bonacich, *Labor Immigration under Capitalism: Asian Workers in the United States before World War II* (Berkeley: University of California Press, 1984), 16–17.

4. P. Starr, *The Social Transformation of American Medicine: The Rise of a Sovereign Profession and the Making of a Vast Industry* (New York: Basic, 1982), 360.

5. H. Shah, interview with author (December 1995).

6. Ghosh, "Some Economic Aspects," 283–84.

7. Ibid.

8. T. Amott and J. Matthaei, *Race, Gender, and Work: A Multicultural Economic History of Women in the United States* (Boston: Beacon, 1991), 211.

9. R. Ballard, "Effects of Labour Migration from Pakistan," in *South Asia*, H. Alari and J. Hariss (eds.) (New York: Monthly Review, 1989), 112–22.

10. U.S. Bureau of the Census, *1990 Census of Population: Social and Economic Characteristics, United States Summary* (Washington, D.C.: Government Printing Office, 1993).

11. U.S. Commission on Civil Rights, *Civil Rights Issues Facing Asian Americans in the 1990s: A Report of the U.S. Commission on Civil Rights* (Washington, D.C.: Government Printing Office, 1992), 131–56.

12. R. T. Takaki, *Strangers from a Different Shore: A History of Asian Americans* (New York: Little, Brown, 1989), 446.

13. U.S. Commission on Civil Rights, *Civil Rights Issues*, 146.

14. Starr, *Social Transformation*, 359–60.

15. Cheng and Bonacich, *Labor Immigration*, 2.

16. Takaki, *Strangers*, 295–97.

17. Ibid., 309.

18. Cheng and Bonacich, *Labor Immigration*, 5.

19. Takaki, *Strangers*, 300.

20. K. Yamanaka and K. McClelland, "Earning the Model Minority Image: Diverse Strategies of Economic Adaptation by Asian American Women," *Ethnic and Racial Studies* 17 (1994): 108.

21. L. McGowan, S. Vosmek, and K. Danaher, "Women and the Global Economy," *Global Exchange* 2 (1995): 2.

22. S. Thaker, "Manager/Wife: Indian Women in the Motel Business," *Committee on South Asian Women Bulletin* 5, no. 1 (1987): 19–20.

23. E. N. Glenn, "From Servitude to Service Work: Historical Continuities in the Racial Division of Paid Reproductive Labor," *Signs* 18, no. 1 (Autumn, 1992): 1. This "reproductive" labor includes purchasing household goods, preparing and serving food, laundering and repairing clothing, maintaining furnishings and appliances, socializing children, providing care and emotional support for adults, and maintaining kin and community ties, none of which is considered part of the economy by traditional economics.

24. McGowan, Vosmek, and Danaher, "Women and the Global Economy," 2.

25. *Ms.* (Nov./Dec. 1995): 43.

26. T. Amott, *Caught in the Crisis: Women and the U.S. Economy Today* (New York: Monthly Review, 1993), 12.

27. S. D. Dasgupta, "Marching to a Different Drummer? Sex Roles of Asian Indian Women in the United States," *Women and Therapy* 5, nos. 2/3 (1986): 297–311.

28. Amott, *Caught in the Crisis*, 85.

29. U.S. Bureau of the Census, *1990 Census*, tables 45, 108, and 110.

30. Ibid.

31. Takaki, *Strangers*, 447.

32. Correspondence with P. Shah.

33. E. N. Glenn, "Cleaning Up/Kept Down: A Historical Perspective on Racial Inequality in 'Women's Work,'" *Stanford Law Review* 43 (July 1991): 1344.

34. J. Anner, ed., *Beyond Identity Politics: Emerging Social Justice Movements in Communities of Color* (Boston: South End, 1996).

35. Ibid.

ABOUT THE CONTRIBUTORS

Jaishri Abichandani was born in Bombay and moved to the United States in 1984. She has been photographing her family and community for four years. Jaishri is the founder of the South Asian Women's Creative Collective and has been using her artistic and organizational work as a tool for empowerment and political self-representation, for herself, her community, and people of color. She has been published in *Contours of the Heart*, the *Times of India*, and *Trikone*, among other publications, and lives with her family in Queens, New York.

Malahat Baig-Amin graduated with a master's of science in social work/ international social welfare from Columbia University. She has worked with the United Nations Children's Fund (UNICEF) in New York and the United Nations High Commissioner for Refugees in East Central Europe (UNHCR), assessing the health needs of women. She has extensive experience working in the area of domestic violence, assisting battered women in the criminal justice system, conducting support groups, counseling individual battered women, and advocating for their children. Malahat is a founding member and project director of the Immigrant Women's Health Project. She is involved in a research study examining domestic violence among South Asian and Arab immigrant women with the Columbia University Social Intervention Group.

Susmita Bando has been an art teacher with the Worcester, Massachusetts, public schools and is working on her master's degree in visual arts, majoring in painting, at the Indiana University of Pennsylvania. After graduating from the Government College of Art in Calcutta twenty years ago, Susmita came to this country. She has held several exhibitions of her paintings here, including one at the Indian Embassy in Washington, D.C. In the future, Susmita plans to go back to her teaching position in Massachusetts and continue with her own work.

Anannya Bhattacharjee is currently working with Workers' Awaaz, which organizes low-wage workers in the South Asian community in New York City. She is the former executive director of the Committee Against Anti-Asian Violence and is a founding member and the former program coordinator of Sakhi for South Asian Women. She is also a founding member and a member of the editorial collective of *SAMAR* magazine. She is a board member of the Brecht Forum and a steering committee member of the Committee on Women, Population, and Environment. She writes and speaks widely on issues concerning women, immigrants, workers, and social change.

Lubna Chaudhry, born in Pakistan, is an assistant professor at the University of Georgia, Athens, with a joint position in Social Foundations of Education and Women's Studies. Her research focuses on the multiple worlds and identities of immigrant communities in the United States.

Shamita Das Dasgupta is an assistant professor in psychology at Rutgers University, Newark, and co-author of *The Demon Slayers and Other Stories*. She is also co-founder of Manavi, the first organization in the United States to focus on violence against South Asian women in this country.

Sayantani DasGupta is an MD/MPH and a freelance writer. Her works have appeared in such magazines as *Ms.*, *A*, and *Z Magazine*, and she has had pieces in anthologies such as *"Bad Girls"/"Good Girls," Our Feet Walk the Sky, Contours of the Heart*, and *Dragon Ladies*. She has co-written a book of folktales with her mother, *The Demon Slayers and Other Stories: Bengali Folktales*, and has a collection of essays, *Love in the Time of Formaldehyde*, forthcoming from Ballantine Books.

Nabila El-Bassel is an associate professor at the Columbia University School of Social Work and the co-director/co-founder of the Social Intervention Group. For the past eight years, she has been conducting basic and intervention research on HIV prevention, substance abuse, and domestic violence among low-income people of color, with funding from NIDA, NIMH, and the CDC. She was recently awarded funding for two large-scale studies. An

NIDA study will examine the interrelationship between HIV risk behavior, domestic violence, and the substance abuse of both perpetrators and victims. An NIMH study will examine the effectiveness of HIV prevention with heterosexual couples in which issues regarding partner abuse will be incorporated into the intervention. Nabila is a founding member of the Immigrant Women's Health Project.

Louisa Gilbert has worked with the Social Intervention Group for nine years. She is an investigator with Nabila El-Bassel on two federally funded research projects that address the issues of HIV prevention, drug use, and domestic violence. Before joining SIG, she worked in India in a development program for rural women. Louisa is also on the board of directors of Sanctuary for Families, a New York–based organization that provides residential legal and counseling services to battered women. She is a founding member of the Immigrant Women's Health Project.

Grace Poore is a feminist lesbian writer and activist whose work deals with ending gender-based violence. She is currently producing and directing a video on incestuous sexual abuse of girls in South Asian communities in India, Sri Lanka, Canada, and the United States. She has published in various journals and anthologies, including *Our Feet Walk the Sky*, *The Very Inside*, *Trikone*, and *Options*.

Naheed Hasnat was born in Chicago but grew up in Saudi Arabia. Returning to the United States for college, she attended the University of California, Berkeley, and worked for two years as a consultant in the San Francisco Bay Area. During this time she continued her interest in writing about and exploring South Asian women's issues, particularly domestic violence. Deciding on a change in fields, she switched coasts and is now attending Columbia University in New York.

Naheed Islam is a Ph.D. candidate in sociology at the University of California, Berkeley. She is writing her dissertation on Bangladeshi immigrants in Los Angeles and how race and racialization affect their experiences. Her upcoming project is a comparison between the experiences of Bangladeshis in the United States and in the UK. Her birth in the United States, adolescent years in Bangladesh, and subsequent life in the United States inspire her work on the transnational politics of race identity and citizenship.

Surina Khan is an associate analyst at Political Research Associates, a national think tank and research center that studies the political right. Her writing has been published in *Trikone, Sojourner, Gay Community News, Boston Phoenix*, and the anthology *Generation Q*.

Satya P. Krishnan is an assistant professor with the Department of Health Studies at New Mexico State University, Las Cruces. She was a postdoctoral fellow at the National Development and Research Institutes, Inc., New York, and her current research interests include domestic violence among Latina and Native American women living in rural communities and HIV/AIDS among migrant farmworkers. She serves on the board of La Casa, Inc., the domestic violence shelter in Southern New Mexico, and is a member of the New Mexico Domestic Violence Advisory Council.

Rinita Mazumdar obtained her Ph.D. in philosophy from the University of Massachusetts. She has also studied at Brock University, Ontario, and the University of Calcutta. She has taught philosophy at different institutions in India, Canada, and the United States. Her research interests include epistemology, postmodernism, postcolonial studies, and women's studies, especially focusing on South Asia. She has several publications in these areas. She is an adjunct professor in Philosophy and Women's Studies at the University of New Mexico.

Sunita Sunder Mukhi is a performance scholar and artist. She is the cultural programs associate at the Asia Society. Her dissertation, "Performing Indianness in New York City," for the Performance Studies Department at New York University focuses on the ways in which Asian Indians in the tristate area express their identities. Her most recent performance works confront the issues of sexuality, identity politics, and women's power, such as "Its a Drag Being an Indian woman," "Cornucopia: Yet Another Interpretation of the Temptation," "Kaleidoscope: A Performance of Poetry," Tagore's "Karna and Kunti," and "From Manila to Manhattan: On Being a Filipino-Indian-American Woman." Her written work has appeared in *Contours of the Heart, Art Spiral*, and *Little India* magazine.

Manisha Roy, a psychological anthropologist and Jungian analyst, is in private practice in Marion, Mass. Born and brought up in India, she was educated at the Universities of Chicago and California. She has taught at the Universities of Chicago, Colorado, and Zurich and has lectured in many countries. Author of many articles, Manisha has also published *Bengali Women*, which is in its third printing and second edition, and co- edited *Cast the First Stone: Ethics in Analytical Practice*. A third book, *The Reckoning Heart*, is under consideration for publication. She also writes fiction in English and in her mother tongue, Bengali.

Sonia Shah is an editor and publisher at South End Press and a freelance writer. She is the editor of the anthology *Dragon Ladies*. Her essays on feminism and Asian-American issues have appeared in *Ms.*, *Sojourner*, *Z Magazine*, *The Indian American*, *Nuclear Times*, and *In These Times* and been anthologized in books, including *Listen Up! The State of Asian America*, *Frontline Feminism, 1975–1995*, *Women Transforming Politics*, *Reconstructing Gender*, *Experiencing Race, Class, and Gender in the United States*, and *Nationalism and Ethnic Conflict*. She is the editor of *Between Fear and Hope* and was formerly managing editor of *Nuclear Times* magazine. She co-founded two South Asian women's groups in the eastern United States.

Anne B. Waters earned her doctoral degree at the University of Michigan in the Interdisciplinary Program in Anthropology and History. Her dissertation was entitled "Predicaments of Women: Family Disputes and Family Violence in the Construction of Subjectivity in Maharashtra, India." She has conducted extensive fieldwork and archival research in South Asia and published articles on women's status in India in both Marathi and English. A visiting assistant professor in anthropology at Mount Holyoke College, she is completing research on women's suicide in contemporary India. Anne is a founding member of the Immigrant Women's Health Project.

INDEX

Abichandani, Jaishri, 223
Abramovitch, Ilana, 192
abuse
    emotional, 150
    physical, 8, 137, 145–159
    physical. *See also* domestic violence
    sexual, 137–138, 150. *See also*
        marital rape
    unwillingness to discuss, 137–138
    verbal, 150
acceptance, social, and self-acceptance,
    85
acquaintance rape, 129
activism, women's, 9, 11–13
    within Islam, 44–45
adolescence, 79, 111
Afrocentrism, 30
Agarwal, P., 16n.15
ajami, 77
Alexander the Great, 141, 200
alien
    lesbian, 66
    as term, 31n.1
alliances and identity politics, 29
Almaguer, Tomas, 85, 90
amnesia, selective, 173. *See also* denial
Amott, Teresa, 211, 216
Anamika (newsletter and collective), 70,
    73, 87
andar-mahal, 117–118, 126

Anderson, Benedict, 175, 180
androgyny, 85
antapura, 78
Apna Ghar, 146, 147
Appadurai, Arjun, 197
approval, need for others', 106
Arundhati, 138–139, 143
Aryan invasion, 77, 200
Asian American, as term, 25–26
Asian and Pacific Islander Lesbian and
        Bisexual Network (APLBN),
        29–30
Asian Indian Ministry, 187
assault, sexual, 118–119. *See also* rape
assistance programs, formal, lack of
        knowledge about, 154
Association of Asian Indians in America
        (AAIA), 166, 183n.7
auparishtaka, 78, 92n.22
autonomy, sexual
    of immigrants' children, 124
    and social class, 119
Ayesha, 12
Ayodhya, Rama's return to, 164

Babar, Mughal emperor, 65
baby-sitting, availability of, 154
"bad fate" and domestic violence, 150–
        151
"bad girls," 116, 124